POETRY OF TH

MARION THAIN was born near Norwich, the younger of two sisters. She rebelled against the scientific pursuits of her family in favour of the arts, and music and literature remain her principal interests. Having gained a First in English at the University of Birmingham, she continued there to write a Master's thesis on Constance Naden, which won the Faculty medal for the best M.Phil submission in 1995. She is currently completing a Ph.D on late nineteenth-century poetry and teaching courses on women's literature at the University of Birmingham. She divides her spare time between Latin-American dancing and playing the cello.

KELSEY THORNTON was born in Huddersfield, the youngest of three brothers. He has been Professor and Head of the School of English in the universities of Newcastle upon Tyne (1987–9) and Birmingham (1989–96). He has written books on Decadence and on Gerard Manley Hopkins and edited work by Clare, Ivor Gurney, Nicholas Hilliard and many of the poets of the 1890s, but feels the best brief life is contained in the stanza:

> How curious to know Kelsey Thornton;
> He is so exceedingly tall.
> His life is of interest to no one
> And he has no achievements at all.

# POETRY OF THE 1890s

*Edited by* R. K. R. THORNTON
*and* MARION THAIN

PENGUIN BOOKS

PENGUIN BOOKS

Published by the Penguin Group
Penguin Books Ltd, 27 Wrights Lane, London w8 5TZ, England
Penguin Books USA Inc., 375 Hudson Street, New York, New York 10014, USA
Penguin Books Australia Ltd, Ringwood, Victoria, Australia
Penguin Books Canada Ltd, 10 Alcorn Avenue, Toronto, Ontario, Canada M4V 3B2
Penguin Books (NZ) Ltd, 182–190 Wairau Road, Auckland 10, New Zealand

Penguin Books Ltd, Registered Offices: Harmondsworth, Middlesex, England

First published in Penguin Classics 1970
Second edition published 1997
1 3 5 7 9 10 8 6 4 2

Set in 10/11.5pt Monotype Ehrhardt
Typeset by Rowland Phototypesetting Ltd, Bury St Edmunds, Suffolk
Printed in England by Clays Ltd, St Ives plc

For Amy Thornton

# CONTENTS

## 1. ALL THE ARTS

## 2. THE MAKING OF THE NEW WOMAN

## 3. *SHE* IS AN ARTIST, TOO

# 4.  LONDON! LONDON! OUR DELIGHT

## 5. LONDON TYPES

# 6. THE HOUND OF HEAVEN

## 7. LOVE AND DEATH

## 10. THE ROSES FALL

# ACKNOWLEDGEMENTS

For permission to publish poems in copyright, thanks are due to the following:

for LAURENCE BINYON; to Mrs Nicolette Gray and the Society of Authors, on behalf of the Laurence Binyon Estate; for OLIVE CUNSTANCE; from *Opals* (The Bodley Head), Random House UK Ltd; for LORD ALFRED DOUGLAS; to Mr Edward Colman, on behalf of the Lord Alfred Douglas Literary Estate; for JOHN GRAY; to the Very Reverend Prior Provincial, O.P., of St Dominic's Priory; for G. A. GREENE; 'Prelude' from *Italian Lyrics of To-day*, to George Allen & Unwin Ltd; for THOMAS HARDY; from *The Collected Poems of Thomas Hardy*, reprinted by permission of the Trustees of the Hardy Estate, Macmillan & Co Ltd, London, the Macmillan Company of Canada Ltd and the Macmillan Company Inc., New York, Copyright © 1925 by the Macmillan Company; for A. E. HOUSMAN; from 'A Shropshire Lad' – authorized edition – from *The Collected Poems of A. E. Housman*. Copyright 1939, 1940, © 1959 by Holt, Rinehart and Winston, Inc. Copyright © 1967, 1968 by Robert E. Symons. Reprinted by permission of Holt, Rinehart and Winston, Inc., and the Society of Authors as the literary representative of the Estate of A. E. Housman, and Jonathan Cape Ltd, publishers of A. E. Housman's *Collected Poems*; for SELWYN IMAGE; from *Poems and Carols*, to George Allen & Unwin Ltd; for RUDYARD KIPLING; from *Barrack-Room Ballads* and *Rudyard Kipling's Verse: Definitive Edition*, to Mrs George Bambridge, Methuen & Co Ltd, Macmillan & Co Ltd and Doubleday & Company, Inc.; for RICHARD LE GALLIENNE; to the Society of Authors as the literary representative of The Estate of Richard Le Gallienne; for ALICE MEYNELL; to Mrs S. Mulvey and the Meynell Family Properties Ltd; for HENRY NEWBOLT from *Poems: New and Old*, published by John Murray, to Mr Peter Newbolt; for VINCENT O'SULLIVAN; from *Poems*, to George Allen & Unwin Ltd; for VICTOR PLARR; from *In the Dorian Mood*, to The Bodley Head; for A. MARY E. ROBINSON; from

*Lyrics Selected from the Works* and *Retrospect and Other Poems*; to A. & C. Black Ltd; for ARTHUR SYMONS; from *The Poems of Arthur Symons*, to William Heinemann Ltd and Dodd, Mead & Company, Inc.; for THEODORE WRATISLAW; to Richards Press Ltd; for W. B. YEATS: from *Collected Poems of W. B. Yeats*, published by Macmillan, to Mr M. B. Yeats and Macmillan & Co Ltd, London.

Every effort has been made to trace copyright holders, but in a few cases this has proved impossible. The publishers would be interested to hear from any copyright holders not here acknowledged.

# INTRODUCTION TO THE
# SECOND EDITION

Revising this anthology for the end of the twentieth century has
brought home how much anthologies are creatures of their time.
The first edition in 1970 attempted to rescue the 1890s from the
simplistic picture of a decade dominated by Decadence or even
divided between Decadence and Anti-decadence. It was for that
reason that Beardsley was not chosen for the cover, since in the
1960s Beardsley had become synonymous with a particular attitude
to the 1890s. The anthology bravely, and as it turns out rashly,
aimed to see the period steadily and see it whole. But the intervening
years have taught us exactly how partial the picture was, and certain
characteristics of the original anthology seem out of date and in
need of revision.

Some minor errors have been corrected and the biographies and
bibliographies have been revised and brought up to date.

The new length available allowed the inclusion of Wilde's *Ballad
of Reading Gaol*, which had been sacrificed to allow space for a
number of minor writers. It now seems right to indicate Wilde's
importance in a period which in some ways he dominated by
including his one poetic work which was new and significant in the
1890s.

But the main area which was in need of revision was that of
women's writing. Poems by four women had been included, and
many more were read and rejected; but the substantial development
of information and interest in women's writing in the last quarter
of this century has made it easier to recognize exactly how much
writing was ignored or undervalued. It is this new perspective,
characteristic perhaps of the end of this century, which has guided
and shaped the most significant changes in this anthology.

It suggested the value of co-operation with a new joint editor,
whose special interest was in women writers of the late nineteenth
century. Having assessed the writers and the shape of the anthology,
we decided to do two things which would use new material to

illuminate the existing sections and selections. As the women's poetry which we selected shared many of the concerns of the poetry included in the first edition, we introduced poems within the existing sections which could expand, balance, reflect on or often undercut the previous selection. However, there were some themes which were important specifically for women poets of the period, and this demanded the creation of two new sections, one dealing with the place of women within the social arena, and the other with the place of women within the literary tradition. The former is centred on women's fight to be set free from restricting social stereotypes, which gave rise to the character of the New Woman. The latter looks at how women writers entered an essentially masculine poetic tradition, the problems they encountered and the revisions they made.

We set the new sections immediately after the first section which establishes an Aesthetic direction, so that the New Woman can stand alongside the dandy, her male equivalent in questioning the confines of gender in a self-conscious and socially challenging way. The woman poet's reflections on her relationship with her art add a new dimension to the concern with artifice dealt with in the first section.

An indication of the substantial shift which the addition of more writing by women made to the anthology is the nature of the new ending. The poetry of the 1890s as it had been portrayed in the first edition was coloured by decline and a sense of foreboding at the end of the century; but many women writers reject this preoccu-pation and look forward to a new century with hope bolstered by a confidence in science and the new theories of evolution. While the anthology begins by stressing the 1890s celebration of artifice, it now ends with a glimpse of the new hope founded on science and nature. The same association with nature which made the celebration of artifice problematic for women, now gives them hope that their day is soon to come.

Having deliberately disturbed the tidiness of our picture of the 1890s with a double ending which looked at both the sense of ending and the sense of beginning, we chose a penultimate poem which acknowledges the reluctance of our picture to be neatly contained within the artificial parameters of the decade. The principle that lies behind our choices is usually that they must be poems which were written in the 1890s or which saw first significant publication at that time. May Kendall's 'Woman's Future' was published in 1887, but demanded inclusion as showing that, before the 1890s and right through the period, women had a new vision which was far from decadent. The book's new shape is the old shape questioned and enriched. Though it begins with the artificial, it ends with the natural, indicating where one could find the optimism of the last line of Thompson's 'Envoy' with which we still conclude.

R. K. R. T.
M. T.

# A NOTE ON THE TEXT

Each poem is followed by the author's name and the name and date of the volume from which the text is taken. This date does not always accurately reflect the date of composition, and details of writing and publishing history must be sought in the books listed in the bibliography. We have omitted some dates given by the poets themselves, to avoid confusion and because they are not always accurate. We have also omitted the dedications which some of the poets placed before their poems, because, although this 1890s fad would give something of a period flavour, the dedications are irrelevant to the poems.

R.K.R.T.
M.T.

# INTRODUCTION TO THE
# FIRST EDITION*

It is common to look at the 1890s as a coherent period; before the nineteenth century had ended, Max Beerbohm had looked back to 'the Beardsley period', and the sense of the decade's form epitomizes its own self-consciousness and self-dramatization. This form has been described in important books about the period: Holbrook Jackson's *The Eighteen Nineties* (1913), Richard Le Gallienne's *The Romantic '90s* (1926), and in particular W. B. Yeats's impressive piece of mythologizing, the *Autobiographies* (1926), of which 'The Tragic Generation' (1922) forms a part; and the form has been illustrated by anthologies, notably those excellent compilations made by A. J. A. Symons (1928) and Martin Secker (1948). Although each book added its own detail, its own angle, there was a large ground of general agreement and the present selection does not try to get rid of the 1890s myth. It does, however, recognize that the myth can be limiting and includes poems which qualify it. The poems, which are after all the chief point and interest of an anthology, were chosen to illustrate not a thesis but a period; but they encouraged a close look at some common generalizations about 1890s writers and their work. This introduction looks at these generalizations and suggests reasons why we might qualify our acceptance of them.

The most common picture of the 'nineties, always good copy and encouraged of late by the boom in Beardsley, is of the sensational type, sees the period as 'Decadent' and usually takes as its central symbol *The Yellow Book*, the publication of which marked a significant step in the crystallization of 'nineties myths. The first volume, in April 1894, was greeted with howls of protest. The *Westminster Gazette* went so far as to say of two of Beardsley's drawings in it that nothing they knew 'would meet the case except a short Act of Parliament to make this kind of thing illegal'. *The Times* said that

---

* Minor amendments in style and detail have been made to conform with the style of the new edition of the book.

'it might be intended to attract by its very repulsiveness and insolence, and in that case it is not unlikely to be successful'. Even in
private the reaction was the same: two women, who wrote poems
and passionate dramas under the name of 'Michael Field' and were
by no means reactionary, had an interest in the publication, since
they had sent a poem for inclusion in the second volume. They
wrote in their diary:

> We have been almost blinded by the glare of hell . . . As we came up to
> the shop we found the whole frontage a hot background of orange-colour
> to sly, roistering heads, silhouetted against it and half-hiding behind masks.
> The window seemed to be gibbering, our eyes to be filled with incurable
> jaundice. *La Réclame*, hideous beyond Duessa or any Witch ever seen by
> the mind's eyes, stood up before us as a shop where contemporary literature
> is sold. One felt as one does when now and then a wholly lost woman stands
> flaming on the pavement with the ghastly laugh of the ribald crowd in the
> air round her. One hates one's eyes for seeing! But the infamous window
> mocked and mowed and fizgiged, saffron and pitchy, till one's eyes were
> arrested like Virgil's before the wind of flame.
>
> And the inside of the book! It is full of cleverness such as one expects
> to find in those who dwell below light and hope and love and aspiration.[1]

Little wonder then that they demanded the return of their poem.

*The Yellow Book* was, in short, a red rag to John Bull. Those who
had produced its daring image (deliberately taking the colour of the
yellow-backed French novels) did their work only too well. Writers,
artists and publishers had learned, usually from France, that there
was much to be gained from outrageous attitudes: the artist could
have his fun at the expense of the bourgeois, on whom he none the
less depended, by laughing at the shocked response which greeted
each new venture; he could feel comfortably superior because of his
more sophisticated and tolerant attitudes; and at the same time he
could further the serious cause of his art. Knowing the power of
advertisement (had not Oscar Wilde been made famous beyond his
talent through parody and shocked fascination?), satirists and players
of the game of *épater les bourgeois* throve on each other, and from the
popularity of some of the productions, even the bourgeois enjoyed
the game. But in the case of *The Yellow Book*, the exercise in shocking

---

1. B.M. Add. MS. 46782, p. 70.

the bourgeois was too successful, especially when the sense of outrage at the immorality of art was strengthened by such equally well-publicized scandals as the case of Oscar Wilde (the yellow-backed French novel he carried at the time of his arrest was reported in the papers as 'Yellow Book'). Because of its success, the one outraged response is often all that is remembered, and the variety of the period is obscured by the assumption that the 1890s can be summed up in one of those favourite adjectives, 'naughty' or 'decadent'.

To balance the caricature Decadent, one finds at the other extreme the Anti-decadent or activist, the muscular moral imperialist. The case is nicely summed up by the first words of Professor J. H. Buckley's preface to his *William Ernest Henley: A Study in the 'Counter-Decadence' of the 'Nineties*:

> By some tacit agreement literary historians of the Victorian period have isolated a picturesque movement dominated by the hero-villain Oscar Wilde and known as the 'decadence' of the 'yellow 'nineties.' The convenience of such a label has led many a reader virtually to ignore the truly vital writing of the English *fin de siècle*. For if there was in the 'nineties a 'decadent' coterie, there was also a far more vigorous 'counter-decadent' group.

This group gathered round the *National Observer* under the editorship of W. E. Henley, and was dubbed by Beerbohm the 'Henley Regatta'. The most obvious example of the type of poetical vigour which this man of passion inspired or attracted to him is Kipling, though Yeats was also among those whose work he published (incidentally revising without Yeats's permission).

Both these caricatures are to be found in the satires of the period itself, although the Decadent was by far the more popular, both because he was simpler to caricature, and because laughter and the desire to mock are more often the province of the vigorous element. Owen Seaman, in *The Battle of the Bays* (1894), which brilliantly parodies poets who might have been considered for the Laureateship on the death of Tennyson, wrote in 'A Ballad of a Bun' of a would-be-popular lady writer seeking the way to success:

> A Decadent was dribbling by;
>   'Lady,' he said, 'you seem undone;
> You need a panacea; try
>   This sample of the Bodley bun.

'It is fulfilled of precious spice,
   Whereof I give the recipe; –
Take common dripping, stew in vice,
   And serve with vertu; taste and see!

'And lo! I brand you on the brow
   As kin to Nature's lowest germ;
You are sister to the microbe now,
   And second-cousin to the worm.'

This parody of Davidson's 'A Ballad of a Nun' (see p. 209) already contains the ingredients of the picture of the Decadent that became so popular. It even includes a reference to the Bodley Head, under which sign John Lane and Elkin Mathews published. Together they began *The Yellow Book*, though Mathews left Lane after the second volume, and they published many of the interesting writers of the decade; their list of 1894 includes Laurence Binyon, John Davidson, 'Michael Field', Herbert Horne, Lionel Johnson, Richard Le Gallienne, Alice Meynell, Dollie Radford, Francis Thompson, Ernest Rhys and Oscar Wilde, not to mention the *Book of the Rhymers' Club* with its contributions by Dowson, Symons and Yeats. Because of the limitations of Lane's list, Seaman called him

a sorry sort of Lane
That hardly ever turns aside,

but he was able to see the value of controversy and published Seaman himself; and he was sufficiently turned aside by the scandal to withdraw Wilde's works from the list. The only other publisher of comparable importance was Leonard Smithers, whose combination of pornography with the best in recent art and literature indicates the place to which public opinion had thrust art in the shocked reaction of the later 1890s. It was Smithers who published *The Savoy* (1896) when *The Yellow Book*, dismissing Beardsley because rumour wrongly associated him with Wilde, lost most of its crusading zeal. *The Savoy*, edited by Arthur Symons and Aubrey Beardsley, was the only English magazine which can justly be called Symbolist, yet in its day it too was lumped with the rest, as in this comment by Ernest Rhys in *The Literary Year-Book* of 1897:

As for the 'Decadence', some of the younger men who have been most freely displaying its colours during the year, as in the derelict 'Savoy', Mr

Symons and (I fear) Mr Yeats, are gone south, only to return, let us hope, under a crescent star! The century's end, then, need not prove quite fatal.

The place of the 1890s in literary history, where it is sometimes regarded as a dead end, is somewhat clarified if one sees the close relationship of Decadence to Symbolism, which had a much wider influence. Symons's *The Symbolist Movement in Literature* (1899), which led Eliot to discover Laforgue and the other French Symbolists, is a later form of a book announced earlier as *The Decadent Movement in Literature*. In the Introduction Symons described how 'the interlude, half a mock-interlude, of Decadence, diverted the attention of the critics while something more serious was in preparation', namely Symbolism.

The Decadent, however, was much more simple to satirize than the Symbolist, and Seaman was not the only one to take advantage of the fact. *Punch* even ran a series of cartoons about 'Our Decadents', and no comic paper could be without its shaft at the popular butt. The character of the Decadent had been established in France in 1884 when J. K. Huysmans wrote *A Rebours*, a novel whose hero, des Esseintes, the last in an aristocratic line, attempts to live a life where, cut off from the outside world and surrounded by art and the artificial, he rather than nature will control his existence. Among the most complete satirical pictures of the Decadent in the 1890s is that by Lionel Johnson, classical scholar, poet and critic of some wit and perception. His essay, 'The Cultured Faun', published in the *Anti-Jacobin* in 1891, summarizes the characteristics of the beast:

Externally, our hero should cultivate a reassuring sobriety of habit, with just a dash of the dandy. None of the wandering looks, the elaborate disorder, the sublime lunacy of his predecessor, the 'apostle of culture'. Externally, then, a precise appearance; internally, a catholic sympathy with all that exists, and 'therefore' suffers, for art's sake. Now art, at present, is not a question of the senses so much as of the nerves. Botticelli, indeed, was very precious, but Baudelaire is very nervous. Gautier was adorably sensuous, but M. Verlaine is pathetically sensitive. That is the point: exquisite appreciation of pain, exquisite thrills of anguish, exquisite adoration of suffering. Here comes in a tender patronage of Catholicism: white tapers upon the high altar, an ascetic and beautiful young priest, the great gilt monstrance, the subtle-scented and mystical incense, the old world accents of the Vulgate, of the Holy Offices; the splendour of the sacred vestments. We kneel at some hour, not too early for our convenience, repeating the solemn Latin, drinking in those Gregorian tones, with plenty of modern French sonnets in memory, should the sermon be dull. But to join the Church! Ah, no! better to dally with the enchanting mysteries, to pass from our dreams of delirium to our dreams of sanctity with no coarse facts to jar upon us. And so these refined persons cherish a double 'passion', the sentiment of repentant yearning and the sentiment of rebellious sin.

To play the part properly a flavour of cynicism is recommended: a scientific profession of materialist dogmas, coupled – for you should forswear consistency – with gloomy chatter about 'The Will to Live' . . . Jumble all these 'impressions' together, your sympathies and your sorrows, your devotion and your despair; carry them about with you in a state of ferment-ation, and finally conclude that life is loathsome yet that beauty is beatific. And beauty – ah, beauty is everything beautiful! Isn't that a trifle obvious, you say? That is the charm of it, it shows your perfect simplicity, your chaste and catholic innocence. Innocence of course: beauty is always innocent, ultimately. No doubt there are 'monstrous' things, terrible pains, the haggard eyes of an *absintheur*, the pallid faces of 'neurotic' sinners; but all that is the portion of our Parisian friends, such and such a 'group of artists', who meet at the Café So-and-So. We like people to think we are much the same, but it isn't true. We are quite harmless, we only concoct strange and subtle verse about it. And, anyway, beauty includes everything; there's another sweet saying for you from our 'impressionist' copy-books. Impres-sions! that is all. Life is mean and vulgar, Members of Parliament are odious, the critics are commercial pedants: we alone know Beauty, and Art, and Sorrow and Sin. Impressions! exquisite, dainty fantasies; fiery-coloured visions; and impertinence straggling into epigram, for 'the true' criticism; *c'est adorable!* And since we are scholars and none of your penny-a-line Bohemians, we throw in occasional doses of 'Hellenism': by which we mean the Ideal of the Cultured Faun. That is to say, a flowery Paganism, such as no 'Pagan' ever had; a mixture of 'beautiful woodland natures', and 'the perfect comeliness of the Parthenon frieze', together with the elegant languors and favourite vices of (let us parade our 'decadent' learning) the *Stratonis Epigrammata*. At this time of day we need not dilate upon the equivocal charm of everything Lesbian. And who shall assail us? – what stupid and uncultured critic, what coarse and narrow Philistine? We are the Elect of Beauty: saints and sinners, devils and devotees, Athenians and Parisians, Romans of the Empire and Italians of the Renaissance. *Fin de siècle! Fin de siècle!* Literature is a thing of beauty, blood, and nerves.

Though it is quite clear that Johnson, like his 'Philistine critic', thinks this creature a 'feeble and foolish beast', he himself is sometimes represented as a similar sort of character.

It is essential to be clear, then, that the Decadent and the Anti-decadent are caricatures, or at best pictures which are only occasionally true to life. Johnson obviously saw the pitfalls too clearly to be himself a Decadent. Yeats, a contributor to the *National Observer*, and even referred to by Henley as 'one of my lads',[2] is often, and with accuracy, associated with the so-called Decadent groups. Richard Le Gallienne, though he tried to dissociate himself from them by writing *English Poems* (1892), *The Religion of a Literary Man* (1893) and satires like 'The Décadent to his Soul', wrote poems which make it simple to include him among Decadent writers. Most poets of the 1890s have at one time or another been called Decadent, though critics who examine their work in greater detail usually remark on the inaccuracy of the term. Even a biographer of Arthur Symons, the writer most closely associated with the movement, insists that 'it would be fallacious to confine him, as has already been done, solely within those narrow limits'.[3] *The Yellow Book* is misleadingly caricatured; Sir Frederick Leighton, P.R.A., Henry James, William Watson and W. B. Yeats, all of whom contributed to the first volume, do not seem 'below light and hope', and time has faded even the most outrageous of the other contributions. Amidst its reputedly hothouse climate grew some very ordinary blooms, just as in the books of the Rhymers' Club, whose atmosphere was recently described by an American Professor as 'hectic and overstrained', one can find a poem like T. W. Rolleston's 'Cycling Song', whose fate as a school song accurately suggests the degree of its exoticism. Yet, though it is a critical commonplace to insist on qualifications of the picture, the simplifications persist; myths and patterns are more powerful than objective truth, and we are unlikely to lose the division between what Lionel Johnson called the pallid school and the school of fresh and vigorous blood.

This is not necessarily a bad thing. The simplifications have their uses; it is convenient to have one's literary history made into a simple pattern, partaking, as Dr Johnson wrote, 'of the spirit of

2. W. B. Yeats, *Autobiographies*, 1955, p. 129.
3. Roger Lhombreaud, *Arthur Symons: A Critical Biography*, 1963, p. 61.

history, which is contrary to minute exactness'. The pattern can often convey the flavour of an age more forcibly than mere pedantic insistence on fact. After all, the myths are influenced, usually created, by men who lived through the period; it is often their lives and their work that we wish to understand, and the meaning of the events is contained in their shaping of them. Thus we have Yeats's description of his friends as 'The Tragic Generation'. Writers about the period support the idea of tragedy with a list of those who died young: Dowson at thirty-two, Johnson at thirty-five, Beardsley at twenty-five, Crackanthorpe at twenty-seven, Wilde at forty-six; one even finds Davidson, a suicide in 1909 at the age of fifty-three, among the young deaths of the 'nineties. It is useless to point to the reasonable survival rate of the Rhymers' Club for example (only three out of thirteen failed to reach the age of sixty); or to compare the loss of poetic talent to the early 1820s when Keats died at twenty-five, Shelley at twenty-nine and Byron at thirty-six. Tragedies are not comparative, and while the latter deaths seem like accidental cutting off of talent, the deaths of the writers of the 1890s seem a sort of fulfilment. Yeats conveyed the sense of decline and tragedy which those deaths symbolize, and the final section of this anthology shows how common the sense of tragedy was, and how it marks the poems as well as the lives of the poets.

Symons too created myths out of the raw material of his friends' lives, most obviously in his account of Dowson, who is often taken as a representative Decadent and typical 1890s poet. The process of Dowson's mythification is instructive, showing the struggle between the truth to fact and the truth to the spirit. Symons's 'A Literary Causerie: on a Book of Verses', in *The Savoy* of August 1896, was a picture of Dowson though it did not mention his name. Treating Dowson almost as if he were already dead, Symons depicted a *poète maudit*, a man of dilapidated appearance, a lover of the sordid in his surroundings, an experimenter with drugs ('At Oxford, I believe, his favourite form of intoxication had been haschisch,' wrote Symons), and a seeker of oblivion, usually through drink. This image of Dowson, reiterated by Symons in his obituary notice of the poet, and in the introduction to an edition of Dowson's poems, was strengthened by Yeats's stories and impressions in his *Autobiographies* and has usually done service as a version of Dowson for the literary histories ever since, influencing also the interpretation of his poems. Friends who knew him better than Symons did and scholars who have studied his life and work have repeatedly tried to rectify the errors in the picture (Edgar Jepson in 1907 and again in 1933, Victor Plarr in 1914, Desmond Flower in 1934, 1950 and 1967, John Gawsworth in 1938, Mark Longaker in 1944 and 1967, and Russell Goldfarb in 1964). The myth persists, attracting readers to his poems, but making misreadings of them too common. Most ironic of all, a letter from Dowson to Symons which has recently come to light suggests that, though Dowson reacted against the description 'dilapidated', he did not object as strongly to the picture as his defenders have. Feeling himself 'fortunate in my chronicler',[4] he was willing to be part of a myth.

Elements of 1890s history and criticism are usefully summarized by using the two caricatured extremes. The trial of Oscar Wilde, for example, can be seen as a debate between Decadent and Anti-decadent literary theory. Wilde had been made to defend at his first trial his aphorism that there was no such thing as a moral or an immoral book, and he contended that a book was either well or badly written. When the Marquess of Queensberry's accusations against Wilde were apparently proved, the Anti-decadent faction of the *National Observer* was among the most vociferous in its denunciation of Wilde and the theory of art he stood for:

There is not a man or woman in the English-speaking world possessed of the treasure of a wholesome mind who is not under a deep debt of gratitude to the Marquess of Queensberry for destroying the High Priest of the Decadents. The obscene impostor, whose prominence has been a social outrage ever since he transferred from Trinity Dublin to Oxford his vices, his follies, and his vanities, has been exposed, and that thoroughly at last. But to the exposure there must be legal and social sequels. There must be another trial at the Old Bailey, or a coroner's inquest – the latter for choice; and of the Decadents, of their hideous conceptions of the meaning of Art, of their worse than Eleusinian mysteries, there must be an absolute end.[5]

These two views explain somewhat the sensation the trial caused in literary circles. Despite the blasts of morality which followed, Arthur

4. Desmond Flower and Henry Maas, eds, *The Letters of Ernest Dowson*, 1967, p. 371.
5. Quoted in *Famous Trials* 7: *Oscar Wilde*, 1962.

Symons stuck to his artistic principles and summarized the position in the preface to the second edition of his *Silhouettes* (1896):

. . . a work of art can be judged from only two standpoints: the standpoint from which its art is measured entirely by its morality, and the standpoint from which its morality is measured entirely by its art.

Symons saw the same sort of division in the use of the word 'Decadence', 'either hurled as a reproach or hurled back as a defiance'. Again the caricature extremes provide a useful way of understanding the term: on the one hand a term of abuse for the Anti-decadent critic, who was hostile, aggressively masculine, anti-French, pro-British, and above all concerned with content and its morality; on the other hand a descriptive term for the Decadent writer, who applied it to style, with which he was most concerned, believing in the irrelevance of morality in artistic matters, inclined to a feminine sensitivity, French-loving. Between the two extremes come the infinite gradations, but the caricatures serve to heighten the distinctions.

One does not always wish to distinguish; if there is a division on the point of morality, there is yet agreement in some respects on the craft of poetry, agreement which can be related to the work of Walter Pater. Pater was perhaps not the man whom one would have expected to inspire seekers after beauty. Beerbohm was so disappointed in Pater's appearance at Oxford that he reported in 'Diminuendo' that 'I nearly went down when they told me that this was Pater'. But speaking of the new generation of writers in the 1890s, Yeats remarked in *The Oxford Book of Modern Verse* that 'one writer . . . had its entire uncritical admiration', and that was Pater. From him came not only a love of learning and a philosophy that helped cause the disasters, but also three important features of the 'nineties aesthetic: the demand for freedom of choice in subject matter, the impressionistic style and the notion of the musicality of verse.

The search for new subject matter was not understood alike by master and disciples. Pater took away the 'Conclusion' to his *Studies in the History of the Renaissance*, fearing that his work 'might possibly mislead some of those young men into whose hands it might fall'. Yeats recorded in his *Autobiographies* how Lionel Johnson, whose word was not always to be trusted, came back from a visit to Pater with the story that, having commented on some books on economics on Pater's shelves, he had been assured by Pater that 'nothing that has interested mankind can ever lose that interest'. However accurate the report, Johnson's story was true to the ideas that Pater put into his criticism. Writers derived a demand for freedom of subject matter and a notion of the amorality of art from such comments in the 'Conclusion' as 'not the fruit of experience, but experience itself, is the end'; or 'art comes to you professing frankly to give nothing but the highest quality to your moments as they pass, and simply for those moments' sake'. Yeats, in the *Autobiographies*, argued along Paterian lines that

> Science, through much ridicule and some persecution has won the right to explore whatever passes before its corporeal eye, and merely because it passes . . . Literature now demands the same right of exploration of all that passes before the mind's eye, and merely because it passes.

Richard Le Gallienne, in *The Romantic '90s*, described Davidson's 'note of revolt against conventional hypocrisies, and his vindication of the free play of human vitality'. Symons too is Paterian at the end of the Introduction to the second edition of *London Nights* (1897), where he claimed that 'whatever has existed has achieved the right of artistic existence'. The question is summed up by Symons in *Silhouettes* (1896) where he wrote, 'If we are to save people's souls by the writing of verses, well and good. But if not, there is no choice but to admit absolute freedom of choice.'

Henley with his hospital poems, Kipling with his ballads of common soldiers, and both in their introduction of a hitherto 'unpoetic' vocabulary, the idiom of the street or the barrack-room, were making advances in new material for poetry, as was Davidson, whose work Eliot saw as an element in his own development. (See the Introduction to section 3 [section 5 of this edition] of this anthology.)

Novelty was sought in both the 'physical life' and the 'inward world of thought and feeling', to use Pater's division. In this era of the early psychoanalysts, both artists and writers were fond of the image of the reflection, and examined the complexities of their own moods and ideas and that 'unseen reality apprehended by the consciousness', which is what Symons said Symbolism attempts to express. One is reminded of Hopkins's novel vocabulary, and his search for the inner nature of an object through exact realization of it.

Catching the exact nature of the thing described is the second feature of 1890s writing that may be owed to Pater, and this more closely unites the two camps. Arnold had written in *On Translating Homer* (1861) that 'of the literature of France and Germany, as of the intellect in Europe in general, the main effort, for now many years, has been a critical effort; the endeavour in all branches of knowledge, theology, philosophy, history, art, science, to see the object as in itself it really is'. Pater, in *The Renaissance*, acknowledged the justice of Arnold's statement, but added that 'in aesthetic criticism the first step towards seeing one's object as it really is, is to know one's own impression as it really is, to discriminate it, to realize it distinctly'. The method of realizing the impression and fixing it is suggested by another comment of Pater that 'the first condition of the poetic way of seeing and presenting things is particularization'. One thus finds theory and practice concerned with the impression. Ernest Dowson wrote in the novel on which he and Arthur Moore collaborated, *Adrian Rome* (1899):

> The fulness of one's life, the fineness of one's impressions, the multiplicity of one's sensations; here it seemed to him, was the rough material out of which grew magnificently the ultimate achievement of one's art.

Symons claimed that Verlaine had achieved the ideal of Decadence, which was 'to fix the last fine shade, the quintessence of things; to fix it fleetingly'.[6] And in the same essay he says of Henley that 'the poetry of Impressionism can go no further, in one direction, than that series of rhymes and rhythms named *In Hospital*'. This is not mere perversity on Symons's part, for Shaw too saw that Henley's chief quality lay in his ability to 'describe anything that was forced on his observation and experience, from a tom-cat in an area to a hospital operation'.[7]

The practice of this style, and its influence, can most simply be seen by looking at a few lines of Symons, and comparing them with some of Eliot. From Symons's 'White Heliotrope':

6. Arthur Symons, 'The Decadent Movement in Literature', *Harper's*, 1893.
7. Letter to Archibald Henderson, quoted in Henderson's *George Bernard Shaw: His Life and Works*, 1911.

> The feverish room and that white bed,
>     The tumbled skirts upon a chair,
>     The novel flung half-open, where
> Hat, hair-pins, puffs, and paints, are spread.

The pictorial arrangement, the eighteenth-century ability to let juxtaposition do the commenting, the impersonality, these are common in Eliot's poems too:

> Out of the window perilously spread
> Her drying combinations touched by the sun's last rays,
> On the divan are piled (at night her bed)
> Stockings, slippers, camisoles, and stays.

Equally important is the idea of the musicality of verse, another feature of 1890s poetry which finds its way into Eliot's poems, as in the *Four Quartets* or 'Rhapsody on a Windy Night'. The idea is expressed mostly famously in Pater's remark in 'The School of Giorgione' that 'all art constantly aspires towards the condition of music'. What he meant was that the arts all attempt to achieve an inseparability of form and content such as one finds in music, an idea developed in the image of the dancer, whose rhythmic movement cannot be separated from her, and who symbolizes a complex set of associated ideas in the poems and paintings of the period. But music, Pater had said, 'is the true measure of perfected art', and, though he may not have followed writers like Baudelaire, who described in his 'Correspondances' how 'perfumes, colours and sounds answer each other', his ideas were echoed by French and English writers. Where Verlaine demanded 'music before all else', Dowson wrote to Arthur Moore that he was writing 'verses making for mere sound, & music, with just a suggestion of sense, or hardly that'.[8] Yeats spoke of Dowson's poems as 'not speech but perfect song, though song for the speaking voice'.

To use the vocabulary of one art for another was common: Beardsley in a letter quoted by his recent biographer wrote of 'story painters and picture writers',[9] John Gray wrote *Silverpoints*, Whistler painted 'Harmonies', Wilde wrote a 'Symphony in Yellow', Henley composed 'London Voluntaries'. Arthur Symons even saw 'The

8. Desmond Flower and Henry Maas, eds, *The Letters of Ernest Dowson*, 1967, p. 190.
9. Stanley Weintraub, *Beardsley*, 1967, p. 95.

World as Ballet', and artists strove to achieve a unified composition
in their lives as well as their art.

Though there are important distinctions between groups of
writers, there is a certain amount of common ground provided
by the three features that I have mentioned. These also suggest
something of the debt to the 'nineties that was felt by later poets.
Pound, for example, whose poem 'The Decadence' is (I hope) a
parody which indicates a thorough understanding of the subject,
wrote the 'Imagist Triad' as a statement of the aims of Imagism:

1. Direct treatment of the 'thing' whether subjective or objective.
2. To use absolutely no word that does not contribute to the presentation.
3. As regarding rhythm: to compose in the sequence of the musical phrase,
not in sequence of a metronome.[10]

Other poets learned from or with the 1890s poets, but there is no
need to justify the latter by suggesting their place in the background
of modern literature; they are themselves sufficiently attractive and
varied to demand the attention of a new anthology.

All this qualification of accepted pictures might lead the reader
to think that I intend to put forward now an anthology providing a
'true likeness'; but one can do no more than provide another version.
I have selected poems published between 1890 and 1900 which
reflect both the quality and the interest of work in the period. A
few of Henley's poems belong to some years earlier, but were
substantially revised and largely made their mark in the 'nineties,
a few were written in the period but not published, such as Dowson's
'Against My Lady Burton', and one, Hardy's 'The Darkling
Thrush', belongs in this company by virtue of its moment of
conception. I have selected only complete poems, feeling that to
select extracts would not reflect the concern with form which marks
the period. Some of the poems are, however, detached from a series.
The poems are divided into eight [ten in this edition] more or less
coherent groups which arise from the poems rather than from an
imposed plan, and their arrangement within the sections is designed
to provide comparisons and contrasts which may be informative; to
place, for example, Yeats among those

10. *Make It New*, 1934.

> Poets with whom I learned my trade,
> Companions of the Cheshire Cheese.[11]

The 'true likeness' is an impossible ideal, and to come near it would require space for poems, plays, short stories, pictures, drawings, photographs, music, song, dance. This selection is merely intended to capture something of the attractiveness of 1890s poetry and convey its pleasures without pinning it out for demonstration like a bright, slightly dusty but completely dead butterfly.

R. K. R. THORNTON

11. 'The Grey Rock'.

# 1. ALL THE ARTS

'The first duty in life is to be as artificial as possible. What the second duty is no one has as yet discovered.' In this typically self-conscious epigram from his 'Phrases and Philosophies for the Use of the Young', Wilde summed up the late nineteenth-century artist's contention that Art is superior to Nature. The same notion was symbolized by his notorious green carnation; flowers were more acceptable if they were artificially aided. Max Beerbohm, flippantly penetrating to the essence of the subject in his 'A Defence of Cosmetics', wrote that 'we are ripe for a new epoch of artifice'. The outraged critics of *The Yellow Book*, where this essay appeared, did not see Beerbohm's satiric purpose, even when he pointed it out in the second volume; for his analysis seemed only too accurate.

Baudelaire, in his 'Éloge du Maquillage', had pointed out the connection between cosmetics and morals, arguing that, whereas crime is natural, virtue is artificial, so that the application of make-up is a praiseworthy attempt to rise above the natural. 'Evil happens effortlessly, naturally, fatally,' wrote Baudelaire; 'good is always the product of some art.' Beerbohm leaned heavily on these ideas when he wrote in the essay mentioned above that

the era of rouge is upon us, and as only in an elaborate era can man by the tangled accrescency of his own pleasures and emotions reach that refinement which is his highest excellence, and by making himself, so to say, independent of Nature, come nearest to God, so only in an elaborate era is woman perfect. Artifice is the strength of the world.

Yeats demonstrated his commitment to the same ideas when he quoted from an early diary of his:

If we cannot imagine ourselves as different from what we are, and try to assume that second self, we cannot impose a discipline upon ourselves though we may accept one from others. Active virtue, as distinguished from the passive acceptance of a code, is therefore theatrical, consciously dramatic, the wearing of a mask.[1]

Make-up, morality, the mask, theatre, music-hall, dancers and the dance, the remaking of the self, all kinds of artifice, thus form an interesting set of interconnected ideas, perhaps clearest in the work of Arthur Symons.

Writers were self-conscious, drawing their images from literature and art as Beardsley did his pictures, and frequently using art or artists as subject matter. 'La Gioconda' for example is one of a book of poems whose starting point is a picture, and incidentally it recalls the passage of Pater which Yeats made the first piece in his *Oxford Book of Modern Verse*. Life itself was also an art. The attitude of the dandy, whether English or French, fact or fiction, whether Baudelaire, Beardsley, Beerbohm, or the des Esseintes of *A Rebours*, was summed up in those words of Wilde that André Gide reported: 'I have put my genius into my life; I have put merely my talent into my work.' Though some were accused of posing, the dandy's concern with creating himself reflects a fundamental part of the aesthetic of many writers of the day, the placing of the artificial above the natural.

1. *Mythologies* (1962), p. 334.

## Villanelle of the Poet's Road

Wine and woman and song,
   Three things garnish our way:
Yet is day over long.

Lest we do our youth wrong,
   Gather them while we may:
Wine and woman and song.

Three things render us strong,
   Vine leaves, kisses and bay;
Yet is day over long.

Unto us they belong,
   Us'the bitter and gay,
Wine and woman and song.

We, as we pass along,
   Are sad that they will not stay;
Yet is day over long.

Fruits and flowers among,
   What is better than they:
Wine and woman and song?
   Yet is day over long.

ERNEST DOWSON
*Decorations* (1899)

## Orchids

Orange and purple, shot with white and mauve,
Such in a greenhouse wet with tropic heat
One sees these delicate flowers whose parents throve
In some Pacific island's hot retreat.

Their ardent colours that betray the rank
Fierce hotbed of corruption whence they rose
Please eyes that long for stranger sweets than prank
Wild meadow-blooms and what the garden shows.

Exotic flowers! How great is my delight
To watch your petals curiously wrought,
To lie among your splendours day and night
Lost in a subtle dream of subtler thought.

Bathed in your clamorous orchestra of hues,
The palette of your perfumes, let me sleep
While your mesmeric presences diffuse
Weird dreams: and then bizarre sweet rhymes shall creep

Forth from my brain and slowly form and make
Sweet poems as a weaving spider spins,
A shrine of loves that laugh and swoon and ache,
A temple of coloured sorrows and perfumed sins!

THEODORE WRATISLAW
*Orchids* (1896)


## Baudelaire

A Paris gutter of the good old times,
    Black and putrescent in its stagnant bed,
    Save where the shamble oozings fringe it red,
Or scaffold trickles, or nocturnal crimes.

It holds dropped gold; dead flowers from tropic climes;
    Gems true and false, by midnight maskers shed;
    Old pots of rouge; old broken phials that spread
Vague fumes of musk, with fumes from slums and slimes.

And everywhere, as glows the set of day,
    There floats upon the winding fetid mire
The gorgeous iridescence of decay:

A wavy film of colour, gold and fire,
   Trembles all through it as you pick your way,
And streaks of purple that are straight from Tyre.

EUGENE LEE-HAMILTON
*Sonnets of the Wingless Hours* (1894)

## Hothouse Flowers

I hate the flower of wood or common field.
I cannot love the primrose nor regret
The death of any shrinking violet,
Nor even the cultured garden's banal yield.

The silver lips of lilies virginal,
The full deep bosom of the enchanted rose
Please less than flowers glass-hid from frosts and snows
For whom an alien heat makes festival.

I love those flowers reared by man's careful art,
Of heady scents and colours: strong of heart
Or weak that die beneath the touch or knife,

Some rich as sin and some as virtue pale,
And some as subtly infamous and frail
As she whose love still eats my soul and life.

THEODORE WRATISLAW
*Orchids* (1896)

## Art and Life

When autumn comes, my orchard trees alone,
Shall bear no fruit to deck the reddening year –
  When apple gatherers climb the branches sere
Only on mine no harvest shall be grown.
For when the pearly blossom first was blown,
  I filled my hands with delicate buds and dear,
  I dipped them in thine icy waters clear,
O well of Art! and turned them all to stone.

Therefore, when winter comes, I shall not eat
Of mellow apples such as others prize:
  I shall go hungry in a magic spring! –
All round my head and bright before mine eyes
The barren, strange, eternal blossoms meet,
  While I, not less an-hungered, gaze and sing.

A. MARY F. ROBINSON
*Lyrics Selected from the Works* (1891)

## Décor de Théâtre

### 1. BEHIND THE SCENES: EMPIRE

The little painted angels flit,
  See, down the narrow staircase, where
The pink legs flicker over it!

Blonde, and bewigged, and winged with gold,
  The shining creatures of the air
Troop sadly, shivering with cold.

The gusty gaslight shoots a thin
  Sharp finger over cheeks and nose
  Rouged to the colour of the rose.

All wigs and paint, they hurry in:
   Then, bid their radiant moment be
   The footlights' immortality!

ARTHUR SYMONS
*London Nights* (2nd edition 1897)

## Prologue

My life is like a music-hall,
   Where, in the impotence of rage,
Chained by enchantment to my stall,
   I see myself upon the stage
Dance to amuse a music-hall.

'Tis I that smoke this cigarette,
   Lounge here, and laugh for vacancy,
And watch the dancers turn; and yet
   It is my very self I see
Across the cloudy cigarette.

My very self that turns and trips,
   Painted, pathetically gay,
An empty song upon the lips
   In make-believe of holiday:
I, I, this thing that turns and trips!

The light flares in the music-hall,
   The light, the sound, that weary us;
Hour follows hour, I count them all,
   Lagging, and loud, and riotous:
My life is like a music-hall.

ARTHUR SYMONS
*London Nights* (2nd edition 1897)

## The Music-hall

The curtain on the grouping dancers falls,
The heaven of colour has vanished from our eyes;
Stirred in our seats we wait with vague surmise
What haply comes that please or that palls.

Touched on the stand the thrice-struck baton calls,
Once more I watch the unfolding curtain rise,
I hear the exultant violins premise
The well-known tune that thrills me and enthralls.

Then trembling in my joy I see you flash
Before the footlights to the cymbals' clash,
With laughing lips, swift feet, and brilliant glance,

You, fair as heaven and as a rainbow bright,
You, queen of song and empress of the dance,
Flower of mine eyes, my love, my heart's delight!

THEODORE WRATISLAW
*Caprices* (1893)

## Maquillage

The charm of rouge on fragile cheeks,
Pearl-powder, and, about the eyes,
The dark and lustrous Eastern dyes;
The floating odour that bespeaks
A scented boudoir and the doubtful night
Of alcoves curtained close against the light.

Gracile and creamy white and rose,
    Complexioned like the flower of dawn,
Her fleeting colours are as those
    That, from an April sky withdrawn,

Fade in a fragrant mist of tears away
When weeping noon leads on the altered day.

ARTHUR SYMONS
*Silhouettes* (2nd edition 1896)

## The White Statue

I love you, silent statue! for your sake
My songs in prayer upreach
Frail hands of flame-like speech
That some mauve-silver twilight you may wake!

I love you more than swallows love the south,
As sunflowers turn and turn
Towards the sun, I yearn
To press warm lips against your cold white mouth!

I love you more than scarlet skirted dawn,
At sight of whose spread wings
The great world wakes and sings;
Forgetful of the long, vague dark withdrawn.

I love you most at purple sunsetting:
When night with feverish eyes
Comes up the fading skies,
I love you with a passion past forgetting.

OLIVE CUSTANCE
*Opals* (1897)

## The Legend of J. J. Jackson the Self-Made Man

He stood upon the bartizan
    Of his new fangled tower,
The proudest and self-madest man
    The moon beheld that hour.

He thought on how he'd made his way,
  On what he'd been before,
And dreamily he murmured: 'J.
  J. Jackson'. Nothing more.

There was no echo that replied,
  Yet his low tone, I wis,
Like a strange summons, seemed to glide
  Through all the edifice.

He gazed around, his blood ran cold.
  What sight could thus appal?
Himself in fresco as of old?
  *But it had left the wall.*

Costly medallions, busts of clay,
  Came looming on afar,
And drearily he murmured: 'J.
  J. Jackson. Here we are!'

Some baneful influence down the stair
  His heavy steps impelled.
At every stage, the Jackson there
  The ghostly concourse swelled.

The green bronze Jackson leaves his stand,
  The green bronze Jackson walks!
The water-colour Jackson, and
  A Jackson done in chalks!

The drawing-room, wide open set,
  His frenzied glance surveyed.
The Parian Jackson statuette
  Was taking off his shade.

Only with bland, benignant air
  The portrait hung the same –
And yet, a form one would not care
  To meet *without* his frame.

Jackson in oils, life size, and all
   Complete. He looked once more.
The frame alone was on the wall,
   The portrait on the floor.

He counted by the moonlight's ray
   The foes he sought to shun,
And bitterly he moaned: '*Twelve* J.
   J. Jacksons against one!'

He turned in mortal horror, yet
   One hope he pondered o'er.
'At least,' he muttered, 'I can get
   Before them to the door!'

Then faltered with a look of dread:
   'The Statue!' That was all.
His alabaster arms outspread
   The Jackson in the hall.

He clasped him in the moonlight grey.
   He banged him on the floor,
He laughed a marble laugh, and J.
   J. Jackson was no more!

And lo! the grisly murmurs run
   From floor to bartizan:
'Why *are* so many portraits done
   Of any self-made man?'

MAY KENDALL
*Songs from Dreamland* (1894)

## By the Statue of King Charles at Charing Cross

Sombre and rich, the skies;
Great glooms, and starry plains.
Gently the night wind sighs;
Else a vast silence reigns.

The splendid silence clings
Around me: and around
The saddest of all kings
Crowned, and again discrowned.

Comely and calm, he rides
Hard by his own Whitehall:
Only the night wind glides:
No crowds, nor rebels, brawl.

Gone, too, his Court: and yet,
The stars his courtiers are:
Stars in their stations set;
And every wandering star.

Alone he rides, alone,
The fair and fatal king:
Dark night is all his own,
That strange and solemn thing.

Which are more full of fate:
The stars; or those sad eyes?
Which are more still and great:
Those brows; or the dark skies?

Although his whole heart yearn
In passionate tragedy:
Never was face so stern
With sweet austerity.

Vanquished in life, his death
By beauty made amends:
The passing of his breath
Won his defeated ends.

Brief life, and hapless? Nay:
Through death, life grew sublime.
*Speak after sentence?* Yea:
And to the end of time.

Armoured he rides, his head
Bare to the stars of doom:
He triumphs now, the dead,
Beholding London's gloom.

Our wearier spirit faints,
Vexed in the world's employ:
His soul was of the saints;
And art to him was joy.

King, tried in fires of woe!
Men hunger for thy grace:
And through the night I go,
Loving thy mournful face.

Yet, when the city sleeps;
When all the cries are still:
The stars and heavenly deeps
Work out a perfect will.

LIONEL JOHNSON
*Poems* (1895)


## *La Gioconda*

### LEONARDO DA VINCI

#### *The Louvre*

Historic, side-long, implicating eyes;
A smile of velvet's lustre on the cheek;
Calm lips the smile leads upward; hand that lies
Glowing and soft, the patience in its rest
Of cruelty that waits and doth not seek
For prey; a dusky forehead and a breast
Where twilight touches ripeness amorously:
Behind her, crystal rocks, a sea and skies

Of evanescent blue on cloud and creek;
Landscape that shines suppressive of its zest
For those vicissitudes by which men die.

MICHAEL FIELD
*Sight and Song* (1892)

## To Milton, – Blind

He who said suddenly, 'Let there be light!'
To thee the dark deliberately gave;
That those full eyes might undistracted be
By this beguiling show of sky and field,
This brilliance, that so lures us from the Truth.
He gave thee back original night, His own
Tremendous canvas, large and blank and free,
Where at each thought a star flashed out and sang.
O blinded with a special lightning, thou
Hadst once again the virgin Dark! and when
The pleasant flowery sight, which had deterred
Thine eyes from seeing, when this recent world
Was quite withdrawn; then burst upon thy view
The elder glory; space again in pangs,
And Eden odorous in the early mist,
That heaving watery plain that *was* the world;
Then the burned earth, and Christ coming in clouds.
Or rather a special leave to thee was given
By the high power, and thou with bandaged eyes
Wast guided through the glimmering camp of God.
Thy hand was taken by angels who patrol
The evening, or are sentries to the dawn,
Or pace the wide air everlastingly.
Thou wast admitted to the presence, and deep
Argument heardest, and the large design
That brings this world out of the woe to bliss.

STEPHEN PHILLIPS
*Poems* (1898)

## Plato in London

The pure flame of one taper fall
Over the old and comely page:
No harsher light disturb at all
This converse with a treasured sage.
Seemly, and fair, and of the best,
  If Plato be our guest,
  Should things befall.

Without, a world of noise and cold:
Here, the soft burning of the fire.
And Plato walks, where heavens unfold,
About the home of his desire.
From his own city of high things,
  He shows to us, and brings,
  Truth of fine gold.

The hours pass; and the fire burns low;
The clear flame dwindles into death:
Shut then the book with care; and so,
Take leave of Plato, with hushed breath:
A little, by the falling gleams,
  Tarry the gracious dreams:
  And they too go.

Lean from the window to the air:
Hear London's voice upon the night!
Thou hast bold converse with things rare:
Look now upon another sight!
The calm stars, in their living skies:
  And then, these surging cries,
  This restless glare!

That starry music, starry fire,
High above all our noise and glare:
The image of our long desire,

The beauty, and the strength, are there.
And Plato's thought lives, true and clear,
    In as august a sphere:
    Perchance, far higher.

LIONEL JOHNSON
*Poems* (1895)

## The Three Musicians

Along the path that skirts the wood,
    The three musicians wend their way,
Pleased with their thoughts, each other's mood,
    Franz Himmel's latest roundelay,
The morning's work, a new-found theme, their breakfast and
        the summer day.

One's a soprano, lightly frocked
    In cool, white muslin that just shows
Her brown silk stockings gaily clocked,
    Plump arms and elbows tipped with rose,
And frills of petticoats and things, and outlines as the warm
        wind blows.

Beside her a slim, gracious boy
    Hastens to mend her tresses' fall,
And dies her favour to enjoy,
    And dies for *réclame* and recall
At Paris and St Petersburg, Vienna and St James's Hall.

The third's a Polish Pianist
    With big engagements everywhere,
A light heart and an iron wrist,
    And shocks and shoals of yellow hair,
And fingers that can trill on sixths and fill beginners with despair.

The three musicians stroll along
    And pluck the ears of ripened corn,
Break into odds and ends of song,

And mock the woods with Siegfried's horn,
And fill the air with Gluck, and fill the tweeded tourist's soul
          with scorn.

  The Polish genius lags behind,
      And, with some poppies in his hand,
  Picks out the strings and wood and wind
      Of an imaginary band,
Enchanted that for once his men obey his beat and understand.

  The charming cantatrice reclines
      And rests a moment where she sees
  Her château's roof that hotly shines
      Amid the dusky summer trees,
And fans herself, half shuts her eyes, and smoothes the frock
          about her knees.

  The gracious boy is at her feet,
      And weighs his courage with his chance;
  His fears soon melt in noonday heat.
      The tourist gives a furious glance,
Red as his guide-book grows, moves on, and offers up a prayer
          for France.

AUBREY BEARDSLEY
In *The Savoy* (1896)

## *The Fiddler of Dooney*

When I play on my fiddle in Dooney,
Folk dance like a wave of the sea;
My cousin is priest in Kilvarnet,
My brother in Moharabuiee.

I passed my brother and cousin:
They read in their books of prayers;
I read in my book of songs
I bought at the Sligo fair.

When we come at the end of time,
To Peter sitting in state,
He will smile on the three old spirits,
But call me first through the gate;

For the good are always the merry,
Save by an evil chance,
And the merry love the fiddle
And the merry love to dance:

And when the folk there spy me,
They will all come up to me,
With 'Here is the fiddler of Dooney!'
And dance like a wave of the sea.

W. B. YEATS
*The Wind Among the Reeds* (1899)


## Javanese Dancers

Twitched strings, the clang of metal, beaten drums,
  Dull, shrill, continuous, disquieting;
And now the stealthy dancer comes
  Undulantly with cat-like steps that cling;

Smiling between her painted lids a smile,
  Motionless, unintelligible, she twines
  Her fingers into mazy lines,
Twining her scarves across them all the while.

One, two, three, four step forth, and, to and fro,
  Delicately and imperceptibly,
Now swaying gently in a row,
  Now interthreading slow and rhythmically,

Still with fixed eyes, monotonously still,
  Mysteriously, with smiles inanimate,
  With lingering feet that undulate,
With sinuous fingers, spectral hands that thrill,

The little amber-coloured dancers move,
  Like little painted figures on a screen,
  Or phantom-dancers haply seen
Among the shadows of a magic grove.

ARTHUR SYMONS
*Silhouettes* (2nd edition 1896)

# 2. THE MAKING OF THE
# NEW WOMAN

The New Woman was as important a figure of the 1890s as the decadent. In fact the New Woman was in some ways the female equivalent of the dandy, striving to rescue herself from the Victorian idea of womanhood and create herself in a new image. Most late Victorians believed – as Linda Dowling phrases it in her article 'The Decadent and the New Woman in the 1890's'[1] – that 'the decadent was new and the New Woman decadent'. Both were seen as aping the opposite sex in a most unbecoming and socially anarchic way: 'a yellow aster, was, after all, nothing more (or less) than the New Woman's green carnation' (again to quote Dowling). The New Woman eschewed the traditional feminine realm of domesticity, passivity and maternity, seeking instead intellectual, sexual and social freedom. She wanted to be physically and mentally active; she wanted the choice of occupations that was available to men; and most of all she wanted real education and a public voice.

Constance Naden and Michael Field were clearly of this type. Naden publicly aligned herself with the dress reformers who rejected the restrictive clothing that wealthy women wore as a signal that they did not – because in those clothes they could not – work. She also lectured on the need for women's suffrage. As president of a ladies' debating society, she argued that the club aimed at 'making us braver, stronger, and more resolute'; and in her inaugural speech she advocated the meetings of the society as a safe arena for women to practise speaking out. 'Education', she proclaimed, 'is given us that we may think for ourselves, feel for ourselves, act for ourselves; why then should we not speak for ourselves?'[2]

The aunt and niece partnership who wrote under the name

1. Linda Dowling, 'The Decadent and the New Woman in the 1890's', *Nineteenth Century Fiction*, 33 (1978–9).
2. 'Inaugural Address of the Session 1883–1884', Presidential address to the Edgbaston Ladies' Debating Society, delivered on 24 October 1883; in the *Third Annual Report* of the Ladies' Debating Society, session 1882–3, 10–27.

Michael Field also declared themselves 'New'. Their biographer, Mary Sturgeon, describes the late nineteenth century as an era when 'Higher Education and Women's Rights and Anti-Vivisection were being indignantly championed, and when "Aesthetic dress" was being very consciously worn – all by the same kind of people. Katharine and Edith were of that kind'.

Many women poets of the 1890s discuss the social position of women, and their writing charts women's gradual assertion of control over their role in society as they escaped the old restricting stereotypes. This process begins with an examination of the limited roles society traditionally allowed Victorian women. For example, the mirror imagery which Naden and Robinson use to complain about the damaging role women were expected to adopt in relation to men is a leitmotif of women's writing of this period. Robinson's use of the garden as an image of the feminine sphere is also typical. Women writers of the period often used the association of women with flowers and the garden – most notoriously expressed by Ruskin in *Sesame and Lilies* (1865) – in order to subvert it. The walled garden became an image of imprisonment, often containing a distressed and lonely inmate.

Humour is an important, and little recognized, strategy for these writers, allowing them explicitly to criticize the roles they are expected to fulfil. In 'The Goose-Girl', for example, Nesbit satirizes the sentimental, fairy-tale vision which the male lover expects the girl to conform to, by having her play him at his own game.

As well as criticizing the traditional roles, these poets also offer new ones. The two Michael Field poems show women actively in control of their fate and the part they play in life. Finally we see the emergence of the New Woman and her struggles to pursue her learning, her art or her career. Allowed to be either a traditional feminine woman or an intellectual but unsexed being, she is forced to weigh up the choice of 'love versus learning'. The result of women's enfranchisement is 'The New Orthodoxy' in which New Woman and confused traditional man try to get it together.

## Love's Mirror

I live with love encompassed round,
    And glowing light that is not mine,
        And yet am sad; for, truth to tell,
        It is not I you love so well;
Some fair Immortal, robed and crowned,
    You hold within your heart's dear shrine.

Cast out the Goddess! let me in;
    Faulty I am, yet all your own,
    But this bright phantom you enthrone
Is such as mortal may not win.

And yet this beauty that you see
    Is like to mine, though nobler far;
Your radiant guest resembles me
    E'en as the sun is like a star.

Then keep her in your heart of hearts,
    And let me look upon her face,
    And learn of that transcendent grace,
Till all my meaner self departs,

And, while I love you more and more,
    My spirit, gazing on the light,
    Becomes, in loveliness and might,
The glorious Vision you adore.

CONSTANCE NADEN
*The Complete Poetical Works* (1894)


## An Oasis

You wandered in the desert waste, athirst;
    My soul I gave you as a well to drink;
    A little while you lingered at the brink,
And then you went, nor either blessed or cursed.

The image of your face, which sank that day
  Into the magic waters of the well,
  Still haunts their clearness, still remains to tell
Of one who looked and drank and could not stay.

The sun shines down, the moon slants over it,
  The stars look in and are reflected not;
  Only your face, unchanged and unforgot,
Shines through the deep, till all the waves are lit.

My soul I gave you as a well to drink,
  And in its depths your face is clearer far
  Than any shine of sun or moon or star –
Since then you pause by many a greener brink.


A. MARY F. ROBINSON
*Lyrics Selected from the Works* (1891)

## The Forest Pool

Lean down and see your little face
  Reflected in the forest pool,
Tall foxgloves grow about the place,
  Forget-me-nots grow green and cool.
Look deep and see the naiad rise
To meet the sunshine of your eyes.

Lean down and see how you are fair,
  How gold your hair, your mouth how red;
See the leaves dance about your hair
  The wind has left unfilleted.
What naiad of them can compare
With you for good and dear and fair?

Ah! look no more – the water stirs,
  The naiad weeps your face to see,
Your beauty is more rare than hers,

And you are more beloved than she.
Fly! fly, before she steals the charms
The pool has trusted to her arms.

EDITH NESBIT
*Songs of Love and Empire* (1898)

## In the Toy Shop

The child had longings all unspoken –
   She was a naughty child.
She had 'a will that must be broken';
   Her brothers drove her wild.
She read the tale, but skipped the moral.
   *She* thought: 'One *might* be good,
If one could never scream and quarrel,
   If one were only wood!'

Meanwhile the doll: 'Ah, fatal chasm!
   Although I've real curls,
I am not made of protoplasm,
   Like other little girls.
You see on every wooden feature
   My animation's nil.
How nice to be a human creature,
   Get cross, and have a will!'

And what may be the real issue
   There's none hath understood;
But some of us are nervous tissue,
   And some of us are wood.
And some to suffering, striving wildly,
   Are never quite resigned;
While we of wood yet murmur mildly
   At being left behind.

MAY KENDALL
*Songs from Dreamland* (1894)

## Celia's Home-Coming

Maidens, kilt your skirts and go
   Down the stormy garden-ways,
Pluck the last sweet pinks that blow,
   Gather roses, gather bays,
Since our Celia comes to-day
That has been too long away.

Crowd her chamber with your sweets –
   Not a flower but grows for her!
Make her bed with linen sheets
   That have lain in lavender;
Light a fire before she come
Lest she find us chill at home.

Ah, what joy when Celia stands
   By the leaping blaze at last
Stooping down to warm her hands
   All benumbèd with the blast,
While we hide her cloak away
To assure us of her stay.

Cyder bring and cowslip wine,
   Fruits and flavours from the East,
Pears and pippins too, and fine
   Saffron loaves to make a feast:
China dishes, silver cups,
For the board where Celia sups!

Then, when all the feasting's done,
   She shall draw us round the blaze,
Laugh, and tell us every one
   Of her far triumphant days –
Celia, out of doors a star,
By the hearth a holier Lar!

A. MARY F. ROBINSON
*Lyrics Selected from the Works* (1891)

## The Barrier

Last night I dreamed I stood once more
    Beneath our garden wall.
I saw the willows bending grey,
    The poplar springing tall.

O paths where oft I plucked the rose,
    O steeple in the sky,
O Common swelling darkly green,
    How glad at heart was I!

My hand I raised to lift the latch,
    But lo, the gate was gone!
And all around, ay, all around
    There ran a wall of stone . . .

O years when oft we plucked the rose,
    When oft we laughed and cried!
Thou hast no gate, O Youth, our Youth,
    When once we stand outside!

A. MARY F. ROBINSON
*Retrospect, and Other Poems* (1893)


## The Last Ditch

Love, through your varied views on Art
    Untiring have I followed you,
Content to know I had your heart
    And was your Art-ideal, too.

As, dear, I was when first we met.
    ('Twas at the time you worshipped Leighton,
And were attempting to forget
    Your Foster and your Noel Paton.)

'Love rhymes with Art,' said your dear voice,
    And, at my crude, uncultured age,
I could but blushingly rejoice
    That you had passed the Rubens stage.

When Madox Brown and Morris swayed
    Your taste, did I not dress and look
Like any Middle Ages maid
    In an illuminated book?

I wore strange garments, without shame,
    Of formless form and toneless tones,
I might have stepped out of the frame
    Of a Rossetti or Burne-Jones.

I stole soft frills from Marcus Stone,
    My waist wore Herkomer's disguise,
My slender purse was strained, I own,
    But – my silk lay as Sargent's lies.

And when you were abroad – in Prague –
    'Mid Cherets I had shone, a star;
Then for your sake I grew as vague
    As Mr Whistler's ladies are.

But now at last you sue in vain,
    For here a life's submission ends:
Not even for you will I grow plain
    As Aubrey Beardsley's 'lady friends.'

Here I renounce your hand – unless
    You find your Art-ideal elsewhere;
I *will not* wear the kind of dress
    That Laurence Housman's people wear!

EDITH NESBIT
*A Pomander of Verse* (1895)

## The Goose-Girl

I wandered lonely by the sea,
　　As is my daily use,
I saw her drive across the lea
　　The gander and the goose.
The gander and the gray, gray goose,
　　She drove them all together;
Her cheeks were rose, her gold hair loose,
　　All in the wild gray weather.

'O dainty maid who drive the geese
　　Across the common wide,
Turn, turn your pretty back on these
　　And come and be my bride.
I am a poet from the town,
　　And, 'mid the ladies there,
There is not one would wear a crown
　　With half your charming air!'

She laughed, she shook her pretty head.
　　'I want no poet's hand;
Go read your fairy-books,' she said,
　　'For this is fairy-land.
My Prince comes riding o'er the leas;
　　He fitly comes to woo,
For I'm a Princess, and my geese
　　Were poets, once, like you!'

EDITH NESBIT
*Songs of Love and Empire* (1898)

## Posies

I made a posy for my love
    As fair as she is soft and fine:
The lilac thrift I made it of,
    And lemon-yellow columbine.

But woe is me for my despair,
    For my pale flowers, woe is me
A bolder man has given her
    A branch of crimson peony!

A. MARY F. ROBINSON
*Lyrics Selected from the Works* (1891)


## A Portrait

### BARTOLOMMEO VENETO

*The Städel'sche Institut at Frankfurt*

A crystal, flawless beauty on the brows
Where neither love nor time has conquered space
On which to live; her leftward smile endows
The gazer with no tidings from the face;
About the clear mounds of the lip it winds with silvery pace
    And in the umber eyes it is a light
Chill as a glowworm's when the moon embrowns an August night.

She saw her beauty often in the glass,
Sharp on the dazzling surface, and she knew
The haughty custom of her grace must pass:
Though more persistent in all charm it grew
As with a desperate joy her hair across her throat she drew
    In crinkled locks stiff as dead, yellow snakes . . .
Until at last within her soul the resolution wakes

She will be painted, she who is so strong
    In loveliness, so fugitive in years:
Forth to the field she goes and questions long
    Which flowers to choose of those the summer bears;
She plucks a violet larkspur, – then a columbine appears
    Of perfect yellow, – daisies choicely wide;
These simple things with finest touch she gathers in her pride.

Next on her head, veiled with well-bleachen white
    And bound across the brow with azure-blue,
    She sets the box-tree leaf and coils it tight
    In spiky wreath of green, immortal hue;
Then, to the prompting of her strange, emphatic insight true,
    She bares one breast, half-freeing it of robe,
And hangs green-water gem and cord beside the naked globe.

    So was she painted and for centuries
    Has held the fading field-flowers in her hand
    Austerely as a sign. O fearful eyes
    And soft lips of the courtesan who planned
To give her fragile shapeliness to art, whose reason spanned
    Her doom, who bade her beauty in its cold
And vacant eminence persist for all men to behold!

    She had no memories save of herself
    And her slow-fostered graces, naught to say
    Of love in gift or boon; her cruel pelf
    Had left her with no hopes that grow and stay;
She found default in everything that happened night or day,
    Yet stooped in calm to passion's dizziest strife
And gave to art a fair, blank form, unverified by life.

    Thus has she conquered death: her eyes are fresh,
    Clear as her frontlet jewel, firm in shade
    And definite as on the linen mesh
    Of her white hood the box-tree's sombre braid,
That glitters leaf by leaf and with the year's waste will not fade.
    The small, close mouth, leaving no room for breath,
In perfect, still pollution smiles – Lo, she has conquered death!

MICHAEL FIELD
*Sight and Song* (1892)

## 'I would not be a fugitive'

I would not be a fugitive
Far in the past amid the olden,
Fond times men labour to recover,
But in the age, ah, verily the golden,
When first a girl dares to become a lover.

How sweeter far it is to give
Than just to rest in the receiving,
Sweeter to sigh than be sighed over,
Sweeter to deal the blow than bear the grieving,
That girl will learn who dares become a lover.

The songs she sings will have the glee,
The laughter of the wind that looses
Wing and breaks from a forest cover;
Freedom of stream that slips its icy nooses
Will be her freedom who becomes a lover.

What Eden unto Eve the tree
Of Life to pluck, to eat unchidden,
Then as a hostess to discover
To man the feast, himself a guest new-bidden,
Now she at last dares to become his lover!

MICHAEL FIELD
*Underneath the Bough* (1893)

## *Love* versus *Learning*

Alas, for the blight of my fancies!
Alas, for the fall of my pride!
I planned, in my girlish romances,
To be a philosopher's bride.

I pictured him learned and witty,
  The sage and the lover combined,
Not scorning to say I was pretty,
  Nor only adoring my *mind*.

No elderly, spectacled Mentor,
  But one who would worship and woo;
Perhaps I might take an inventor,
  Or even a poet would do.

And tender and gay and well-favoured,
  My fate overtook me at last:
I saw, and I heard, and I wavered,
  I smiled, and my freedom was past.

He promised to love me for ever,
  He pleaded, and what could I say?
I thought he must surely be clever,
  For he is an Oxford M.A.

But now, I begin to discover
  My visions are fatally marred;
Perfection itself as a lover,
  He's neither a sage nor a bard.

He's mastered the usual knowledge,
  And says it's a terrible bore;
He formed his opinions at college,
  Then why should he think any more?

My logic he sets at defiance,
  Declares that my Latin's no use,
And when I begin to talk Science
  He calls me a dear little goose.

He says that my lips are too rosy
  To speak in a language that's dead,
And all that is dismal and prosy
  Should fly from so sunny a head.

He scoffs at each grave occupation,
   Turns everything off with a pun;
And says that his sole calculation
   Is how to make two into one.

He says Mathematics may vary,
   Geometry cease to be true,
But scorning the slightest vagary
   He still will continue to woo.

He says that the sun may stop action,
   But he will not swerve from his course;
For love is his law of attraction,
   A smile his centripetal force.

His levity's truly terrific,
   And often I think we must part,
But compliments so scientific
   Recapture my fluttering heart.

Yet sometimes 'tis very confusing,
   This conflict of love and of lore –
But hark! I must cease from my musing,
   For that is his knock at the door!

CONSTANCE NADEN
*The Complete Poetical Works* (1894)


## A Legend

The setting sun an aureole made
About her hair. With eyes that strayed
Not from the book – 'Lord God,' she prayed,

And ended not – for in the door
Her women beckoned – 'Lady, sore
In need three pilgrims alms implore.'

And she fared forth those three to greet,
And set before them wine and meat,
And bathed and kissed their way-worn feet,

In honour of three that, angel-told,
Took their long journey – one growing old –
One weeping she could not warmer fold
Her little Babe that wept for cold.

Dying was the sunset fire and flare
When at length she, climbing again the stair,
Returned untroubled to her prayer.

'Lord God,' began she – and from the hall
Came sudden shrilling clamour and call
Of her young children playing at ball,

With wrath of two, and tears of one,
And in the door her eldest son,
Breathless and beckoning, urged her, 'Run,

'Sweet mother of mine! for sturdy blow
My brothers each on each bestow,
And stint not —' Then, with no least show

Or of reluctance or annoy,
In honour of one whose dear employ
Was to tend God, a little Boy –
Whom God called Mother and served with joy,

Descending, she, with gentlest word,
Sweetly through all the outcry heard,
Chid softly two and kissed the third,

And hushed and healed their strife perplexed,
And up and down played with them next,
And to her prayer returned unvexed.

Red glory of the west was gone –
The first star white in the lattice shone –
'Lord God,' she prayed – and on the stone

Rang steps, and she was 'ware, before
The next word, of her husband in the door,
And blood that trickled to the floor.

'My half-tamed falcon,' said he, 'missed
The prey I tossed, and, ere I wist,
'Twixt rage and sport she rent my wrist –

'Wilt balsam bring to cure the smart?
None virtue hath as thine, dear heart.'
Unfretted she set her book apart,

In honour of him, whom Mary Maid
And Mother and Queen herself obeyed,
At bidding of whom she went or stayed,
Nor murmured once nor once delayed.

Washed she and bound his hurt with care,
Nor time did count, nor labour spare,
And yet again turned back to her prayer.

Dusk was the lattice – and behold!
On the page the Collect still untold
Stood written in letters of pure gold.

MAY PROBYN
*Pansies* (1895)

## The Sister of Mercy

Speak not of passion, for my heart is tired,
I should but grieve thee with unheeding ears;
Speak not of hope, nor flash thy soul inspired
In haggard eyes, that do but shine with tears.
Think not I weep because my task is o'er;
This is but weakness – I must rest to-day:
Nay, let me bid farewell and go my way,
Then shall I soon be patient as before.

Yes, thou art grateful, that I nursed thee well;
This is not love, for love comes swift and free:
Yet might I long with one so kind to dwell,
Cared for as in thy need I cared for thee:
And sometimes when at night beside thy bed
I sat and held thy hand, or bathed thy head,
And heard the wild delirious words, and knew
Even by these, how brave thou wert, and true,
Almost I loved – but many valiant men
These hands have tended, and shall tend again;
And now thou art not fevered or distressed
I hold thee nothing dearer than the rest.
Nay, tell me not thy strong young heart will break
If to thy prayer such cold response I make;
It will not break – hearts cannot break, I know,
Or this weak heart had broken long ago.
Ah no! I would not love thee, if I could;
And when I cry, in some rebellious mood,
'To live for others is to live alone;
Oh, for a love that is not gratitude,
Oh, for a little joy that is my own!'
Then shall I think of thee, and shall be strong,
Knowing thee noblest, best, yet undesired:
Ah, for what other, by what passion fired,
Could I desert my life-work, loved so long?
I marvel grief like thine can move me still,
Who have seen death, and worse than death, ere now –
Nay, look not glad, rise up; thou shalt not bow
Thy knee, as if these tears thy hope fulfil:
Farewell! I am not bound by any vow;
This is the voice of mine own steadfast will.

CONSTANCE NADEN
*The Complete Poetical Works* (1894)

## Love, Death, and Art

Lord, give me Love! give me the silent bliss
Of meeting souls, of answering eyes and hands;
The comfort of one heart that understands;
The thrill and rapture of Love's sealing kiss.

Or grant me – lest I weary of all this –
The quiet of Death's unimagined lands,
Wherein the longed-for Tree of Knowledge stands,
Where Thou art, Lord – and the great mysteries.

Nay, let me sing, my God, and I'll forego,
Love's smiling mouth, Death's sweetlier smiling eyes.
Better my life long mourn in glorious woe,
Than love unheard in a mute Paradise –

For no grief, no despair, can quail me long,
While I can make these sweet to me in song.

A. MARY F. ROBINSON
*Lyrics Selected from the Works* (1891)

## Love and the Muse

Struck down by Love in cruel mood,
That ever I met Love I rued,
    Bleeding and bruised I lay,
Wet was my face as with the salt sea spray.

A lovely Muse on sparkling wing
A painless elemental thing,
    Free as a bird did float,
Swift flames of song light leaping from her throat.

And being more pitiful that Love
Stooped glowing from her path above.
    And an unearthly kiss
Laid on my lips: Muse, answer, what is this?

In dreams or drunkenness divine
My life is all transfused with thine;
  Like bubbles swept along,
My tears dissolve on cataracts of song.

MATHILDE BLIND
*The Poetical Works* (1900)

## *The New Orthodoxy*

So, dear Fred, you're not content
Though I quote the books you lent,
And I've kept that spray you sent
  Of the milk-white heather;
For you fear I'm too 'advanced'
To remember all that chanced
In the old days, when we danced,
  Walked, and rode together.

Trust me, Fred, beneath the curls
Of the most 'advanced' of girls,
Many a foolish fancy whirls,
  Bidding Fact defiance,
And the simplest village maid
Needs not to be much afraid
Of her sister, sage and staid,
  Bachelor of Science.

Ah! while yet our hope was new
Guardians thought 'twould never do
That Sir Frederick's heir should woo
  Little Amy Merton:
So the budding joy they snatched
From our hearts, so meetly matched –
You to Oxford they despatched,
  Me they sent to Girton.

Were the vows all writ in dust?
No – you're one-and-twenty – just –
And you write – 'We will, we must
   Now, at once, be married!'
Nay, you plan the wedding trip!
Softly, sir! there's many a slip
Ere the goblet to the lip
   Finally is carried.

Oh, the wicked tales I hear!
Not that you at Ruskin jeer,
Nor that at Carlyle you sneer
   With his growls dyspeptic:
But that, having read in vain
Huxley, Tyndall, Clifford, Bain,
All the scientific train –
   You're a hardened sceptic!

Things with fin, and claw, and hoof
Join to give us perfect proof
That our being's warp and woof
   We from near and far win;
Yet your flippant doubts you vaunt,
And – to please a maiden aunt –
You've been heard to say you can't
   Pin your faith to Darwin!

Then you jest, because Laplace
Said this Earth was nought but gas
Till the vast rotating mass
   Denser grew and denser:
Something worse they whisper too,
But I'm sure it *can't* be true –
For they tell me, Fred, that you
   Scoff at Herbert Spencer!

Write – or telegraph – or call!
Come yourself and tell me all:
No fond hope shall me enthrall,

No regret shall sway me:
Yet – until the worst is said,
Till I know your faith is dead,
I remain, dear doubting Fred,
  Your believing
                    AMY

CONSTANCE NADEN
*The Complete Poetical Works* (1894)

# 3. *SHE* IS AN ARTIST, TOO

The New Woman won the right to pursue her learning and art. But she was soon to realize that the battle was only just begun. For the women who chose to write, the struggle with a poetic tradition which presumed the masculinity of the writer was intense. In the Romantic tradition of poetry inherited by the Victorians, the poet is, in Wordsworth's words, 'man speaking to men'; the dialectic which underpinned the poetics was that between a masculine poet and a feminine muse or model. The tradition of poetry available to these Victorian women poets was one in which they were the silent object to be looked at and written about. The position of the speaking subject was not one they, as women, could easily occupy.

One only has to read some of the critics of the age to see that Victorian poetics allowed women to be poems but not poets. This conviction is manifest in the (unintentionally) highly amusing preface which Eric Robertson wrote to his anthology *English Poetesses* in 1883 – which includes the work of Constance Naden and A. Mary F. Robinson, among others. He writes, with what he no doubt considers the height of generosity, that 'Children are the best poems Providence meant women to produce'. Robertson finds this a suitable compensation for his conviction that 'women have always been inferior to men as writers of poetry; and they always will be' (p. xv). Women's true contribution to poetry, he concludes, is 'the beauty of noble lives led by pure and able women' (p. xvi).

A prominent subject in the work of the women poets of the 1890s is the discussion, explicitly or implicitly, of their relationship with their art, and the problems they encounter in dealing with a masculine poetic tradition. The woman writer's alienation from the poetic tradition is figured again and again. In A. Mary F. Robinson's work, it is the world of Apollo and classical Greek myth which represents the masculine literary tradition with which she feels she is not in sympathy. The things she wants to say cannot be expressed through traditional poetic imagery. In a very different way, the two rather odd poems by Caroline Lindsay are expressive of a similar predicament. By stopping abruptly half-way through a narrative she indicates the lack of power and her own sense of inarticulacy to which working within the traditional poetics condemns her; the narrative voice is prematurely silenced.

Claiming the authoritative voice which was necessary to produce poetry was, for women of the nineteenth century, a highly problematic enterprise. The aim Naden voiced for a ladies' debating society, described in the previous section, shows how alien public expression was to the feminine role. Naden's poem 'Speech and Silence' and Robinson's 'Taking Possession' can be seen as reflections on this theme.

However, for all the problems encountered in attempting to write as women and as poets, these poets did develop strategies which would enable the two concepts to come together. Images of writing poetry as spinning and weaving typically occur in the poetry of women as they 'feminize' the activity, and pull it into their sphere. 'The Sonnet' is an explicit attempt to claim the association of poetry with a specifically female heritage. 'The Two Artists' is a witty poem which has this serious message at its heart.

Women poets developed their own feminine tradition of poetry with their own muse figures, their own methods of composition, and a focus on what are socially considered specifically 'feminine' qualities. The double-text, for example, which appears in the dual authorship gestured towards in 'A Girl' and in the palimpsest of 'The Ballad of the Flag Painter' is a recurring motif in the writing of women. This doubleness has become a key motif of the feminine in the twentieth-century feminist theory of Luce Irigaray. For her, while masculinity is phallocentric, feminity is multiple and diverse: woman is the sex 'which is not one'. Irigaray believes that 'we haven't been taught, nor allowed, to express multiplicity', but that to do so is to use a feminine form of expression.[1] The poetry of the 1890s is not only a moment sealed in history, but is also part of a progression which was already reaching out towards the modern literary landscape.

1. Luce Irigaray, *This Sex Which is Not One*, translated by Catherine Porter with Carolyn Burke (Ithaca, NY, 1985), p. 210.

## Going South

A little grey swallow,
    I fled to the vales
    Of the nightingales
And the haunts of Apollo.

Behind me lie the sheer white cliffs, the hollow
    Green waves that break at home, the northern gales,
    The oaks above the homesteads in the vales,
For all my home is far, and cannot follow.

            O nightingale voices!
            O lemons in flower!
            O branches of laurel!

You all are here, but ah not here my choice is:
    Fain would I pluck one pink-vein'd bloom of sorrel,
Or watch the wrens build in our hazel bower.

A. MARY F. ROBINSON
*Lyrics Selected from the Works* (1891)

## Foam Fancy

Over the sea,
In days long ago,
There came a white ship
From a land of snow.

It brought to the children
A bushel of toys,
It brought to the grown folks
Sweet blessings and joys.

It brought to all sad hearts
A message of peace,
And to some weary pilgrims
A word of release.

It brought to the poet
The song he loved best –
So begins the old legend;
I know not the rest.

CAROLINE LINDSAY
*Lyrics and Other Poems* (1890)

## A Romance

A little maid sat sewing,
    On the doorstep sewèd she:
'I'll bide me here till the hot noon's near,
    And my love rides back to me.'

He came. It was chilly evening;
    The tears from her eyelids fell;
But when he drew nigh the teardrops grew dry –
    And there's nothing more to tell.

CAROLINE LINDSAY
*Lyrics and Other Poems* (1890)

## A Classic Landscape

This wood might be some Grecian heritage
    Of the antique world, this hoary ilex wood;
    So broad the shade, so deep the solitude,
    So grey the air where Oread fancies brood.

Beyond, the fields are tall with purple sage;
    The sky bends downward like a purple sheet –
    A purple wind-filled sail – i' the noonday heat;
    And past the river shine the fields of wheat.

O tender wheat, O starry saxifrage,
   O deep-red tulips, how the fields are fair!
   Far off the mountains pierce the quivering air,
   Ash-coloured, mystical, remote, and bare.

How far they look, the Mountains of Mirage
   Or northern Hills of Heaven, how far away!
   In front the long paulonia-blossoms sway
   From leafless boughs across that dreamy grey.

O world, how worthy of a golden age!
   How might Theocritus have sung and found
   The Oreads here, the Naiads gathering round,
   Their pallid locks still dripping to the ground!

For me, O world, thou art how mere a stage,
   Whereon the human soul must act alone,
   In a dead language, with the plot unknown,
   Nor learn what happens when the play is done.

A. MARY F. ROBINSON
*Lyrics Selected from the Works* (1891)


## Old Songs

This song I wrote – ah me, how long ago!
   When up the stair of Heaven and down again
   (For even then I could not long remain),
With happy feet I used to come and go.

This ode I sang beneath a laurel bough
   Where I had sought for Truth among the dead;
   This little verse (and still the page is red),
To soothe some easier pang forgotten now.

I took the dew of lilies grown apart;
   The scanty wine of amphoras; and, bright
And clear, the blood that flows from trivial scars;

But with the bitter ink of mine own heart
   I have not written and I must not write,
      Let rust and acid dim the eternal stars.

A. MARY F. ROBINSON
*Lyrics Selected from the Works* (1891)

## Inspiration

I wandered in the enchanted wood,
   And as I wandered there, I sang
A song I never understood,
   Though sweet the music rang.

I held a lily white and fair,
   Its perfume was a song divine,
A song like moonlight and clear air,
   No rose-hued cloud like mine.

Beneath pale moon and wind-winged skies
   My lips were dumb as one drew near,
Folded warm wings across my eyes
   And whispered in my ear.

He left a flame-flower in my hand,
   And bade me sing as heretofore
The song I could not understand;
   But I can sing no more.

His secret seals my dumb lips fast,
   My lily withered 'neath his wing;
But now I understand at last
   The song I used to sing.

EDITH NESBIT
*A Pomander of Verse* (1895)

## Speech and Silence

When some sweet voice flows forth in foreign speech,
   The soul shines through the words, and makes them clear,
   And all we see interprets all we hear,
For smiles and frowns have wondrous power to teach:
And voiceless grief our inmost heart can reach,
   With calm, deep gaze, too sad for hope or fear:
   Our eyes are wet for those who shed no tear,
And lips that Death has silenced, yet may preach.

In stillness we must win our deepest lore,
   Or 'mid the speechless chant of earth and sea:
   Truth is a spirit, bodiless and free;
Imaged in words, 'tis perfect truth no more,
   For all our lofty visions fade and flee,
And song begins, when ecstasy is o'er.

CONSTANCE NADEN
*The Complete Poetical Works* (1894)

## Taking Possession

When, in the wastes of old, the Arabian Sheikh
   Beheld a sudden peace amid the sands,
   With springing waters and green pasture lands,
Fringed with the waving palm and cactus-spike,

Think ye he stayed to fashion fence or dyke?
   Nay! for he called into his hollowed hands
   Till all his hounds came trooping swift in bands:
Sheep-dog and wolf-hound, terrier, cur, and tyke,

They bayed with deep, full voices on the calm.
   Then he: 'So far as the last echoes die
The land is mine, pasture and spring and palm!'

So men who watch afar the Hope Divine
    Rally a pack of sectaries and cry:
'Behold the Land of Promise: ours, not thine!'

A. MARY F. ROBINSON
*Retrospect and Other Poems* (1893)

## The Two Artists

'Edith is fair,' the painter said,
    'Her cheek so richly glows,
My palette ne'er could match the red
    Of that pure damask rose.

'Perchance, the evening rain-drops light,
    Soft sprinkling from above,
Have caught the sunset's colour bright,
    And borne it to my love.

'In distant regions I must seek
    For tints before unknown,
Ere I can paint the brilliant cheek
    That blooms for me alone.'

All this his little sister heard,
    Who frolicked by his side;
To check such theories absurd,
    That gay young sprite replied:

'Oh, I can tell you where to get
    That pretty crimson bloom,
For in a bottle it is set
    In Cousin Edith's room.

'I'm sure that I could find the place,
    If you want some to keep;
I watched her put it on her face –
    She didn't see me peep!

'So nicely she laid on the pink,
    As well as *you* could do,
And really, I almost think
    *She* is an artist, too.'

The maddened painter tore his hair,
    And vowed he ne'er would wed,
And never since, to maiden fair,
    A tender word has said.

Bright ruby cheeks, and skin of pearl,
    He knows a shower may spoil,
And when he wants a blooming girl
    Paints one himself in oil.

CONSTANCE NADEN
*The Complete Poetical Works* (1894)

## The Song Spinner

Safe in my golden room of thought,
    I hear outside the rush and sweep
Of travel wearied wings of sin:
    I hear the tears of those that weep . . .
My musings are with visions fraught:
    To catch Love's voice my soul stands mute,
    Around me speechless memories flute
Vague threads of music to weave in
The songs of life I sit and spin.

I sit and spin the songs of life . . .
    About my knees proud flowers press,
Their leaves fold round me like soft wings,
    Their colours soothe as the caress
Of cool slim hands, and, like a knife
    Too sharp to hurt, their keen fresh scent
    Stabs through my senses to the pent
And passionate soul beyond that sings
Of mortal and immortal things . . .

Frail mystic perfume men call 'praise'!
  Star-sandaled memories moving slow . . .
Angels of hope with shimmerous hair . . .
  Pale dreams that waver to and fro:
By such as these are aureoled days
  Of song encompassed from rose-dawn
  To languorous drift of light out-worn . . .
The while I strive with fervid care . . .
Slow spinning the poem fabric fair!

OLIVE CUSTANCE
*Opals* (1897)


## The Sonnet

Sonnet, be not rebellious in my hands
  That ply the spindle oftener than the lute:
  Without our woman's singing thou wert mute,
O sonnet, born of us in sunnier lands!

Think, how the singing-women trooped in bands
  To seek the greenwood, dancing to the flute!
  Hast thou forgot the refrain dissolute?
The circling dance, the chant, the ivied wands?

Sonnet, a thousand years ago to-day
  Thou wast indeed the wild instinctive song
That women chaunted for the Feast of May!

But now, O solemn mirror of the mind,
  Now it is I am weak, and thou art strong,
Keep me a coign of clearness and be kind!

A. MARY F. ROBINSON
*Retrospect and Other Poems* (1893)

## *A Pastoral of Parnassus*

*'Ma io perchè venirvi? O chi'l concede?'*

At morning dawn I left my sheep
   And sought the mountains all aglow;
The shepherds said, 'The way is steep:
      Ah, do not go!'

I left my pastures fresh with rain,
   My water-courses edged with bloom,
A larger breathing space to gain
      And singing room.

Then of a reed I wrought a flute,
   And as I went I sang and played.
But though I sang, my heart was mute
      And sore afraid.

Because the great hill and the sky
   Were full of glooms and glorious
Beyond all light or dark that I
      Imagined thus.

A sudden sense, a second sight,
   Showed God, who burns in every briar.
Then sudden voices, strong and bright,
      Flashed up like fire.

And turning where that music rang
   I saw aloft, and far away,
The watching poets; and they sang
      Through night and day.

And very sweet – ah, sweet indeed –
   Their voices sounded high and deep.
I blew an echo on my reed
      As one asleep.

I heard. My heart grew cold with dread,
    For what would happen if they heard?
Would not these nightingales strike dead
        Their mocking-bird?

Then from the mountain's steepest crown,
    Where white cliffs pierce the tender grass,
I saw an arm reach slowly down,
        Heard some word pass.

'The end is come,' I thought, 'and still
    I am more happy, come what may,
To die upon Parnassus-hill
        Than live away.'

Then hands and faces luminous
    And holy voices grew one flame –
'Come up, poor singer, and sing with us!'
        They sang; I came.

So ended all my wandering;
    This is the end and this is sweet –
All night, all day, to listen and sing
        Below their feet.

A. MARY F. ROBINSON
*Lyrics Selected from the Works* (1891)


### 'Apollo and the Muses'

Τοῖς μὲν ἀοιδὰς, τοῖς δ' αὖ δακρύων
Βίον αμβλωπὸν παρέχουσαι.

Apollo and the Muses taught thee not
Thy mighty strain, enchantment to the mind,
Thralling the heart by spell of holy fears;

Awful thou sought'st Erinys' sacred grot;
And the Eternal Goddess, well-inclin'd,
Hath given thee songs, for the dull life of tears.

MICHAEL FIELD
*Underneath the Bough* (1893)

## 'A Girl'

A girl,
   Her soul a deep-wave pearl
Dim, lucent of all lovely mysteries;
   A face flowered for heart's ease,
   A brow's grace soft as seas
   Seen through faint forest-trees:
   A mouth, the lips apart,
Like aspen-leaflets trembling in the breeze

From her tempestuous heart.
Such: and our souls so knit,
I leave a page half-writ –
   The work begun
Will be to heaven's conception done,
   If she come to it.

MICHAEL FIELD
*Underneath the Bough* (1893)

## Illusions

Not in the heavens alone is Truth renowned;
   Sad human hearts, that seem to love her less,
   Even in mutiny her power confess:
We speak in fables, and are compassed round

With poesy, distilling song from sound,
   Colour from light, and hope from happiness;
   Subliming weakness, yearning, and distress,
To that high faith wherewith our life is crowned.

All fair deceits are prophets of the truth,
   E'en as the desert mirage tells a tale
     Of palms and wells, real, though far away:
The star-bright hopes that light the world's dim youth
   Are not too brilliant, but too silvery pale,
     To sparkle still, when dawns the golden day.

CONSTANCE NADEN
*The Complete Poetical Works* (1894)


## The Ballad of the Flag Painter

In a wideawake not worn for show
   He passes every day.
He's an artist, like myself, I know,
   But *he* is an R.A.

And a thousand pounds if *I* could make
   By painting some great lord,
I think a better wideawake
   I'd manage to afford!

Small difference between our tiles!
   Only my coat's in rags,
And it is canvas that *he* spiles,
   I merely spile the flags.

His reputation is immense –
   I never liked him less.
He's often flung a few odd pence
   To a comrade in distress.

And however green his hat may look
    Of tin he must be flush –
They say he always has a duke
    Or duchess neath his brush!

His portraits in a gallery
    I've seen, but for my part,
Though painted very skilfully,
    I didn't call it *art!*

Devoid of beauty or of mirth,
    They only seemed to stare
As if they wondered who on earth
    The *other* portraits were.

No need of galleries for me,
    My works of art to hold!
Because the new ones, don't you see,
    I paint upon the old.

See how the silvery moonbeams fall
    On this forsaken pile
And ruined bridge – that's what I call
    The true poetic style!

Only – a shower will come some day,
    And spoil my pictures, when
I cannot see them washed away,
    Or paint them in again.

They'll run together, blue and pink,
    And sea and shore and sky,
There'll never be a soul to think
    Of keeping the things dry.

The flags, for me, will stay quite clean.
    But when I'm dead and gone,
*His* duchesses will smile serene
    Posterity upon.

And so he'll win – but I confess,
   I've very little doubt,
Some of his dukes and duchesses
   Had better be washed out!

MAY KENDALL
*Songs from Dreamland* (1894)

# 4. LONDON! LONDON!
## OUR DELIGHT

It was inevitable that artists and writers who subscribed to a theory which placed the artificial above the natural should come to paint and write of the city, seeing it as a central symbol of man's shaping of his world. This love of artificial things is in a sense a complete reversal of the Romantic idea of the beauty of Nature and the corrupting influence of man. Wits like Whistler and Wilde delighted in standing this familiar idea on its head and asserting that Nature imitates Art. When a woman said that a landscape reminded her of his work, Whistler replied, 'Yes madam, Nature is creeping up.' And Vivian in Wilde's 'The Decay of Lying' insists that 'the extraordinary change that has taken place in the climate of London during the past ten years is entirely due to a particular school of Art'. Beardsley, borrowing these ideas and the manner of Beerbohm, wrote with some glee in the *New Review* that

London will soon be resplendent with advertisements, and against a leaden sky skysigns will trace their formal arabesque. Beauty has laid siege to the city, and telegraph wires shall no longer be the sole joy of our aesthetic perceptions.[1]

Symons put a less extreme case more calmly in the preface to the second edition of his *Silhouettes* (1896).

There is no necessary difference in artistic value between a good poem about a flower in the hedge and a good poem about the scent in a sachet. I am always charmed to read beautiful poems about nature in the country. Only, personally, I prefer town to country; and in the town we have to find for ourselves, as best we may, the *décor* which is the town equivalent of the great natural *décor* of fields and hills. Here it is that artificiality comes in; and if any one sees no beauty in the effects of artificial light, in all the variable, most human, and yet most factitious town landscape, I can only pity him, and go on my own way.

1. Quoted by Stanley Weintraub in *Aubrey Beardsley* (1967).

Whether the influence to write urban poetry came, as Richard Le Gallienne suggested, from Robert Buchanan's *London Poems* (1866), or from French ideas, or from the vast influx of people into the towns, or a combination of these and other reasons, the popularity of the subject is demonstrated by Amy Levy's *A London Plane-Tree* (1889), W. E. Henley's *London Types* (1898) and *London Voluntaries* (1893), Laurence Binyon's two series of *London Visions* (1896 and 1899), Ernest Rhys's *A London Rose* (1894), John Davidson's *Fleet Street Eclogues* (1893) and Arthur Symons's *London Nights* (1895), to name only those books whose titles indicate their interest.

It is not only the city which is celebrated, but also those chance, casual or fleeting encounters which are characteristic of modern city life, and had formed such a key motif in French poetry.

Twentieth-century poetry has tended to be predominantly urban, though the Georgians for example would prefer semi-rural subjects, and Eliot acknowledged his debt to 1890s writers (see section 5). And though Yeats, unlike his friends, rarely put London into his poems, he understood the significance of the city; for it occurs in his later poems, transformed into the 'holy city of Byzantium', where Yeats comes, to borrow Beerbohm's words (see section 1), 'nearest to God' in that climactic use of the idea of the superiority of the artificial to the natural:

> gather me
> Into the artifice of eternity.

## A Ballad of London

Ah, London! London! our delight,
Great flower that opens but at night,
Great City of the Midnight Sun,
Whose day begins when day is done.

Lamp after lamp against the sky
Opens a sudden beaming eye,
Leaping alight on either hand,
The iron lilies of the Strand.

Like dragonflies, the hansoms hover,
With jewelled eyes, to catch the lover;
The streets are full of lights and loves,
Soft gowns, and flutter of soiled doves.

The human moths about the light
Dash and cling close in dazed delight,
And burn and laugh, the world and wife,
For this is London, this is life!

Upon thy petals butterflies,
But at thy root, some say, there lies
A world of weeping trodden things,
Poor worms that have not eyes or wings.

From out corruption of their woe
Springs this bright flower that charms us so,
Men die and rot deep out of sight
To keep this jungle-flower bright.

Paris and London, World-Flowers twain
Wherewith the World-Tree blooms again,
Since Time hath gathered Babylon,
And withered Rome still withers on.

Sidon and Tyre were such as ye,
How bright they shone upon the Tree!
But Time hath gathered, both are gone,
And no man sails to Babylon.

Ah, London! London! our delight,
For thee, too, the eternal night,
And Circe Paris hath no charm
To stay Time's unrelenting arm.

Time and his moths shall eat up all.
Your chiming towers proud and tall
He shall most utterly abase,
And set a desert in their place.

RICHARD LE GALLIENNE
*Robert Louis Stevenson: an Elegy, and Other Poems* (1895)


## London in July

What ails my senses thus to cheat?
    What is it ails the place,
That all the people in the street
    Should wear one woman's face?

The London trees are dusty-brown
    Beneath the summer sky;
My love, she dwells in London town,
    Nor leaves it in July.

O various and intricate maze,
    Wide waste of square and street;
Where, missing through unnumbered days,
    We twain at last may meet!

And who cries out on crowd and mart?
    Who prates of stream and sea?
The summer in the city's heart —
    That is enough for me.

AMY LEVY
*A London Plane-Tree* (1889)

## London

Athwart the sky a lowly sigh
    From west to east the sweet wind carried;
The sun stood still on Primrose Hill;
    His light in all the city tarried:
The clouds on viewless columns bloomed
Like smouldering lilies unconsumed.

'Oh sweetheart, see! how shadowy,
    Of some occult magician's rearing,
Or swung in space of heaven's grace
    Dissolving, dimly reappearing,
Afloat upon ethereal tides
St Paul's above the city rides!'

A rumour broke through the thin smoke
    Enwreathing abbey, tower, and palace,
The parks, the squares, the thoroughfares,
    The million-peopled lanes and alleys,
An ever-muttering prisoned storm,
The heart of London beating warm.

JOHN DAVIDSON
*Ballads and Songs* (1894)

## Impression de Nuit

### LONDON

See what a mass of gems the city wears
Upon her broad live bosom! row on row
Rubies and emeralds and amethysts glow.
See! that huge circle like a necklace, stares

With thousands of bold eyes to heaven, and dares
The golden stars to dim the lamps below,
And in the mirror of the mire I know
The moon has left her image unawares.

That's the great town at night: I see her breasts,
Pricked out with lamps they stand like huge black towers,
I think they move! I hear her panting breath.
And that's her head where the tiara rests.
And in her brain, through lanes as dark as death,
Men creep like thoughts . . . The lamps are like pale flowers.

LORD ALFRED DOUGLAS
*The City of the Soul* (1899)


## Sunset in the City

Above the town a monstrous wheel is turning,
    With glowing spokes of red,
Low in the west its fiery axle burning;
    And, lost amid the spaces overhead,
A vague white moth, the moon, is fluttering.

Above the town an azure sea is flowing,
    'Mid long peninsulas of shining sand,
From opal unto pearl the moon is growing,
    Dropped like a shell upon the changing strand.

Within the town the streets grow strange and haunted,
    And, dark against the western lakes of green,
The buildings change to temples, and unwonted
    Shadows and sounds creep in where day has been.

Within the town, the lamps of sin are flaring,
    Poor foolish men that know not what ye are!
Tired traffic still upon his feet is faring –
    Two lovers meet and kiss and watch a star.

RICHARD LE GALLIENNE
*English Poems* (1892)

## City Nights

### 1. IN THE TRAIN

The train through the night of the town,
　　Through a blackness broken in twain
　　　　By the sudden finger of streets;
Lights, red, yellow, and brown,
　　From curtain and window-pane,
　　　　The flashing eyes of the streets.

Night, and the rush of the train,
　　A cloud of smoke through the town,
　　　　Scaring the life of the streets;
And the leap of the heart again,
　　Out into the night, and down
　　　　The dazzling vista of streets!

### 2. IN THE TEMPLE

The grey and misty night,
　　Slim trees that hold the night among
　　Their branches, and, along
The vague Embankment, light on light.

The sudden, racing lights!
　　I can just hear, distinct, aloof,
　　The gaily clattering hoof
Beating the rhythm of festive nights.

The gardens to the weeping moon
　　Sigh back the breath of tears.
　　O the refrain of years on years
'Neath the weeping moon!

ARTHUR SYMONS
*Silhouettes* (2nd edition 1896)

## A Northern Suburb

Nature selects the longest way,
   And winds about in tortuous grooves;
A thousand years the oaks decay;
   The wrinkled glacier hardly moves.

But here the whetted fangs of change
   Daily devour the old demesne –
The busy farm, the quiet grange,
   The wayside inn, the village green.

In gaudy yellow brick and red,
   With rooting pipes, like creepers rank,
The shoddy terraces o'erspread
   Meadow, and garth, and daisied bank.

With shelves for rooms the houses crowd,
   Like draughty cupboards in a row –
Ice-chests when wintry winds are loud,
   Ovens when summer breezes blow.

Roused by the fee'd policeman's knock,
   And sad that day should come again,
Under the stars the workmen flock
   In haste to reach the workmen's train.

For here dwell those who must fulfil
   Dull tasks in uncongenial spheres,
Who toil through dread of coming ill,
   And not with hope of happier years –

The lowly folk who scarcely dare
   Conceive themselves perhaps misplaced,
Whose prize for unremitting care
   Is only not to be disgraced.

JOHN DAVIDSON
*New Ballads* (1897)

## The Phantom Train

These unbefriended city drudges,
    At last they break away;
Not all the juries and the judges
    Could force their longer stay.
There's not a Philistine who grudges
    The hard won holiday.

Fades all the city's hurly-burly,
    They choose their bournes at will,
Yon grimy porter, rough and surly,
    Is bound for heath and hill.
The shop girl toiling late and early
    Lights at a hamlet still.

The dry old scholar, grey with learning,
    Methought, no friends had he,
And yet some kindly face discerning
    He surely seems to be!
The wind to welcome his returning
    Is blowing from the sea.

The April sunshine has departed,
    The city's bleak and drear –
Who gaily on your revel started,
    Alas, what do you here,
You passengers so heavy-hearted
    That were so light of cheer?

A dream before the ledger flitted,
    A dream before the brain;
Ah, yet the toil is unremitted,
    The journeying is vain!
The train the city never quitted,
    'Twas but a phantom train!

MAY KENDALL
*Songs from Dreamland* (1894)

## London Voluntaries

### 3
### *Scherzando*

Down through the ancient Strand
The spirit of October, mild and boon
And sauntering, takes his way
This golden end of afternoon,
As though the corn stood yellow in all the land
And the ripe apples dropped to the harvest-moon.

Lo! the round sun, half-down the western slope –
Seen as along an unglazed telescope –
Lingers and lolls, loth to be done with day:
Gifting the long, lean, lanky street
And its abounding confluences of being
With aspects generous and bland;
Making a thousand harnesses to shine
As with new ore from some enchanted mine,
And every horse's coat so full of sheen
He looks new-tailored, and every 'bus feels clean,
And never a hansom but is worth the feeing;
And every jeweller within the pale
Offers a real Arabian Night for sale;
And even the roar
Of the strong streams of toil, that pause and pour
Eastward and westward, sounds suffused –
Seems as it were bemused
And blurred, and like the speech
Of lazy seas on a lotus-haunted beach –
With this enchanted lustrousness,
This mellow magic, that (as a man's caress
Brings back to some faded face, beloved before,
A heavenly shadow of the grace it wore
Ere the poor eyes were minded to beseech)
Old things transfigures, and you hail and bless
Their looks of long-lapsed loveliness once more:
Till Clement's, angular and cold and staid,

Gleams forth in glamour's very stuffs arrayed;
And Bride's, her aëry, unsubstantial charm
Through flight on flight of springing, soaring stone
Grown flushed and warm,
Laughs into life full-mooded and fresh-blown;
And the high majesty of Paul's
Uplifts a voice of living light, and calls –
Calls to his millions to behold and see
How goodly this his London Town can be!

For earth and sky and air
Are golden everywhere,
And golden with a gold so suave and fine
The looking on it lifts the heart like wine.
Trafalgar Square
(The fountains volleying golden glaze)
Shines like an angel-market. High aloft
Over his couchant Lions in a haze
Shimmering and bland and soft,
A dust of chrysoprase,
Our Sailor takes the golden gaze
Of the saluting sun, and flames superb
As once he flamed it on his ocean round.
The dingy dreariness of the picture-place,
Turned very nearly bright,
Takes on a luminous transiency of grace,
And shows no more a scandal to the ground.
The very blind man pottering on the kerb,
Among the posies and the ostrich feathers
And the rude voices touched with all the weathers
Of the long, varying year,
Shares in the universal alms of light.
The windows, with their fleeting, flickering fires,
The height and spread of frontage shining sheer,
The quiring signs, the rejoicing roofs and spires –
'Tis El Dorado – El Dorado plain,
The Golden City! And when a girl goes by,
Look! as she turns her glancing head,
A call of gold is floated from her ear!

Golden, all golden! In a golden glory,
Long-lapsing down a golden coasted sky,
The day not dies but seems
Dispersed in wafts and drifts of gold, and shed
Upon a past of golden song and story
And memories of gold and golden dreams.

W. E. HENLEY
*Poems* (1898)


## London Voluntaries

### 4
#### *Largo e mesto*

Out of the poisonous East,
Over a continent of blight,
Like a maleficent Influence released
From the most squalid cellarage of hell,
The Wind-Fiend, the abominable –
The Hangman Wind that tortures temper and light –
Comes slouching, sullen and obscene,
Hard on the skirts of the embittered night;
And in a cloud unclean
Of excremental humours, roused to strife
By the operation of some ruinous change
Wherever his evil mandate run and range
Into a dire intensity of life,
A craftsman at his bench, he settles down
To the grim job of throttling London Town.

So, by a jealous lightlessness beset
That might have oppressed the dragons of old time
Crunching and groping in the abysmal slime,
A cave of cut-throat thoughts and villainous dreams,
Hag-rid and crying with cold and dirt and wet,
The afflicted City, prone from mark to mark
In shameful occultation, seems

A nightmare labyrinthine, dim and drifting,
With wavering gulfs and antic heights, and shifting,
Rent in the stuff of a material dark,
Wherein the lamplight, scattered and sick and pale,
Shows like the leper's living blotch of bale:
Uncoiling monstrous into street on street
Paven with perils, teeming with mischance,
Where man and beast go blindfold and in dread,
Working with oaths and threats and faltering feet
Somewhither in the hideousness ahead;
Working through wicked airs and deadly dews
That make the laden robber grin askance
At the good places in his black romance,
And the poor, loitering harlot rather choose
Go pinched and pined to bed
Than lurk and shiver and curse her wretched way
From arch to arch, scouting some threepenny prey.

Forgot his dawns and far-flushed afterglows,
His green garlands and windy eyots forgot,
The old Father-River flows,
His watchfires cores of menace in the gloom,
As he came oozing from the Pit, and bore,
Sunk in his filthily transfigured sides,
Shoals of dishonoured dead to tumble and rot
In the squalor of the universal shore:
His voices sounding through the gruesome air
As from the Ferry where the Boat of Doom
With her blaspheming cargo reels and rides:
The while his children, the brave ships,
No more adventurous and fair,
Nor tripping it light of heel as home-bound brides,
But infamously enchanted,
Huddle together in the foul eclipse,
Or feel their course by inches desperately,
As through a tangle of alleys murder-haunted,
From sinister reach to reach out – out – to sea.

And Death the while –
Death with his well-worn, lean, professional smile,
Death in his threadbare working trim –
Comes to your bedside, unannounced and bland,
And with expert, inevitable hand
Feels at your windpipe, fingers you in the lung,
Or flicks the clot well into the labouring heart:
Thus signifying unto old and young,
However hard of mouth or wild of whim,
'Tis time – 'tis time by his ancient watch - to part
From books and women and talk and drink and art.
And you go humbly after him
To a mean suburban lodging: on the way
To what or where
Not Death, who is old and very wise, can say:
And you – how should you care
So long as, unreclaimed of hell,
The Wind-Fiend, the insufferable,
Thus vicious and thus patient, sits him down
To the black job of burking London Town?

W. E. HENLEY
*Poems* (1898)


## A March Day in London

The east wind blows in the street to-day;
The sky is blue, yet the town looks grey.
'Tis the wind of ice, the wind of fire,
Of cold despair and of hot desire,
Which chills the flesh to aches and pains,
And sends a fever through all the veins.

From end to end, with aimless feet,
All day long have I paced the street.
My limbs are weary, but in my breast
Stirs the goad of a mad unrest.

I would give anything to stay
The little wheel that turns in my brain;
The little wheel that turns all day,
That turns all night with might and main.

What is the thing I fear, and why?
Nay, but the world is all awry –
The wind's in the east, the sun's in the sky.
The gas-lamps gleam in a golden line;
The ruby lights of the hansoms shine,
Glance, and flicker like fire-flies bright;
The wind has fallen with the night,
And once again the town seems fair
Thwart the mist that hangs i' the air.

And o'er, at last, my spirit steals
A weary peace; peace that conceals
Within its inner depths the grain
Of hopes that yet shall flower again.

AMY LEVY
*A London Plane-Tree* (1889)

## In the Isle of Dogs

While the water-wagon's ringing showers
Sweetened the dust with a woodland smell,
'Past noon, past noon, two sultry hours,'
Drowsily fell
From the schoolhouse clock
In the Isle of Dogs by Millwall Dock.

Mirrored in shadowy windows draped
With ragged net or half-drawn blind
Bowsprits, masts, exactly shaped
To woo or fight the wind,

Like monitors of guilt
By strength and beauty sent,
Disgraced the shameful houses built
To furnish rent.

From the pavements and the roofs
In shimmering volumes wound
The wrinkled heat;
Distant hammers, wheels and hoofs,
A turbulent pulse of sound,
Southward obscurely beat,
The only utterance of the afternoon,
Till on a sudden in the silent street
An organ-man drew up and ground
The Old Hundredth tune.

Forthwith the pillar of cloud that hides the past
Burst into flame,
Whose alchemy transmuted house and mast,
Street, dockyard, pier and pile:
By magic sound the Isle of Dogs became
A northern isle –
A green isle like a beryl set
In a wine-coloured sea,
Shadowed by mountains where a river met
The ocean's arm extended royally.

There also in the evening on the shore
An old man ground the Old Hundredth tune,
An old enchanter steeped in human lore,
Sad-eyed, with whitening beard, and visage lank:
Not since and not before,
Under the sunset or the mellowing moon,
Has any hand of man's conveyed
Such meaning in the turning of a crank.

Sometimes he played
As if his box had been
An organ in an abbey richly lit;
For when the dark invaded day's demesne,
And the sun set in crimson and in gold;

When idlers swarmed upon the esplanade,
And a late steamer wheeling towards the quay
Struck founts of silver from the darkling sea,
The solemn tune arose and shook and rolled
Above the throng,
Above the hum and tramp and bravely knit
All hearts in common memories of song.
Sometimes he played at speed;
Then the Old Hundredth like a devil's mass
Instinct with evil thought and evil deed,
Rang out in anguish and remorse. Alas!
That men must know both Heaven and Hell!
Sometimes the melody
Sang with the murmuring surge;
And with the winds would tell
Of peaceful graves and of the passing bell.
Sometimes it pealed across the bay
A high triumphal dirge,
A dirge
For the departing undefeated day.

A noble tune, a high becoming mate
Of the capped mountains and the deep broad firth;
A simple tune and great,
The fittest utterance of the voice of earth.

JOHN DAVIDSON
*The Last Ballad* (1899)


## Impression

The pink and black of silk and lace,
    Flushed in the rosy-golden glow
Of lamplight on her lifted face;
Powder and wig, and pink and lace,

And those pathetic eyes of hers;
    But all the London footlights know
The little plaintive smile that stirs
The shadow in those eyes of hers.

Outside, the dreary church-bell tolled,
    The London Sunday faded slow;
Ah, what is this? what wings unfold
In this miraculous rose of gold?

ARTHUR SYMONS
*Silhouettes* (2nd edition 1896)


## Ideal

We are not sundered for we never met.
We only passed each other in the throng,
We moved together but not long . . . not long . . .
You were indifferent . . . and I may forget
Your profound eyes, your heavy hair, your voice
So clear, yet deep and low with tenderness,
That lingered on my ears like a caress
And roused my heart to make a futile choice.

O! Poet that passed me carelessly in the throng –
O! Soul that clamoured unto God in song!
How should I lose you thus and lack regret?

OLIVE CUSTANCE
*Opals* (1897)

## At the Cavour

Wine, the red coils, the flaring gas,
   Bring out a brighter tone in cheeks
That learn at home before the glass
   The flush that eloquently speaks.

The blue-grey smoke of cigarettes
   Curls from the lessening ends that glow;
The men are thinking of the bets,
   The women of the debts, they owe.

Then their eyes meet, and in their eyes
   The accustomed smile comes up to call,
A look half miserably wise,
   Half heedlessly ironical.

ARTHUR SYMONS
*Silhouettes* (2nd edition 1896)

## Etchings

### 3
### At the Empire

The low and soft luxurious promenade,
Electric-light, pile-carpet, the device
Of gilded mirrors that repeat you thrice;
The crowd that lounges, strolls from yard to yard;

The calm and brilliant Circes who retard
Your passage with the skirts and rouge that spice
The changeless programme of insipid vice,
And stun you with a languid strange regard;

Ah! what are these, the perfume and the glow,
The ballet that coruscates down below,
The glittering songstress and the comic stars,

Ah! what are these, although we sit withdrawn
Above our sparkling tumblers and cigars,
To us so like to perish with a yawn?

THEODORE WRATISLAW
*Orchids* (1896)

# 5. LONDON TYPES

Three things combined to make London types a popular subject for poetry. First, the interest in London itself (see the previous section; though the Edinburgh of Henley's hospital, or the Paris of Symons's music-hall would do as well); second, the tradition of the dramatic monologue and depiction of character, which the poets learned from Browning and Tennyson (Symons's first book had been *An Introduction to the Study of Browning*, 1886) and which they passed on to Pound and Eliot; third, the rising interest in the rights of the ordinary man and woman, as exemplified in the socialist and suffragist movements. Though present in some novels and factual reports, these types had tended to be unacceptable in poetry, only appearing transformed into the sentimental heroes and heroines of poets like G. R. Sims. And they were not always acceptable in prose. W. T. Stead had published a series of articles called 'The Maiden Tribute of Modern Babylon', where he told how he had been able to buy for £5 a girl of just over thirteen, ostensibly for vicious purposes. His aim, in which he was successful, was to secure the passing of the Criminal Law Amendment Bill (1885), but he so shocked the nation that he was gaoled for three months, and W. H. Smith refused to sell the paper which carried his articles. Smith's also refused to sell George Moore's *Esther Waters* (1894), a novel which describes the difficult life of a servant girl.

Now both the actions and the voice of the ordinary man and woman began to find a place in poetry; once more back to a language really used by men. T. S. Eliot wrote in the preface to Maurice Lindsay's *John Davidson, a Selection of his Poems* (1961) that

*Thirty Bob a Week* seems to me the only poem in which Davidson freed himself completely from the poetic diction of English verse of his time (just as *Non Sum Qualis Eram* seems to me the one poem in which, by a slight shift of rhythm, Ernest Dowson freed himself). But I am sure that I found inspiration in the content of the poem, and in the complete fitness of content and idiom: for I also had a good many dingy urban images to reveal. Davidson had a great theme, and also found an idiom which elicited the greatness of the theme, which endowed this thirty-bob-a-week clerk with a dignity that would not have appeared if a more conventional poetic diction had been employed. The personage that Davidson created in this poem has haunted me all my life, and the poem is to me a great poem for ever.

Others were finding this idiom: Kipling, for example, or Henley, who was not only writing his *London Types* but also helping throughout the 1890s to compile and edit a dictionary of *Slang and its Analogues*.

Some held aloof from these matters and from social upheavals. Yeats wrote that 'we poets continued to write verse and read it out at "The Cheshire Cheese", convinced that to take part in such movements would be only less disgraceful than to write for the newspapers'.[1]

Like the city itself, dancers were both symbol and substance, and Symons, an ardent admirer of dancers in the flesh, also states very clearly the symbolic role of the dancer, which is seen also in the poems of Davidson and Binyon. Again it is Yeats who, much later, makes fullest use of this symbol, as in 'Byzantium'.

1. *The Oxford Book of Modern Verse* (1936), p. xi.

## Thirty Bob a Week

I couldn't touch a stop and turn a screw,
    And set the blooming world a-work for me,
Like such as cut their teeth – I hope, like you –
    On the handle of a skeleton gold key;
I cut mine on a leek, which I eat it every week:
    I'm a clerk at thirty bob as you can see.

But I don't allow it's luck and all a toss;
    There's no such thing as being starred and crossed;
It's just the power of some to be a boss,
    And the bally power of others to be bossed:
I face the music, sir; you bet I ain't a cur;
    Strike me lucky if I don't believe I'm lost!

For like a mole I journey in the dark,
    A-travelling along the underground
From my Pillar'd Halls and broad Suburbean Park,
    To come the daily dull official round;
And home again at night with my pipe all alight,
    A-scheming how to count ten bob a pound.

And it's often very cold and very wet,
    And my missis stitches towels for a hunks;
And the Pillar'd Halls is half of it to let –
    Three rooms about the size of travelling trunks.
And we cough, my wife and I, to dislocate a sigh,
    When the noisy little kids are in their bunks.

But you never hear her do a growl or whine,
    For she's made of flint and roses, very odd;
And I've got to cut my meaning rather fine,
    Or I'd blubber, for I'm made of greens and sod:
So p'r'aps we are in Hell for all that I can tell,
    And lost and damn'd and served up hot to God.

I ain't blaspheming, Mr Silver-tongue;
    I'm saying things a bit beyond your art:
Of all the rummy starts you ever sprung,

Thirty bob a week's the rummiest start!
With your science and your books and your the'ries about
     spooks,
  Did you ever hear of looking in your heart?

I didn't mean your pocket, Mr, no:
  I mean that having children and a wife,
With thirty bob on which to come and go,
  Isn't dancing to the tabor and the fife:
When it doesn't make you drink, by Heaven! it makes
     you think,
  And notice curious items about life.

I step into my heart and there I meet
  A god-almighty devil singing small,
Who would like to shout and whistle in the street,
  And squelch the passers flat against the wall;
If the whole world was a cake he had the power to take,
  He would take it, ask for more, and eat it all.

And I meet a sort of simpleton beside,
  The kind that life is always giving beans;
With thirty bob a week to keep a bride
  He fell in love and married in his teens:
At thirty bob he stuck; but he knows it isn't luck:
  He knows the seas are deeper than tureens.

And the god-almighty devil and the fool
  That meet me in the High Street on the strike,
When I walk about my heart a-gathering wool,
  Are my good and evil angels if you like.
And both of them together in every kind of weather
  Ride me like a double-seated bike.

That's rough a bit and needs its meaning curled.
  But I have a high old hot un in my mind –
A most engrugious notion of the world,
  That leaves your lightning 'rithmetic behind:
I give it at a glance when I say 'There ain't no chance,
  Nor nothing of the lucky-lottery kind.'

And it's this way that I make it out to be:
   No fathers, mothers, countries, climates – none;
Not Adam was responsible for me,
   Nor society, nor systems, nary one:
A little sleeping seed, I woke – I did, indeed –
   A million years before the blooming sun.

I woke because I thought the time had come;
   Beyond my will there was no other cause;
And everywhere I found myself at home,
   Because I chose to be the thing I was;
And in whatever shape of mollusc or of ape
   I always went according to the laws.

I was the love that chose my mother out;
   I joined two lives and from the union burst;
My weakness and my strength without a doubt
   Are mine alone for ever from the first:
It's just the very same with a difference in the name
   As 'Thy will be done.' You say it if you durst!

They say it daily up and down the land
   As easy as you take a drink, it's true;
But the difficultest go to understand,
   And the difficultest job a man can do,
Is to come it brave and meek with thirty bob a week,
   And feel that that's the proper thing for you.

It's a naked child against a hungry wolf;
   It's playing bowls upon a splitting wreck;
It's walking on a string across a gulf
   With millstones fore-and-aft about your neck;
But the thing is daily done by many and many a one;
   And we fall, face forward, fighting, on the deck.

JOHN DAVIDSON
*Ballads and Songs* (1894)

## Tommy

I went into a public-'ouse to get a pint o' beer,
The publican 'e up an' sez, 'We serve no red-coats here.'
The girls be'ind the bar they laughed an' giggled fit to die,
I outs into the street again an' to myself sez I:
　　　O it's Tommy this, an' Tommy that, an' 'Tommy, go away';
　　　But it's 'Thank you, Mister Atkins,' when the band begins
　　　　　to play,
　　　The band begins to play, my boys, the band begins to play,
　　　O it's 'Thank you, Mister Atkins,' when the band begins to
　　　　　play.

I went into a theatre as sober as could be,
They gave a drunk civilian room, but 'adn't none for me;
They sent me to the gallery or round the music-'alls,
But when it comes to fightin', Lord! they'll shove me in the stalls!
　　　For it's Tommy this, an' Tommy that, an' 'Tommy, wait
　　　　　outside';
　　　But it's 'Special train for Atkins' when the trooper's on the
　　　　　tide,
　　　The troopship's on the tide, my boys, the troopship's on the
　　　　　tide,
　　　O it's 'Special train for Atkins' when the trooper's on the tide.

Yes, makin' mock o' uniforms that guard you while you sleep
Is cheaper than them uniforms, an' they're starvation cheap;
An' hustlin' drunken soldiers, when they're goin' large a bit
Is five times better business than paradin' in full kit.
　　　Then it's Tommy this, an' Tommy that, an' 'Tommy, 'ow's
　　　　　yer soul?'
　　　But it's 'Thin red line of 'eroes' when the drums begin to roll,
　　　The drums begin to roll, my boys, the drums begin to roll,
　　　O it's 'Thin red line of 'eroes' when the drums begin to roll.

We aren't no thin red 'eroes, nor we aren't no blackguards too,
But single men in barricks, most remarkable like you;
An' if sometimes our conduck isn't all your fancy paints,
Why, single men in barricks don't grow into plaster saints;

While it's Tommy this, an' Tommy that, an' 'Tommy, fall
    be'ind,'
But it's 'Please to walk in front, sir,' when there's trouble in
    the wind,
There's trouble in the wind, my boys, there's trouble in the
    wind,
O it's 'Please to walk in front, sir,' when there's trouble in
    the wind.

You talk o' better food for us, an' schools, an' fires, an' all:
We'll wait for extry rations if you treat us rational.
Don't mess about the cook-room slops, but prove it to our
face
The Widow's Uniform is not the soldier-man's disgrace.
    For it's Tommy this, an' Tommy that, an' 'Chuck him out,
      the brute!'
    But it's 'Saviour of 'is country' when the guns begin to
      shoot;
    An' it's Tommy this, an' Tommy that, an' anything you
      please;
    An' Tommy ain't a bloomin' fool – you bet that Tommy
      sees!

RUDYARD KIPLING
*Barrack-Room Ballads* (1892)

## Any Bar

Though, if you ask her name, she says ELISE,
Being plain ELIZABETH, e'en let it pass,
And own that, if her aspirates take their ease,
She ever makes a point, in washing glass,
Handling the engine, turning taps for tots,
And countering change, and scorning what men say,
Of posing as a dove among the pots,
Nor often gives her dignity away.
Her head's a work of art, and, if her eyes

Be tired and ignorant, she has a waist;
Cheaply the mode she shadows; and she tries
From penny novels to amend her taste;
   And, having mopped the zinc for certain years,
   And faced the gas, she fades and disappears.

W. E. HENLEY
*London Types* (1898)

## *In Hospital*

### 9
### LADY-PROBATIONER

Some three, or five, or seven, and thirty years;
A Roman nose; a dimpling double-chin;
Dark eyes and shy that, ignorant of sin,
Are yet acquainted, it would seem, with tears;
A comely shape; a slim, high-coloured hand,
Graced, rather oddly, with a signet ring;
A bashful air, becoming everything;
A well-bred silence always at command.
Her plain print gown, prim cap, and bright steel chain
Look out of place on her, and I remain
Absorbed in her, as in a pleasant mystery.
Quick, skilful, quiet, soft in speech and touch . . .
'Do you like nursing?' 'Yes, Sir, very much.'
Somehow, I rather think she has a history.

W. E. HENLEY
*Poems* (1898)

## In Hospital

### 10
### STAFF-NURSE: NEW STYLE

Blue-eyed and bright of face but waning fast
Into the sere of virginal decay,
I view her as she enters, day by day,
As a sweet sunset almost overpast.
Kindly and calm, patrician to the last,
Superbly falls her gown of sober gray,
And on her chignon's elegant array
The plainest cap is somehow touched with caste.
She talks BEETHOVEN; frowns disapprobation
At BALZAC's name, sighs it at 'poor GEORGE SAND's';
Knows that she has exceeding pretty hands;
Speaks Latin with a right accentuation;
And gives at need (as one who understands)
Draught, counsel, diagnosis, exhortation.

W. E. HENLEY
*Poems* (1898)

## Holiday at Hampton Court

Scales of pearly cloud inlay
    North and south the turquoise sky,
While the diamond lamp of day
    Quenchless burns, and time on high
A moment halts upon his way
    Bidding noon again good-bye.

Gaffers, gammers, huzzies, louts,
    Couples, gangs, and families
Sprawling, shake, with Babel-shouts

Bluff King Hal's funereal trees;
And eddying groups of stare-abouts
   Quiz the sandstone Hercules.

When their tongues and tempers tire,
   Harry and his little lot
Condescendingly admire
   Lozenge-bed and crescent-plot,
Aglow with links of azure fire,
   Pansy and forget-me-not.

Where the emerald shadows rest
   In the lofty woodland aisle,
Chaffing lovers quaintly dressed
   Chase and double many a mile,
Indifferent exiles in the west
   Making love in cockney style.

Now the echoing palace fills;
   Men and women, girls and boys
Trample past the swords and frills,
   Kings and Queens and trulls and toys;
Or listening loll on window-sills,
   Happy amateurs of noise!

That for pictured rooms of state!
   Out they hurry, wench and knave,
Where beyond the palace-gate
   Dusty legions swarm and rave,
With laughter, shriek, inane debate,
   Kentish fire and comic stave.

Voices from the river call;
   Organs hammer tune on tune;
Larks triumphant over all
   Herald twilight coming soon,
For as the sun begins to fall
   Near the zenith gleams the moon.

JOHN DAVIDSON
*The Last Ballad* (1899)

## Ballade of a Special Edition

He comes; I hear him up the street –
  Bird of ill omen, flapping wide
The pinion of a printed sheet,
  His hoarse note scares the eventide.
Of slaughter, theft, and suicide
  He is the herald and the friend;
Now he vociferates with pride –
  A double murder in Mile End!

A hanging to his soul is sweet;
  His gloating fancy 's fain to bide
Where human-freighted vessels meet,
  And misdirected trains collide.
With Shocking Accidents supplied,
  He tramps the town from end to end.
How often have we heard it cried –
  A double murder in Mile End.

War loves he; victory or defeat,
  So there be loss on either side.
His tale of horrors incomplete,
  Imagination's aid is tried.
Since no distinguished man has died,
  And since the Fates, relenting, send
No great catastrophe, he's spied
  This double murder in Mile End.

Fiend, get thee gone! no more repeat
  Those sounds which do mine ears offend.
It is apocryphal, you cheat,
  Your double murder in Mile End.

AMY LEVY
*A London Plane-Tree* (1889)

## In the Season

Her insolent carriage shines down Rotten Row,
Her beauty shaded from the sun of June
Outblazes even the dazzling afternoon;
Her heart is hard and hot with triumph; though
Her eyelids droop too languid to bestow
A glance upon the crowd that drives or stands,
She feels the reins of conquest in her hands,
Exulting in the senses' overthrow.

The champing horses bear her down the mile,
And as all eyes go after her a smile
Dawns and is gone upon the clear-cut face:

She leans back on the cushions to recall
The night's long list of dinner, theatre, ball,
In languors of premeditated grace.

THEODORE WRATISLAW
*Caprices* (1893)

## Hammersmith

'LIZA's *old man*'s perhaps a little *shady*,
'LIZA's *old woman*'s prone to *booze* and cringe;
But 'LIZA deems herself *a perfect lady*,
And proves it in her feathers and her fringe.
For 'LIZA has a *bloke* her heart to cheer,
With *pearlies* and a *barrer* and a *jack*,
So all the vegetables of the year
Are duly represented on her back.

Her boots are sacrifices to her hats,
Which knock you speechless – *like a load of bricks!*
Her summer velvets dazzle WANSTEAD FLATS,
And cost, at times, a good eighteen-and-six.
    Withal, outside the gay and giddy whirl,
      'LIZA's a stupid, straight, hard-working girl.

W. E. HENLEY
*London Types* (1898)

## Papillons du Pavé

A butterfly, a queer red thing,
Comes drifting idly down the street:
Ah, do not now the cool leaves swing,
That you must brave the city's heat?

A butterfly, a poet vain,
Whose life is weeping in his mind,
And all the dreaming of his brain
Is blighted by the dusty wind.

A painted butterfly sits there,
Who sickens of the café chaff;
And down the sultry evening air
She flings her sudden weary laugh.

VINCENT O'SULLIVAN
*Poems* (1896)

## Nora on the Pavement

As Nora on the pavement
Dances, and she entrances the grey hour
Into the laughing circle of her power,
The magic circle of her glances,
As Nora dances on the midnight pavement;

Petulant and bewildered,
Thronging desires and longing looks recur,
And memorably re-incarnate her,
As I remember that old longing,
A footlight fancy, petulant and bewildered;

There where the ballet circles,
See her, but ah! not free her from the race
Of glittering lines that link and interlace;
This colour now, now that, may be her,
In the bright web of those harmonious circles.

But what are these dance-measures,
Leaping and joyous, keeping time alone
With Life's capricious rhythm, and all her own,
Life's rhythm and hers, long sleeping,
That wakes, and knows not why, in these dance-measures?

It is the very Nora;
Child, and most blithe, and wild as any elf,
And innocently spendthrift of herself,
And guileless and most unbeguiled,
Herself at last, leaps free the very Nora.

It is the soul of Nora,
Living at last, and giving forth to the night,
Bird-like, the burden of its own delight,
All its desire, and all the joy of living,
In that blithe madness of the soul of Nora.

ARTHUR SYMONS
*Silhouettes* (2nd edition 1896)

## Mari's Saturday Nights

### 2

### OCTOBER: THE PHILOSOPHY OF
### THE PAVEMENT

What if my face be pale, she said:
　　For I can buy it colour.
What if my virtue's frail, she said:
　　Since life gets dull and duller,
Let it go fast and faster, till I'm dead!

And if I die so soon, she said,
　　Far better, dead and buried,
Than living this wild life, she said,
　　Where women are so wearied,
Upon the endless pavement that they tread.

And if God is so great, she said,
　　He still may stoop and save me!
And if it be but fate, she said,
　　These eyes and red lips, gave me?
What use is left in praying, then? she said.

But if we had our way, she said,
　　With men, – then we would love them,
Not as for everyday, she said,
　　But with God's stars above them,
And flowers below, to dress the day! she said.

Then hardest hearted men, she said,
　　Would only love for kindness;
And all sad women then, she said,
　　Should end their tears and blindness:
And Christ save Mari Magdalen! she said.

ERNEST RHYS
*Welsh Ballads* (1898)

## The Little Dancers

Lonely, save for a few faint stars, the sky
Dreams; and lonely, below, the little street
Into its gloom retires, secluded and shy.
Scarcely the dumb roar enters this soft retreat;
And all is dark, save where come flooding rays
From a tavern window: there, to the brisk measure
Of an organ that down in an alley merrily plays,
Two children, all alone and no one by,
Holding their tattered frocks, through an airy maze
Of motion, lightly threaded with nimble feet,
Dance sedately: face to face they gaze,
Their eyes shining, grave with a perfect pleasure.

LAURENCE BINYON
*London Visions* (1896)

## Décor de Théâtre

### 4
#### LA MÉLINITE: MOULIN ROUGE

Olivier Metra's Waltz of Roses
    Sheds in a rhythmic shower
    The very petals of the flower;
And all is roses,
    The rouge of petals in a shower.

Down the long hall the dance returning
    Rounds the full circle, rounds
    The perfect rose of lights and sounds,
The rose returning
    Into the circle of its rounds.

Alone, apart, one dancer watches
  Her mirrored, morbid grace;
  Before the mirror, face to face,
Alone she watches
  Her morbid, vague, ambiguous grace.

Before the mirror's dance of shadows
  She dances in a dream,
  And she and they together seem
A dance of shadows;
  Alike the shadows of a dream.

The orange-rosy lamps are trembling
  Between the robes that turn;
  In ruddy flowers of flame that burn
The lights are trembling:
  The shadows and the dancers turn.

And, enigmatically smiling,
  In the mysterious night,
  She dances for her own delight,
A shadow smiling
  Back to a shadow in the night.

ARTHUR SYMONS
*London Nights* (2nd edition 1897)


## Selene Eden

My dearest lovers know me not;
  I hide my life and soul from sight;
I conquer all whose blood is hot;
  My mystery is my mail of might.

I had a troupe who danced with me:
  I veiled myself from head to foot;
My girls were nude as they dared be;
  They sang a chorus, I was mute.

But now I fill the widest stage
    Alone, unveiled, without a song;
And still with mystery I engage
    The aching senses of the throng.

A dark-blue vest with stars of gold,
    My only diamond in my hair,
An Indian scarf about me rolled:
    That is the dress I always wear.

And first the sensuous music whets
    The lustful crowd; the dim-lit room
Recalls delights, recalls regrets;
    And then I enter in the gloom.

I glide, I trip, I run, I spin,
    Lapped in the lime-light's aureole.
Hushed are the voices, hushed the din,
    I see men's eyes like glowing coal.

My loosened scarf in odours drenched
    Showers keener hints of sensual bliss;
The music swoons, the light is quenched,
    Into the dark I blow a kiss.

Then, like a long wave rolling home,
    The music gathers speed and sound;
I, dancing, am the music's foam,
    And wilder, fleeter, higher bound,

And fling my feet above my head;
    The light grows, none aside may glance;
Crimson and amber, green and red,
    In blinding baths of these I dance.

And soft, and sweet, and calm, my face
    Looks pure as unsunned chastity,
Even in the whirling triple pace:
    That is my conquering mystery.

JOHN DAVIDSON
*In a Music-Hall* (1891)

## To One in Bedlam

With delicate, mad hands, behind his sordid bars,
Surely he hath his posies, which they tear and twine;
Those scentless wisps of straw, that miserably line
His strait, caged universe, whereat the dull world stares,
Pedant and pitiful. O, how his rapt gaze wars
With their stupidity! Know they what dreams divine
Lift his long, laughing reveries like enchaunted wine,
And make his melancholy germane to the stars'?

O lamentable brother! if those pity thee,
Am I not fain of all thy lone eyes promise me;
Half a fool's kingdom, far from men who sow and reap,
All their days, vanity? Better than mortal flowers,
Thy moon-kissed roses seem: better than love or sleep,
The star-crowned solitude of thine oblivious hours!

ERNEST DOWSON
*Verses* (1896)


## Waiting

Within unfriendly walls
    We starve – or starve by stealth.
Oxen fatten in their stalls;
    You guard the harrier's health:
They never can be criminals,
    And can't compete for wealth.
        From the mansion and the palace
            Is there any help or hail
        For the tenants of the alleys,
            Of the workhouse and the jail?

Though lands await our toil,
   And earth half-empty rolls,
Cumberers of English soil,
   We cringe for orts and doles –
Prosperity's accustomed foil,
   Millions of useless souls.
      In the gutters and the ditches
         Human vermin festering lurk –
      We, the rust upon your riches;
         We, the flaw in all your work.

Come down from where you sit;
   We look to you for aid.
Take us from the miry pit,
   And lead us undismayed:
Say, 'Even you, outcast, unfit,
   Forward with sword and spade!'
      And myriads of us idle
         Would thank you through our tears,
      Though you drove us with a bridle,
         And a whip about our ears!

From cloudy cape to cape
   The teeming waters seethe;
Golden grain and purple grape
   The regions overwreathe.
Will no one help us to escape?
   We scarce have room to breathe.
      You might try to understand us:
         We are waiting night and day
      For a captain to command us,
         And the word we must obey.

JOHN DAVIDSON
*The Last Ballad* (1899)

# 6. THE HOUND OF HEAVEN

Barbey d'Aurevilly wrote in 1884 in a review of *A Rebours* that 'after such a book, there is nothing left for the author but to choose between the muzzle of a pistol and the foot of the cross'. Huysmans wrote in 1903 that the choice was made, having become a devout Roman Catholic. Many of the poets of the 1890s, concerned with problems similar to those which faced the author and the hero of 'the breviary of the Decadence', as Symons called *A Rebours*, found themselves faced with a similar dilemma. Their choice was commonly the same as Huysmans': 'Some turned Catholic,' wrote Yeats in *The Oxford Book of Modern Verse*, '. . . that too was a tradition.'[1] Beardsley, Olive Custance, Lord Alfred Douglas, Dowson, Johnson, both women who signed themselves 'Michael Field' and Oscar Wilde, became Catholics; Francis Thompson, who had been brought up in a Catholic family, had been intended for the priesthood, and his religious inclinations never left him; John Gray, a Catholic convert, became a priest; in fact rumour had it that 'during the 'nineties there had been so many converts to Catholicism that the Pope had decreed that John Gray, on receiving holy orders, must not return to England!'[2]

For women poets, inspired by writers like Christina Rossetti, the dilemma expressed itself in the tradition of convent poems that Angela Leighton has identified. These poems typically emphasize the choice between the security of religion and the stress of the world, between vocation and desire, and ultimately between allegiance to the father and to the mother.

What Barbey d'Aurevilly had so acutely analysed in Huysmans and his hero, des Esseintes, was not only their disgust with the world and its aims but also the inability of art to answer the problems of existence, and their consequent turning to religion for the answers.

1. *The Oxford Book of Modern Verse*, p. x.
2. *Two Friends*, ed. Fr. Brocard Sewell (1963).

An equally perceptive critic might have found the same need in the writers of the 1890s. Shaw did write, in the first number of *The Savoy* (January 1896), that society needed 'refreshment and recreation' and, though he perhaps meant it a little differently from the ordinary man, added that 'in the church alone can our need be truly met'. Yeats points out that 'there are "stars" in poem after poem of certain writers of the 'nineties as though to symbolize an aspiration towards what is inviolate and fixed'.[3] The fixedness of religion, of Catholicism in particular, was attractive, as was the ritual: 'Life must be a ritual' was a phrase of Johnson's that stuck in Yeats's mind. And though the superficial and decorative aspects were no doubt suited to their taste, their religion was by no means insincere. Perhaps the most unconventional in religious matters were Symons, the son of a Methodist minister, and Davidson, the son of a minister in the Evangelical Union.

But there were accusations of insincerity. Le Gallienne, who later conducted a long correspondence in the *Daily Chronicle* on the subject 'Is Christianity played out?' and published it as *The Religion of a Literary Man* (1893), complained of the Decadent who 'used his soul / As bitters to the over dulcet sins'. Certainly the refusal to be moral in the Victorian sense and the tendency to make art a religion left poets open to complaint; but many are fairly conventional in their religion, much more so than Yeats, whose mystical visions foreshadow his later and more completely worked-out beliefs. The religious synthesis was as necessary for these poets as it had been for Tennyson, Robert Browning and Christina Rossetti, and as it was to be for Eliot.

3. *The Oxford Book of Modern Verse*, p. xix.

## Benedictio Domini

Without, the sullen noises of the street!
   The voice of London, inarticulate,
Hoarse and blaspheming, surges in to meet
   The silent blessing of the Immaculate.

Dark is the church, and dim the worshippers,
   Hushed with bowed heads as though by some old spell,
While through the incense-laden air there stirs
   The admonition of a silver bell.

Dark is the church, save where the altar stands,
   Dressed like a bride, illustrious with light,
Where one old priest exalts with tremulous hands
   The one true solace of man's fallen plight.

Strange silence here: without, the sounding street
   Heralds the world's swift passage to the fire:
O Benediction, perfect and complete!
   When shall men cease to suffer and desire?

ERNEST DOWSON
*Verses* (1896)

## Magic

2

They wrong with ignorance a royal choice,
Who cavil at my loneliness and labour:
For them, the luring wonder of a voice,
The viol's cry for them, the harp and tabour:
     For me divine austerity,
     And voices of philosophy.

Ah! light imaginations, that discern
No passion in the citadel of passion:
Their fancies lie on flowers; but my thoughts turn
To thoughts and things of an eternal fashion:
    The majesty and dignity
    Of everlasting verity.

Mine is the sultry sunset, when the skies
Tremble with strange, intolerable thunder:
And at the dead of an hushed night, these eyes
Draw down the soaring oracles winged with wonder:
    From the four winds they come to me,
    The Angels of Eternity.

Men pity me; poor men, who pity me!
Poor, charitable, scornful souls of pity!
I choose laborious loneliness: and ye
Lead Love in triumph through the dancing city:
    While death and darkness girdle me,
    I grope for immortality.

LIONEL JOHNSON
*Ireland, with Other Poems* (1897)


## The Hound of Heaven

I fled Him, down the nights and down the days;
    I fled Him, down the arches of the years;
I fled Him, down the labyrinthine ways
    Of my own mind; and in the mist of tears
I hid from Him, and under running laughter.
      Up vistaed hopes I sped;
      And shot, precipitated
Adown Titanic glooms of chasmed fears,
  From those strong Feet that followed, followed after.
      But with unhurrying chase,
      And unperturbèd pace,

Deliberate speed, majestic instancy,
    They beat – and a Voice beat
    More instant than the Feet –
'All things betray thee, who betrayest Me.'

        I pleaded, outlaw-wise,
By many a hearted casement, curtained red,
    Trellised with intertwining charities;
(For, though I knew His love Who followèd,
        Yet was I sore adread
Lest, having Him, I must have naught beside)
But, if one little casement parted wide,
    The gust of His approach would clash it to.
    Fear wist not to evade, as Love wist to pursue.
Across the margent of the world I fled,
    And troubled the gold gateways of the stars,
    Smiting for shelter on their changèd bars;
        Fretted to dulcet jars
And silvern chatter the pale ports o' the moon.
I said to dawn: Be sudden – to eve: Be soon;
        With thy young skiey blossoms heap me over
        From this tremendous Lover!
Float thy vague veil about me, lest He see!
    I tempted all His servitors, but to find
My own betrayal in their constancy,
In faith to Him their fickleness to me,
    Their traitorous trueness, and their loyal deceit.
To all swift things for swiftness did I sue;
    Clung to the whistling mane of every wind.
        But whether they swept, smoothly fleet,
        The long savannahs of the blue;
        Or whether, Thunder-driven,
        They clanged his chariot 'thwart a heaven,
Plashy with flying lightnings round the spurn o' their feet: –
    Fear wist not to evade as Love wist to pursue.
        Still with unhurrying chase,
        And unperturbèd pace,
        Deliberate speed, majestic instancy,

Came on the following Feet,
And a Voice above their beat –
'Naught shelters thee, who wilt not shelter Me.'

I sought no more that, after which I strayed,
In face of man or maid;
But still within the little children's eyes
Seems something, something that replies,
*They* at least are for me, surely for me!
I turned me to them very wistfully;
But just as their young eyes grew sudden fair
With dawning answers there,
Their angel plucked them from me by the hair.
'Come then, ye other children, Nature's – share
With me' (said I) 'your delicate fellowship;
Let me greet you lip to lip,
Let me twine with you caresses,
Wantoning
With our Lady-Mother's vagrant tresses,
Banqueting
With her in her wind-walled palace,
Underneath her azured daïs,
Quaffing, as your taintless way is,
From a chalice
Lucent-weeping out of the dayspring.'
So it was done:
*I* in their delicate fellowship was one –
Drew the bolt of Nature's secrecies.
*I* knew all the swift importings
On the wilful face of skies;
I knew how the clouds arise
Spumèd of the wild sea-snortings;
All that's born or dies
Rose and drooped with – made them shapers
Of mine own moods, or wailful or divine –
With them joyed and was bereaven.
I was heavy with the even,
When she lit her glimmering tapers

Round the day's dead sanctities.
I laughed in the morning's eyes.
I triumphed and I saddened with all weather,
        Heaven and I wept together,
And its sweet tears were salt with mortal mine;
Against the red throb of its sunset-heart
        I laid my own to beat,
        And share commingling heat;
But not by that, by that, was eased my human smart.
In vain my tears were wet on Heaven's grey cheek.
For ah! we know not what each other says,
        These things and I; in sound *I* speak –
*Their* sound is but their stir, they speak by silences.
Nature, poor stepdame, cannot slake my drouth;
        Let her, if she would owe me,
Drop yon blue bosom-veil of sky, and show me
        The breasts o' her tenderness:
Never did any milk of hers once bless
        My thirsting mouth.
        Nigh and nigh draws the chase,
        With unperturbèd pace
    Deliberate speed, majestic instancy;
        And past those noisèd Feet
        A Voice comes yet more fleet –
    'Lo! naught contents thee, who content'st not Me.'

Naked I wait Thy love's uplifted stroke!
My harness piece by piece Thou hast hewn from me,
        And smitten me to my knee;
        I am defenceless utterly.
        I slept, methinks, and woke,
And, slowly gazing, find me stripped in sleep.
In the rash lustihead of my young powers,
        I shook the pillaring hours
And pulled my life upon me; grimed with smears,
I stand amid the dust o' the mounded years –
My mangled youth lies dead beneath the heap.
My days have crackled and gone up in smoke,

Have puffed and burst as sun-starts on a stream.
     Yea, faileth now even dream
The dreamer, and the lute the lutanist;
Even the linked fantasies, in whose blossomy twist
I swung the earth a trinket at my wrist,
Are yielding; cords of all too weak account
For earth with heavy griefs so overplussed.
     Ah! is Thy love indeed
A weed, albeit an amaranthine weed,
Suffering no flowers except its own to mount?
     Ah! must –
     Designer infinite! –
Ah! must Thou char the wood ere Thou canst limn with it?
My freshness spent its wavering shower i' the dust;
And now my heart is as a broken fount,
Wherein tear-drippings stagnate, spilt down ever
     From the dank thoughts that shiver
Upon the sighful branches of my mind.
     Such is; what is to be?
The pulp so bitter, how shall taste the rind?
I dimly guess what Time in mists confounds;
Yet ever and anon a trumpet sounds
From the hid battlements of Eternity,
Those shaken mists a space unsettle, then
Round the half-glimpsèd turrets slowly wash again;
     But not ere him who summoneth
     I first have seen, enwound
With glooming robes purpureal, cypress-crowned;
His name I know, and what his trumpet saith.
Whether man's heart or life it be which yields
     Thee harvest, must Thy harvest fields
     Be dunged with rotten death?
       Now of that long pursuit
       Comes on at hand the bruit;
     That Voice is round me like a bursting sea:
       'And is thy earth so marred,
       Shattered in shard on shard?
     Lo, all things fly thee, for thou fliest Me!

'Strange, piteous, futile thing!
Wherefore should any set thee love apart?
Seeing none but I makes much of naught' (He said),
'And human love needs human meriting:
    How hast thou merited –
Of all man's clotted clay the dingiest clot?
    Alack, thou knowest not
How little worthy of any love thou art!
Whom wilt thou find to love ignoble thee,
    Save Me, save only Me?
All which I took from thee I did but take,
    Not for thy harms,
But just that thou might'st seek it in My arms.
    All which thy child's mistake
Fancies as lost, I have stored for thee at home:
    Rise, clasp My hand, and come.'

    Halts by me that footfall:
    Is my gloom, after all,
Shade of His hand, outstretched caressingly?
    'Ah, fondest, blindest, weakest,
    I am He Whom thou seekest!
Thou dravest love from thee, who dravest Me.'

FRANCIS THOMPSON
*Poems* (1893)


### 'Lord, if thou art not present'

Lord, if thou art not present, where shall I
Seek thee the absent? If thou art everywhere,
How is it that I do not see thee nigh?

Thou dwellest in a light remote and fair.
How can I reach that light, Lord? I beseech
Thee, teach my seeking, and thyself declare

Thyself the sought to me. Unless thou teach
Me, Lord, I cannot seek; nor can I find
Thee, if thou wilt not come within my reach.

Lord, let me seek, with sturdy heart and mind,
In passion of desire and longingly.
Let me desire thee, seeking thee; and find . . .

Loving thee, find thee; love thee, finding thee.

JOHN GRAY
*Spiritual Poems* (1896)


## The Silent Heavens

Here I wander about, and here I mournfully ponder:
    Weary to me is the sun, weary the coming of night:
Here is captivity still, there would be captivity yonder:
    Like to myself are the rest, smitten is all with a blight.

Much I complain of my state to my own heart heavily
      beating:
    Much to the stars I complain: much to the universe
      cold;
The stars that of old were fixed, in spheres their courses
      repeating;
    Solidly once were they fixed, and with them their
      spheres were rolled.

Then through the space of the spheres to the steadfast
      empyrean
    Echo on echo to Earth answered her manifold cries:
Earth was the centre of things, and the threne of all, or the
      pæan,
    Bearing hell in her heart, on her bosom all life that
      dies.

If they were fixed, as of old, in their firmament solid and
    vaulted,
    Then might the echo of woe or of laughter
      reverberate thence:
Nor my voice alone, but to them all voices exalted,
    Should with due answer be met, murmuring sweet to
      the sense.

But they roll on their way through the void, the inane
    unretentive:
    Past them all voices stream into the echoless space.
Where is the pitying grace, that once was prayer's
    incentive,
    Where is the ear that heard, and the face that once
      answered to face?

R. W. DIXON
*The Last Poems of Richard Watson Dixon, D.D.* (1905)

## Veni Creator

So humble things Thou hast borne for us, O God,
Left'st Thou a path of lowliness untrod?
Yes, one, till now; another Olive-Garden.
For we endure the tender pain of pardon, –
One with another we forbear. Give heed,
Look at the mournful world Thou hast decreed.
The time has come. At last we hapless men
Know all our haplessness all through. Come, then,
Endure undreamed humility: Lord of Heaven,
Come to our ignorant hearts and be forgiven.

ALICE MEYNELL
*Poems* (1898)

## The Dark Angel

Dark Angel, with thine aching lust
To rid the world of penitence:
Malicious Angel, who still dost
My soul such subtile violence!

Because of thee, no thought, no thing,
Abides for me undesecrate:
Dark Angel, ever on the wing,
Who never reachest me too late!

When music sounds, then changest thou
Its silvery to a sultry fire:
Nor will thine envious heart allow
Delight untortured by desire.

Through thee, the gracious Muses turn
To Furies, O mine Enemy!
And all the things of beauty burn
With flames of evil ecstasy.

Because of thee, the land of dreams
Becomes a gathering place of fears:
Until tormented slumber seems
One vehemence of useless tears.

When sunlight glows upon the flowers,
Or ripples down the dancing sea:
Thou, with thy troop of passionate powers,
Beleaguerest, bewilderest, me.

Within the breath of autumn woods,
Within the winter silences:
Thy venomous spirit stirs and broods,
O Master of impieties!

The ardour of red flame is thine,
And thine the steely soul of ice:
Thou poisonest the fair design
Of nature, with unfair device.

Apples of ashes, golden bright;
Waters of bitterness, how sweet!
O banquet of a foul delight,
Prepared by thee, dark Paraclete!

Thou art the whisper in the gloom,
The hinting tone, the haunting laugh:
Thou art the adorner of my tomb,
The minstrel of mine epitaph.

I fight thee, in the Holy Name!
Yet, what thou dost, is what God saith:
Tempter! should I escape thy flame,
Thou wilt have helped my soul from Death:

The second Death, that never dies,
That cannot die, when time is dead:
Live Death, wherein the lost soul cries,
Eternally uncomforted.

Dark Angel, with thine aching lust!
Of two defeats, of two despairs:
Less dread, a change to drifting dust,
Than thine eternity of cares.

Do what thou wilt, thou shalt not so,
Dark Angel! triumph over me:
*Lonely, unto the Lone I go;*
*Divine, to the Divinity.*

LIONEL JOHNSON
*Poems* (1895)


## Insomnia

He wakened quivering on a golden rack
    Inlaid with gems: no sign of change, no fear
    Or hope of death came near;
Only the empty ether hovered black

About him stretched upon his living bier,
Of old by Marlin's Master deftly wrought:
  Two Seraphim of Gabriel's helpful race
  In that far nook of space
With iron levers wrenched and held him taut.

The Seraph at his head was Agony;
  Delight, more terrible, stood at his feet:
  Their sixfold pinions beat
The darkness, or were spread immovably,
  Poising the rack, whose jewelled fabric meet
To strain a god, did fitfully unmask
  With olive light of chrysoprases dim
  The smiling Seraphim
Implacably intent upon their task.

JOHN DAVIDSON
*The Last Ballad* (1899)


## The Veil of Light

Here, where the vague winds, tired, come to sleep,
Here, where they hide when hunted by the rain;
From this point whence the world looks far and deep,
We gaze triumphant on the earth's dull plain.

How hardly won! – but now this comely peace:
Even the sea-tang in the mellow air
Breathes harshly, and its strength disturbs the ease
Of yon thin cloud soft falling from God's Hair.

Ah, that bright cloud! – a curtain from the sky;
That shifting filmy thing, that drifting gauze:
The dooms that 'neath its trembling shadows lie,
Though suns be in our hearts, must give us pause.

All down the valleys of the universe,
Through firmaments to where the tall stars end,
The terror lurks, and stabs us like a curse,
Whom Fear binds close together, O my friend!

Blank dreams are there that make a mock of life;
And all of sinister that round the bed
Crawl in dark hours, alive and wet with strife;
And all the thoughts when no more words are said.

And what unknown is there to mar our way?
What more, O Blessèd Lord! what vile thing more
Lies hid behind that mass of whitened grey?
What furtive venom is there still in store?

Hear, in Thy lofty place, Thy children calling!
Dead leaves, we ride upon the wings of night:
Remove, Lord God most High, this shroud appalling –
This hard, intolerable Veil of Light!

VINCENT O'SULLIVAN
*Poems* (1896)

## A Shropshire Lad

### 43
#### THE IMMORTAL PART

When I meet the morning beam,
Or lay me down at night to dream,
I hear my bones within me say,
'Another night, another day.

'When shall this slough of sense be cast,
This dust of thought be laid at last,
The man of flesh and soul be slain
And the man of bone remain?

'This tongue that talks, these lungs that shout,
These thews that hustle us about,
This brain that fills the skull with schemes,
And its humming hive of dreams, –

'These to-day are proud in power
And lord it in their little hour:
The immortal bones obey control
Of dying flesh and dying soul.

''Tis long till eve and morn are gone:
Slow the endless night comes on,
And late to fulness grows the birth
That shall last as long as earth.

'Wanderers eastward, wanderers west,
Know you why you cannot rest?
'Tis that every mother's son
Travails with a skeleton.

'Lie down in the bed of dust;
Bear the fruit that bear you must;
Bring the eternal seed to light,
And morn is all the same as night.

'Rest you so from trouble sore,
Fear the heat o' the sun no more,
Nor the snowing winter wild,
Now you labour not with child.

'Empty vessel, garment cast,
We that wore you long shall last.
– Another night, another day.'
So my bones within me say.

Therefore they shall do my will
To-day while I am master still,
And flesh and soul, now both are strong,
Shall hale the sullen slaves along,

Before this fire of sense decay,
This smoke of thought blow clean away,
And leave with ancient night alone
The stedfast and enduring bone.

A. E. HOUSMAN
*A Shropshire Lad* (1896)


## Quisque suos manes

What have you seen, eyes of strange fire! What have you seen,
Far off, how far away! long since, so long ago!
To fill you with this jewel flame, this frozen glow:
Haunted and hard, still eyes, malignant and serene?
In what wild place of fear, what Pan's wood, have you been,
That struck your lustrous rays into a burning snow?
What agonies were yours? What never equalled woe?
Eyes of strange fire, strange eyes of fire! on what dread scene?

Smitten and purged, you saw the red deeps of your sin:
You saw there death in life; you will see life in death.
The sunlight shrank away, the moon came wan and thin,
Among the summer trees the sweet winds held their breath.
Now those celestial lights, which you can never win,
Haunt you, and pierce, and blind. The Will of God so saith.

LIONEL JOHNSON
*Ireland, with Other Poems* (1897)


## The Secret Rose

Far off, most secret, and inviolate Rose,
Enfold me in my hour of hours; where those
Who sought thee in the Holy Sepulchre,
Or in the wine vat, dwell beyond the stir

And tumult of defeated dreams; and deep
Among pale eyelids, heavy with the sleep
Men have named beauty. Thy great leaves enfold
The ancient beards, the helms of ruby and gold
Of the crowned Magi; and the king whose eyes
Saw the Pierced Hands and Rood of elder rise
In druid vapour and make the torches dim;
Till vain frenzy awoke and he died; and him
Who met Fand walking among flaming dew
By a grey shore where the wind never blew,
And lost the world and Emer for a kiss;
And him who drove the gods out of their liss,
And till a hundred morns had flowered red,
Feasted and wept the barrows of his dead;
And the proud dreaming king who flung the crown
And sorrow away, and calling bard and clown
Dwelt among wine-stained wanderers in deep woods;
And him who sold tillage, and house, and goods,
And sought through lands and islands numberless years,
Until he found with laughter and with tears,
A woman, of so shining loveliness,
That men threshed corn at midnight by a tress,
A little stolen tress. I, too, await
The hour of thy great wind of love and hate.
When shall the stars be blown about the sky,
Like the sparks blown out of a smithy, and die?
Surely thine hour has come, thy great wind blows,
Far off, most secret, and inviolate Rose?

W. B. YEATS
*The Wind Among the Reeds* (1899)

## Nuns of the Perpetual Adoration

Calm, sad, secure; behind high convent walls,
  These watch the sacred lamp, these watch and pray:
And it is one with them when evening falls,
  And one with them the cold return of day.

These heed not time; their nights and days they make
  Into a long, returning rosary,
Whereon their lives are threaded for Christ's sake:
  Meekness and vigilance and chastity.

A vowed patrol, in silent companies,
  Life-long they keep before the living Christ:
In the dim church, their prayers and penances
  Are fragrant incense to the Sacrificed.

Outside, the world is wild and passionate;
  Man's weary laughter and his sick despair
Entreat at their impenetrable gate:
  They heed no voices in their dream of prayer.

They saw the glory of the world displayed;
  They saw the bitter of it, and the sweet;
They knew the roses of the world should fade,
  And be trod under by the hurrying feet.

Therefore they rather put away desire,
  And crossed their hands and came to sanctuary;
And veiled their heads and put on coarse attire:
  Because their comeliness was vanity.

And there they rest; they have serene insight
  Of the illuminating dawn to be:
Mary's sweet Star dispels for them the night,
  The proper darkness of humanity.

Calm, sad, secure; with faces worn and mild:
  Surely their choice of vigil is the best?
Yea! for our roses fade, the world is wild;
  But there, beside the altar, there, is rest.

ERNEST DOWSON
*Verses* (1896)

## The Carmelite Nun

Silence is mine, and everlasting peace;
  My heart is empty, waiting for its Lord;
All hope, all passion, all desire shall cease,
  And loss of self shall be my last reward.

For I would lose my life, my thought, my will;
  The love and hate, the grief and joy of earth:
I watch and pray, and am for ever still;
  So shall I find the death, which yet is birth.

Yet once I loved to hear the wild birds sing,
  I knew the hedge-row blossoms all by name;
Keen sight was mine, to trace the budding spring,
  Clear voice, for songs of joy when summer came.

Too dear I held each earthly sight and sound,
  Too well I loved each fair created thing,
And when I prayed to Him I had not found,
  I called Him in my heart 'the mountains' King.'

All, all is past – gone, every vain delight;
  No beauty tempts me in this lonely cell:
Yet why, O Lord, were earth and sky so bright,
  Winning the soul that in Thyself should dwell?

Often my heart recalls the sacred time
  When fell the tresses of my nut-brown hair;
But then will come – O God, forgive the crime! –
  That guilty question – Can I still be fair?

I cannot quite forget that I am young;
   I sometimes long to see my mother's face:
Oh, when I left her, how she wept, and clung
   About my neck in agonized embrace!

And there was one – Ah, no, the thought is sin –
   Why come these thronging forms of earthly grace?
Close, close, my heart! Thou shalt not let them in,
   To break the stillness of this holy place.

Oh, Mary, Mother, help me to endure!
   I am a woman, with a heart like thine:
But no – thy nature is too high and pure
   Thou canst not feel these low-born pangs of mine.

Oh, for the vision of the Master's face!
   Oh, for the music of the heavenly throng!
I have but lived on earth a little space,
   And yet I cry, 'How long, O Lord, how long?'

CONSTANCE NADEN
*Complete Poetical Works* (1894)

## Sœur Louise de la Miséricorde

### (LOUISE DE LA VALLIÈRE)

Scourge, and cilice, and feet unshod,
And Office, and fast, and the love of God.

The grille, and the cell, and the sweet Vows three,
And the holy habit – for me! for me!

For me, who at first in the state of grace,
Blushed when the great sin looked in my face –

Who housed desire of it unconfessed
In the bosom that once received God for its Guest –

Who, with peril and guilt of it all to me known,
Drank of it, laved in it, made it mine own.

Oh! God of mine, nailed up on the Rood,
Why hast Thou waited? oh! Kind – oh! Good –

God of my heart, on the bitter Tree
Waiting, when I would not hear of Thee.

My sin loaded the scourge that tore
To pieces the Body that Mary bore –

My sin launched the blows and disgrace
To change and to mar all Thy beautiful Face –

And I, when for ever from pain Thou didst part,
Clove to Its Centre Thy dear dead Heart –

My All! my Jesus! still can it be,
Thy Heart and the holy habit – for me?

Through the sorrows of Mary Thy Mother, who stood
With the sword in her soul beneath the Rood,

Through the added sorrow her grief brought Thee
Assoil Thou those that have sinned through me . . .

Chimes! . . . and another to-morrow near –
And after to-morrow year on year . . .

Lord, for such as I used to be
I have given my body to grief and Thee,

To broken sleep, and girdle of iron,
And scourgings to blood, and the flags to lie on –

Wait, wait but for them as for me Thou didst wait,
Who came unwilling, and came so late –

Oh! Kind – oh! Gentle – I chose not Thee –
My Jesus, why hast Thou chosen me?

Chimes . . . and the long night going its way
Till the next chime bringeth another day –

Penance, and fast, and the feet unshod,
And a living death, and the love of God.

MAY PROBYN
*Pansies* (1895)

## Ballade

### A DOUBLE REFRAIN

There was a tree where the lilies grew tall
   In the happy Garden, and carried freight
So fair that it seemed like a festival
   When the apple of Death Eve plucked and ate.
   And Tree there was on a hill desolate,
Gibbet-planted, without the wall
   Of the city, and under in sword-stricken state
Mary, consenting to save us all.

'As gods shall ye be,' said the Angel, whose fall
   Had dragged half Heaven through the Beautiful Gate;
And Adam made haste at her shrill, sweet call
   When the apple of Death Eve plucked and ate.
   And an Angel it was who was bidden to wait
For Yea or for Nay in the chamber small,
   When spoke without doubt and without debate
Mary, consenting to save us all.

Like lamps 'mid the leaves hung the gold-fruit ball
   And the red, where the birds whistled each to its mate;
On high, doves built as in flower-domed hall
   When the apple of Death Eve plucked and ate.
   But for Him lifted up, while the Wounds grew more great
That held Him, the savour of myrrh and gall,
   And for crown of His sorrow to contemplate
Mary, consenting to save us all.

### ENVOI

   Jesus! to rescue us scheming straight
   When the apple of Death Eve plucked and ate,
Thou wouldst have by the Rood as erst in the Stall
Mary, consenting to save us all.

MAY PROBYN
*Pansies* (1895)

## Good Friday

He hangs a dead corpse on the tree,
   Who made the whole world's life to spring:
   And, as some outcast, shameful, thing
The Lord of all we see.

Darkness falls thick to shroud the time:
   Nature herself breaks up, and cries:
   Even from the grave shocked ghosts arise,
At this tremendous crime.

Speak not: no human voice may tell
   The secrets, which these hours enfold:
   By treacherous hands to traitors sold,
God yields Himself to Hell.

Speak not, draw close: through stricken heart
   Drink in the sense of all that's here:
   The shame, the cross, the nails, the spear,
Rending His soul apart.

Ah! and far crueller, far, than they,
   (Tools, and mere symbols these) our sin!
   Breathe to thyself, soul, deep within,
''Twas I, that caused this day.'

Speak not: He speaks not: no reproach
   Falls from Those dying lips on thee:
   No vengeance, muttering ills to be,
Bars thy devout approach.

Stricken, unmurmuring, dead, divine,
   This day He hangs, as He hung of old:
   Only the dire sight cries, 'Behold!
Was ever love like Mine?'

SELWYN IMAGE
*Poems and Carols* (1894)

## A Carol for Christmas Eve

We are but of such mortal mould,
   *Nos exaudi, Domine!*
That the night can scarce withhold
   In its shroud our sins from Thee.

That night comes, when Thou shalt come,
   *Nos exaudi, Domine!*
From Thy home to this sad home,
   And die for us upon the tree.

If then the stars shine out so bright,
   *Nos exaudi, Domine!*
That Thou seest by their light,
   How great our sins and many be;

Thou wilt come, as they were not,
   *Nos exaudi, Domine!*
Or as they were all forgot,
   Or forgiven, Lord, by Thee.

HERBERT HORNE
*Diversi Colores* (1891)

## A Meditation for Christmas

Consider, O my soul, what morn is this!
   Whereon the eternal Lord of all things made,
For us, poor mortals, and our endless bliss,
   Came down from heaven; and, in a manger laid,
   The first, rich, offerings of our ransom paid:
Consider, O my soul, what morn is this!

Consider what estate of fearful woe
   Had then been ours, had He refused this birth;
From sin to sin tossed vainly to and fro,

Hell's playthings, o'er a doomed and helpless earth!
Had He from us withheld His priceless worth,
Consider man's estate of fearful woe!

Consider to what joys He bids thee rise,
    Who comes, Himself, life's bitter cup to drain!
Ah! look on this sweet Child, Whose innocent eyes,
    Ere all be done, shall close in mortal pain,
    That thou at last Love's Kingdom may'st attain:
Consider to what joys He bids thee rise!

Consider all this wonder, O my soul:
    And in thine inmost shrine make music sweet!
Yea, let the world, from furthest pole to pole,
    Join in thy praises this dread birth to greet;
    Kneeling to kiss thy Saviour's infant feet!
Consider all this wonder, O my soul!

SELWYN IMAGE
*Poems and Carols* (1894)


## The Church of a Dream

Sadly the dead leaves rustle in the whistling wind,
Around the weather-worn, gray church, low down the vale:
The Saints in golden vesture shake before the gale;
The glorious windows shake, where still they dwell enshrined;
Old Saints, by long dead, shrivelled hands, long since designed:
There still, although the world autumnal be, and pale,
Still in their golden vesture the old saints prevail;
Alone with Christ, desolate else, left by mankind.

Only one ancient Priest offers the Sacrifice,
Murmuring holy Latin immemorial:
Swaying with tremulous hands the old censer full of spice,

In gray, sweet incense clouds; blue, sweet clouds mystical:
To him, in place of men, for he is old, suffice
Melancholy remembrances and vesperal.

LIONEL JOHNSON
*Poems* (1895)


## To the Rose upon the Rood of Time

Red Rose, proud Rose, sad Rose of all my days!
Come near me, while I sing the ancient ways:
Cuhoollin battling with the bitter tide;
The Druid, gray, wood-nurtured, quiet-eyed,
Who cast round Fergus dreams, and ruin untold;
And thine own sadness, whereof stars, grown old
In dancing silver sandalled on the sea,
Sing in their high and lonely melody.
Come near, that no more blinded by man's fate,
I find under the boughs of love and hate,
In all poor foolish things that live a day,
Eternal Beauty wandering on her way.

Come near, come near, come near – Ah, leave me still
A little space for the rose-breath to fill!
Lest I no more hear common things that crave;
The weak worm hiding down in its small cave,
The field mouse running by me in the grass,
And heavy mortal hopes that toil and pass;
But seek alone to hear the strange things said
By God to the bright hearts of those long dead,
And learn to chaunt a tongue men do not know.
Come near; I would, before my time to go,
Sing of old Eire and the ancient ways:
Red Rose, proud Rose, sad Rose of all my days.

W. B. YEATS
*Poems* (1899)

## Enthusiasts

Let your swords flash, and wound the golden air of God:
Bright steel, to meet and cleave the splendour of His sun!
Now is a war of wars in majesty begun:
Red shall the cornfields ripen, where our horses trod,
Where scythe nor sickle swept, but smote war's iron rod:
Where the stars rose and set, and saw the blood still run.
So shall men tell of us, and dread our deeds, though done:
New annals yet shall praise time's fiercest period.
Let your swords flash, and wound the glowing air: now play
A glorious dance of death, with clash and gleam of sword.
Did Syrian sun and moon stand still on Israel's day?
Those orbs halt over Ajalon at Joshua's word?
Of us, who ride for God, shall Christian children say:
*To battle, see! flash by armed angels of the Lord.*

LIONEL JOHNSON
*Poems* (1895)

## The Valley of the Black Pig

The dews drop slowly and dreams gather: unknown spears
Suddenly hurtle before my dream-awakened eyes,
And then the clash of fallen horsemen and the cries
Of unknown perishing armies beat about my ears.
We who still labour by the cromlec on the shore,
The grey cairn on the hill, when day sinks drowned in dew,
Being weary of the world's empires, bow down to you
Master of the still stars and of the flaming door.

W. B. YEATS
*The Wind Among the Reeds* (1899)

## Extreme Unction

Upon the eyes, the lips, the feet,
    On all the passages of sense,
The atoning oil is spread with sweet
    Renewal of lost innocence.

The feet, that lately ran so fast
    To meet desire, are soothly sealed;
The eyes, that were so often cast
    On vanity, are touched and healed.

From troublous sights and sounds set free;
    In such a twilight hour of breath,
Shall one retrace his life, or see,
    Through shadows, the true face of death?

Vials of mercy! Sacring oils!
    I know not where nor when I come,
Nor through what wanderings and toils,
    To crave of you Viaticum.

Yet, when the walls of flesh grow weak,
    In such an hour, it well may be,
Through mist and darkness, light will break,
    And each anointed sense will see.

ERNEST DOWSON
*Verses* (1896)

## Epilogue: Credo

Each, in himself, his hour to be and cease
    Endures alone, but who of men shall dare,
    Sole with himself, his single burden bear,
All the long day until the night's release?

Yet, ere night falls, and the last shadows close,
  This labour of himself is each man's lot;
  All he has gained of earth shall be forgot,
Himself he leaves behind him when he goes.

If he has any valiancy within,
  If he has made his life his very own,
  If he has loved or laboured, and has known
A strenuous virtue, or a strenuous sin;

Then, being dead, his life was not all vain,
  For he has saved what most desire to lose,
  And he has chosen what the few must choose,
Since life, once lived, shall not return again.

For of our time we lose so large a part
  In serious trifles, and so oft let slip
  The wine of every moment, at the lip
Its moment, and the moment of the heart.

We are awake so little on the earth,
  And we shall sleep so long, and rise so late,
  If there is any knocking at that gate
Which is the gate of death, the gate of birth.

ARTHUR SYMONS
*London Nights* (2nd edition 1897)

# 7. LOVE AND DEATH

There is no evidence that poets of the 1890s loved or died more frequently than those of any other period. There was certainly nothing new in the traditional poetic subjects of love and death, and many of the poems are of the period because of their style rather than their content.

None the less, some poets sang of loves quite distinct from traditional types. Le Gallienne, reviewing John Gray's *Silverpoints* (1893), greets Gray's line 'What bonny hair our child will have' with the comment: 'Is not this absurdly domestic in a decadent? Really Mr Gray must check these natural impulses.' Certainly bought love, casual love, unfaithful love and the 'love that dare not speak its name' (though it seems to have written it in both gay and lesbian contexts) were being claimed as subject matter for poetry. It had been done before, even in the Victorian period; Dante Gabriel Rossetti had written of

> Lazy laughing languid Jenny,
> Fond of a kiss and fond of a guinea;

Swinburne's poems had hymned a variety of loves, and Wilde had described 'The Harlot's House'. But Dowson could still feel nervous about his 'Cynara': 'I have just seen the proofs of my "Cynara" poem for the April Hobby. It looks less indecent in print, but I am still nervous! though I admire Horne's audacity.'[1]

The insistence on the more perverse type of subject was a combination of a striving for freedom in choice of subject matter, a desire to shock and a love of the artificial or unnatural. It was also a reaction against the hypocrisy of the Victorian pretence of rectitude, the true superficiality of which has been demonstrated by Steven Marcus's *The Other Victorians*. But freedom of subject matter often meant concentration on the perverse or erotic, a fact recognized by

1. *The Letters of Ernest Dowson*, ed. Desmond Flower and Henry Maas (1967).

parodists. Symons, in the person of Arthur in Owen Seaman's 'A Vigo-Street Eclogue', admits his propensities:

> What's Nature's law compared with women's?
> *John:*    For this enigma go to S-m-ns;
>           He is the –
> *Arthur:*              Yes, I am, I know,
>           The devil of a Romeo!

And Lionel Johnson, in the following parody from his short story 'Incurable' (from *The Pageant* of 1896), catches the more extreme of the lyrics of Symons or Wratislaw (like the latter's 'The Conquest of Sense').

> Sometimes, in very joy of shame,
> Our flesh becomes one living flame:
> And she and I
> Are no more separate, but the same.

> Ardour and agony unite;
> Desire, delirium, delight:
> And I and she
> Faint in the fierce and fevered night.

> Her body music is: and ah,
> The accords of lute and viola,
> When she and I
> Play on live limbs love's opera!

More problematic than the straightforward objectification of the female beloved is the disturbing connection between love and death, where the most lovely and beloved woman is a dead one. This is indeed a pertinent comment on the feminine ideal.

Women poets attempted to avoid the caricature and objectification of conventional love poetry, sometimes by undercutting or specifically criticizing those conventions, as in 'A Woman's Story', sometimes by replacing them with new images and new psychological honesty, as in 'Love Without Wings'. These revolutionary attitudes also explain their more optimistic and humorous tone, which contrasts strikingly with the notion of decline which colours much other poetry of the 1890s.

## A Question and an Answer

*The Question:*  What is Love? Is Love in this,
That flies between us, in a kiss?
Nay, what is Love? Is Love the zest,
That wakes, when I unloose my breast?
But what is Love? Say now: who knows,
Or where he lurks, or how he shows?

*The Answer:*  Dearest, Truth is stern, I fear:
Love, as yet, can scarce be here.

Love is poor; nay, Love is sorry;
    Tears, not kisses, chiefly stay him:
His sad weeds best tell his story;
    Vain delights befool, bewray him.

Truth, alas! is hard to bear:
Know, as yet, Love is not here.

But, when the evil days are come,
    If those same lips, which kiss you now,
Still make your tearful eyes their home,
    And chide the sorrow from your brow;

Then say to your own heart, my Dear:
Abide, poor heart, for Love is here.

Love is a light, in darkened ways;
    Love is a path, in pathless lands;
Love is a fire, in winter days;
    A staff, in chill, unsteady hands.

Speak to your heart, my own, my Dear;
Say: this is Love, and Love is here.

HERBERT HORNE
*Diversi Colores* (1891)

## Nerves

The modern malady of love is nerves.
Love, once a simple madness, now observes
The stage of his passionate disease,
And is twice sorrowful because he sees,
Inch by inch entering, the fatal knife.
O health of simple minds, give me your life,
And let me, for one midnight, cease to hear
The clock for ever ticking in my ear,
The clock that tells the minutes in my brain.
It is not love, nor love's despair, this pain
That shoots a witless, keener pang across
The simple agony of love and loss.
Nerves, nerves! O folly of a child who dreams
Of heaven, and, waking in the darkness, screams.

ARTHUR SYMONS
Dated by Symons 1897
Reprinted in *Collected Works* (1924)

## White Heliotrope

The feverish room and that white bed,
    The tumbled skirts upon a chair,
    The novel flung half-open, where
Hat, hair-pins, puffs, and paints, are spread;

The mirror that has sucked your face
    Into its secret deep of deeps,
    And there mysteriously keeps
Forgotten memories of grace;

And you, half dressed and half awake,
    Your slant eyes strangely watching me,
    And I, who watch you drowsily,
With eyes that, having slept not, ache;

This (need one dread? nay, dare one hope?)
   Will rise, a ghost of memory, if
   Ever again my handkerchief
Is scented with White Heliotrope.

ARTHUR SYMONS
*London Nights* (2nd edition 1897)

## Spring-Song

Ah love, the sweet spring blossoms cling
To many a broken wind-tossed bough,
And young birds among branches sing
That mutely hung till now.

The little new-born things which lie
In dewy meadows, sleep and dream
Beside the brook that twinkles by
To some great lonely stream.

And children, now the day is told,
From many a warm and cosy nest,
Look up to see the young moon hold
The old moon to her breast.

Dear love, my pulses throb and start
To-night with longings sweet and new,
And young hopes beat within a heart
Grown old in loving you.

DOLLIE RADFORD
*A Light Load* (1891)

## A Woman's Story

Ay, 'twas thirty year ago –
All the garden was aglow:
Ruddy holyoaks, red roses,
Marigold and salvia posies,
Stately sunflow'rs, humble pansies –
'Heart's-ease true as little Nan's is,'
Quoth my lover, speaking low.
In the orchard trilled a robin.
Ah me! how my heart was throbbin',
Those long happy years ago!

Well, the tale's been often told:
Two things, pure love and pure gold,
Do not wane with passing fashion.
Life's cold without human passion.
Pick me that blue pansy yonder –
Thoughts for pansies, say you? – fonder
Grow our thoughts as we wax old.
Haply, as the rough path steepens,
And our feet lag, true love deepens –
Just because the tale's retold.

CAROLINE LINDSAY
*Lyrics and Other Poems* (1890)


## A Shropshire Lad

### 13

When I was one-and-twenty
    I heard a wise man say,
'Give crowns and pounds and guineas
    But not your heart away;

Give pearls away and rubies
    But keep your fancy free.'
But I was one-and-twenty,
    No use to talk to me.

When I was one-and-twenty
    I heard him say again,
'The heart out of the bosom
    Was never given in vain;
'Tis paid with sighs a plenty
    And sold for endless rue.'
And I am two-and-twenty,
    And oh, 'tis true, 'tis true.

A. E. HOUSMAN
*A Shropshire Lad* (1896)

## Down by the Salley Gardens

Down by the salley gardens my love and I did meet;
She passed the salley gardens with little snow-white feet.
She bid me take love easy, as the leaves grow on the tree;
But I, being young and foolish, with her would not agree.

In a field by the river my love and I did stand,
And on my leaning shoulder she laid her snow-white hand.
She bid me take life easy, as the grass grows on the weirs;
But I was young and foolish, and now am full of tears.

W. B. YEATS
*Poems* (1899)

## Plymouth Harbour

### A SONG

Oh, what know they of harbours
   Who toss not on the sea!
They tell of fairer havens,
   But none so fair there be

As Plymouth town outstretching
   Her quiet arms to me;
Her breast's broad welcome spreading
   From Mewstone to Penlee.

Ah, with this home-thought, darling,
   Come crowding thoughts of thee.
Oh, what know they of harbours
   Who toss not on the sea!

ERNEST RADFORD
*Old and New* (1895)

## Saint Germain-en-Laye

### (1887–1895)

Through the green boughs I hardly saw thy face,
They twined so close: the sun was in mine eyes;
And now the sullen trees in sombre lace
Stand bare beneath the sinister, sad skies.

O sun and summer! Say in what far night,
The gold and green, the glory of thine head,
Of bough and branch have fallen? Oh, the white
Gaunt ghosts that flutter where thy feet have sped,

Across the terrace that is desolate,
And rang then with thy laughter, ghost of thee,
That holds its shroud up with most delicate,
Dead fingers, and behind the ghost of me,

Tripping fantastic with a mouth that jeers
At roseal flowers of youth the turbid streams
Toss in derision down the barren years
To death the host of all our golden dreams.

ERNEST DOWSON
*Decorations* (1899)

## Aedh Wishes for the Cloths of Heaven

Had I the heavens' embroidered cloths,
Enwrought with golden and silver light,
The blue and the dim and the dark cloths
Of night and light and the half light,
I would spread the cloths under your feet:
But I, being poor, have only my dreams;
I have spread my dreams under your feet;
Tread softly because you tread on my dreams.

W. B. YEATS
*The Wind Among the Reeds* (1899)

## A Mésalliance

(TRIOLET)

Is she mine, – and for life, –
        And drinks tea from her saucer!
She eats with her knife –
Is she mine – and for life?

When I asked her to wife
    All her answer was 'Lor', sir!'
Is she mine? and for life?
    And drinks tea from her saucer!

MAY PROBYN
*Pansies* (1895)

## The Two Trees

Beloved, gaze in thine own heart,
The holy tree is growing there;
From joy the holy branches start,
And all the trembling flowers they bear.
The changing colours of its fruit
Have dowered the stars with merry light;
The surety of its hidden root
Has planted quiet in the night;
The shaking of its leafy head
Has given the waves their melody,
And made my lips and music wed,
Murmuring a wizard song for thee.
There, through bewildered branches, go
Winged Loves borne on in gentle strife,
Tossing and tossing to and fro
The flaming circle of our life.
When looking on their shaken hair,
And dreaming how they dance and dart,
Thine eyes grow full of tender care:
Beloved, gaze in thine own heart.

Gaze no more in the bitter glass
The demons, with their subtle guile,
Lift up before us when they pass,
Or only gaze a little while;
For there a fatal image grows,
With broken boughs, and blackened leaves,

And roots half hidden under snows
Driven by a storm that ever grieves.
For all things turn to barrenness
In the dim glass the demons hold,
The glass of outer weariness,
Made when God slept in times of old.
There, through the broken branches, go
The ravens of unresting thought;
Peering and flying to and fro,
To see men's souls bartered and bought.
When they are heard upon the wind,
And when they shake their wings; alas!
Thy tender eyes grow all unkind:
Gaze no more in the bitter glass.

W. B. YEATS
*Poems* (1899)


## *Les Demoiselles de Sauve*

Beautiful ladies through the orchard pass;
Bend under crutched-up branches, forked and low;
Trailing their samet palls o'er dew-drenched grass.

Pale blossoms, looking on proud Jacqueline,
Blush to the colour of her finger tips,
And rosy knuckles, laced with yellow lace.

High-crested Berthe discerns, with slant, clinched eyes,
Amid the leaves pink faces of the skies;
She locks her plaintive hands Sainte-Margot-wise.

Ysabeau follows last, with languorous pace;
Presses, voluptuous, to her bursting lips,
With backward stoop, a bunch of eglantine.

Courtly ladies through the orchard pass;
Bow low, as in lords' halls; and springtime grass
Tangles a snare to catch the tapering toe.

JOHN GRAY
*Silverpoints* (1893)


## 'Through hazels and apples'

Through hazels and apples
    My love I led,
Where the sunshine dapples
    The strawberry-bed:
Did we pluck and eat
    That morn, my sweet?

And back by the alley
    Our path I chose,
That we might dally
    By one rare rose:
Did we smell at the heart,
    And then depart?

A lover, who grapples
    With love, doth live
Where roses and apples
    Have naught to give:
Did I take my way
    Unfed that day?

MICHAEL FIELD
*Underneath the Bough* (1893)

## Paradise Walk

She is living in Paradise Walk,
With the dirt and the noise of the street;
And heaven flies up, if she talk,
With Paradise down at her feet.

She laughs through a summer of curls;
She moves in a garden of grace:
Her glance is a treasure of pearls,
How saved from the deeps of her face!

And the magical reach of her thigh
Is the measure, with which God began
To build up the peace of the sky,
And fashion the pleasures of man.

With Paradise down at her feet,
While heaven flies up if she talk;
With the dirt and the noise of the street,
She is living in Paradise Walk.

HERBERT HORNE
*Diversi Colores* (1891)

## Song

In the first light of the morning,
    When the thrush sang loud and clear,
And the black-bird hailed day's dawning,
    How I wished my love could hear.

When the sun shone on the sand there,
    And the roses bloomed above,
And the blue waves kissed the land there,
    How I longed to see my love.

Now the birds good-night are calling,
   And the moonbeams come and go,
And my tears are falling, falling,
   Because I want him so.

DOLLIE RADFORD
*A Light Load* (1891)


## *A Shropshire Lad*

### 21
#### BREDON HILL

In summertime on Bredon
   The bells they sound so clear;
Round both the shires they ring them
   In steeples far and near,
   A happy noise to hear.

Here of a Sunday morning
   My love and I would lie,
And see the coloured counties,
   And hear the larks so high
   About us in the sky.

The bells would ring to call her
   In valleys miles away:
'Come all to church, good people;
   Good people, come and pray.'
   But here my love would stay.

And I would turn and answer
   Among the springing thyme,
'Oh, peal upon our wedding,
   And we will hear the chime,
   And come to church in time.'

But when the snows at Christmas
    On Bredon top were strown,
My love rose up so early
    And stole out unbeknown
    And went to church alone.

They tolled the one bell only,
    Groom there was none to see,
The mourners followed after,
    And so to church went she,
    And would not wait for me.

The bells they sound on Bredon,
    And still the steeples hum,
'Come all to church, good people.' –
    Oh, noisy bells, be dumb;
    I hear you, I will come.

A. E. HOUSMAN
*A Shropshire Lad* (1896)

## 'Cease smiling, Dear! a little while be sad'

*Dum nos fata sinunt, oculos satiemus Amore*
PROPERTIUS

Cease smiling, Dear! a little while be sad,
    Here in the silence, under the wan moon;
Sweet are thine eyes, but how can I be glad,
    Knowing they change so soon?

For Love's sake, Dear, be silent! Cover me
    In the deep darkness of thy falling hair;
Fear is upon me and the memory
    Of what is all men's share.

O could this moment be perpetuate!
    Must we grow old, and leaden-eyed and gray,
And taste no more the wild and passionate
      Love sorrows of to-day?

Grown old, and faded, Sweet! and past desire,
    Let memory die, lest there be too much ruth,
Remembering the old, extinguished fire
      Of our divine, lost youth.

O red pomegranate of thy perfect mouth!
    My lips' life-fruitage, might I taste and die,
Here in thy garden, where the scented south
      Wind chastens agony;

Reap death from thy live lips in one long kiss,
    And look my last into thine eyes and rest:
What sweets had life to me sweeter than this
      Swift dying on thy breast?

Or, if that may not be, for Love's sake, Dear!
    Keep silence still, and dream that we shall lie,
Red mouth to mouth, entwined, and always hear
      The south wind's melody,

Here in thy garden, through the sighing boughs,
    Beyond the reach of time and chance and change,
And bitter life and death, and broken vows,
      That sadden and estrange.

ERNEST DOWSON
*Verses* (1896)


## A Summer's Day

Overhead a sapphire sky;
    Blossom of the may-trees round:
    On the warm, lush, meadow-ground,
Where the sorrel blooms, we lie.

Psyche-winged, in gold and white,
   Butterflies float past: the earth,
    'Neath the charm of summer's birth,
Thrills with delicate delight.

Softly breathes a southern wind;
   Sings for joy a lark above:
    Oh! what paradise of love
Fairer may our spirits find!

Far away is London town,
   As a world unknown, forgot:
    Misery and sins are not!
Nothing now for tears or frown!

Lean, my Dearest, lean your head
   Quietly against me. So!
    Listen, while I whisper low
Words, that hardly may be said.

Nay, your spirit lifts the veil
   From love, trembling to confess:
    In this summer peacefulness
Silence better tells his tale.

Your free senses have discerned,
   Ere his stamm'ring lips can part,
    That, for which but heart to heart
Knows a language, yet unlearned.

Lean, my Dearest, lean your head
   Quietly against me: lay
    Little hand in mine, to say,
'Thus, indeed, the heart is sped.'

Ah! a cloud across the sun!
   Ah! a chill within the breeze!
    Ah! a shiver through the trees!
And the flower-land is dun!

Nothing! see the light return,
  Clearer from the gray eclipse!
  And the smile about your lips
Tells a spirit's unconcern.

Foolish, verily, was I
  Dreaming you should thus divine
  Secrets of this heart of mine.
Love for you comes by-and-by.

Here, enough, to-day you feel
  This bland summer hour's content;
  Magic music, colour, scent,
Through your happy senses steal.

Only, Dearest, lean your head
  Quietly against me. So!
  Leave me, when these moments go,
Ah! what memories instead!

SELWYN IMAGE
*Poems and Carols* (1894)

## O Mors! quam amara est memoria tua homini pacem habenti in substantiis suis

Exceeding sorrow
  Consumeth my sad heart!
Because to-morrow
  We must depart,
Now is exceeding sorrow
  All my part!

Give over playing,
  Cast thy viol away:
Merely laying
  Thine head my way:
Prithee, give over playing,
  Grave or gay.

Be no word spoken;
  Weep nothing: let a pale
Silence, unbroken
  Silence prevail!
Prithee, be no word spoken,
  Lest I fail!

Forget to-morrow!
  Weep nothing: only lay
In silent sorrow
  Thine head my way:
Let us forget to-morrow,
  This one day!

ERNEST DOWSON
*Verses* (1896)


## Transition

A little while to walk with thee, dear child;
  To lean on thee my weak and weary head;
Then evening comes: the winter sky is wild,
  The leafless trees are black, the leaves long dead.

A little while to hold thee and to stand,
  By harvest-fields of bending golden corn:
Then the predestined silence, and thine hand,
  Lost in the night, long and weary and forlorn.

A little while to love thee, scarcely time
  To love thee well enough; then time to part,
To fare through wintry fields alone and climb
  The frozen hills, not knowing where thou art.

Short summer-time and then, my heart's desire,
  The winter and the darkness: one by one
The roses fall, the pale roses expire
Beneath the slow decadence of the sun.

ERNEST DOWSON
*Decorations* (1899)

## *Song from* The Tragic Mary

Ah me, if I grew sweet to man
It was but as a rose that can
No longer keep the breath that heaves
And swells among its folded leaves.

The pressing fragrance would unclose
The flower, and I became a rose,
That unimpeachable and fair
Planted its sweetness in the air.

No art I used men's love to draw;
I lived but by my being's law,
As roses are by heaven designed
To bring the honey to the wind.

MICHAEL FIELD
*Underneath the Bough* (1893)

## *Return of the Troops*

The town is very gay to-day,
  And down our busy street
Flags wave, and all the balconies
  Are filled, our men to greet.

One night, not very long ago,
  I heard them marching down
To where their ship lay, and the sound
  So filled the silent town

With farewell voices that I wept
  To know no word or deed
Of mine had stirred the sleeping night,
  To bid our men God-speed.

The town is very gay to-day,
  And in our busy street,
My eyes are dim with tears for those
  I neither sped nor greet.

DOLLIE RADFORD
*A Light Load* (1891)

## *A Shropshire Lad*

### 22

The street sounds to the soldiers' tread,
  And out we troop to see:
A single redcoat turns his head,
  He turns and looks at me.

My man, from sky to sky's so far,
  We never crossed before;
Such leagues apart the world's ends are,
  We're like to meet no more;

What thoughts at heart have you and I
  We cannot stop to tell;
But dead or living, drunk or dry,
  Soldier, I wish you well.

A. E. HOUSMAN
*A Shropshire Lad* (1896)

## The Travelling Companion

Into the silence of the empty night
I went, and took my scornèd heart with me,
And all the thousand eyes of heaven were bright;
But Sorrow came and led me back to thee.

I turned my weary eyes towards the sun,
Out of the leaden East like smoke came he.
I laughed and said, 'The night is past and done';
But Sorrow came and led me back to thee.

I turned my face towards the rising moon,
Out of the south she came most sweet to see,
She smiled upon my eyes that loathed the noon;
But Sorrow came and led me back to thee.

I bent my eyes upon the summer land,
And all the painted fields were ripe for me,
And every flower nodded to my hand;
But Sorrow came and led me back to thee.

O Love! O Sorrow! O desired Despair!
I turn my feet towards the boundless sea,
Into the dark I go and heed not where,
So that I come again at last to thee.

LORD ALFRED DOUGLAS
*The City of the Soul* (1899)

## Idealism

I know the woman has no soul, I know
    The woman has no possibilities
        Of soul or mind or heart, but merely is
The masterpiece of flesh: well, be it so.
It is her flesh that I adore; I go
    Thirsting afresh to drain her empty kiss.

I know she cannot love: it is not this
My vanquished heart implores in overthrow.
Tyrannously I crave, I crave alone,
  Her perfect body, Earth's most eloquent
    Music, divinest human harmony;
  Her body now a silent instrument,
    That 'neath my touch shall wake and make for me
The strains I have but dreamed of, never known.

ARTHUR SYMONS
*London Nights* (2nd edition 1897)


## 'Ερος δ'αῦτε...

Crimson nor yellow roses, nor
The savour of the mounting sea
Are worth the perfume I adore
That clings to thee.

The languid-headed lilies tire,
The changeless waters weary me.
I ache with passionate desire
Of thine and thee.

There are but these things in the world –
Thy mouth of fire,
Thy breasts, thy hands, thy hair upcurled,
And my desire!

THEODORE WRATISLAW
*Orchids* (1896)

## *Stella Maris*

Why is it I remember yet
You, of all women one has met
In random wayfare, as one meets
The chance romances of the streets,
The Juliet of a night? I know
Your heart holds many a Romeo.
And I, who call to mind your face
In so serene a pausing-place,
Where the bright pure expanse of sea,
The shadowy shore's austerity,
Seem a reproach to you and me,
I too have sought on many a breast
The ecstasy of love's unrest,
I too have had my dreams, and met
(Ah me!) how many a Juliet.
Why is it, then, that I recall
You, neither first nor last of all?
For, surely as I see to-night
The phantom of the lighthouse light,
Against the sky, across the bay,
Fade, and return, and fade away,
So surely do I see your eyes
Out of the empty night arise.
Child, you arise and smile to me
Out of the night, out of the sea,
The Nereid of a moment there,
And is it seaweed in your hair?

O lost and wrecked, how long ago,
Out of the drowning past, I know
You come to call me, come to claim
My share of your delicious shame.
Child, I remember, and can tell
One night we loved each other well,
And one night's love, at least or most,
Is not so small a thing to boast.

You were adorable, and I
Adored you to infinity,
That nuptial night too briefly borne
To the oblivion of morn.
Ah! no oblivion, for I feel
Your lips deliriously steal
Along my neck, and fasten there;
I feel the perfume of your hair,
I feel your breast that heaves and dips,
Desiring my desirous lips,
And that ineffable delight
When souls turn bodies, and unite
In the intolerable, the whole
Rapture of the embodied soul.

That joy was ours, we passed it by;
You have forgotten me, and I
Remember you thus strangely, won
An instant from oblivion.
And I, remembering, would declare
That joy, not shame, is ours to share,
Joy that we had the frank delight
To choose the chances of one night,
Out of vague nights, and days at strife,
So infinitely full of life.
What shall it profit me to know
Your heart holds many a Romeo?
Why should I grieve, though I forget
How many another Juliet?
Let us be glad to have forgot
That roses fade, and loves are not,
As dreams, immortal, though they seem
Almost as real as a dream.
It is for this I see you rise,
A wraith, with starlight in your eyes,

Where calm hours move, for such a mood
Solitude out of solitude;
For this, for this, you come to me
Out of the night, out of the sea.

ARTHUR SYMONS
*London Nights* (2nd edition 1897)


## *Non sum qualis eram bonae sub regno Cynarae*

Last night, ah, yesternight, betwixt her lips and mine
There fell thy shadow, Cynara! thy breath was shed
Upon my soul between the kisses and the wine;
And I was desolate and sick of an old passion,
   Yea, I was desolate and bowed my head:
I have been faithful to thee, Cynara! in my fashion.

All night upon mine heart I felt her warm heart beat,
Night-long within mine arms in love and sleep she lay;
Surely the kisses of her bought red mouth were sweet;
But I was desolate and sick of an old passion,
   When I awoke and found the dawn was gray:
I have been faithful to thee, Cynara! in my fashion.

I have forgot much, Cynara! gone with the wind,
Flung roses, roses riotously with the throng,
Dancing, to put thy pale, lost lilies out of mind;
But I was desolate and sick of an old passion,
   Yea, all the time, because the dance was long:
I have been faithful to thee, Cynara! in my fashion.

I cried for madder music and for stronger wine,
But when the feast is finished and the lamps expire,
Then falls thy shadow, Cynara! the night is thine;

And I am desolate and sick of an old passion,
    Yea hungry for the lips of my desire:
I have been faithful to thee, Cynara! in my fashion.

ERNEST DOWSON
*Verses* (1896)

## 'Say, if a gallant rose my bower doth scale'

Say, if a gallant rose my bower doth scale,
    Higher and higher,
And, tho' she twine the other side the pale,
    Toward me doth sigh her
    Perfume, her damask mouth –
    *Roses will love the south* –
    Can I deny her?

I have a lady loves me in despite
    Of bonds that tie her,
And bid her honest Corin's flame requite;
    When I espy her,
    Kisses are near their birth –
    *Love cannot live in dearth* –
    Say, shall I fly her?

MICHAEL FIELD
*Underneath the Bough* (1893)

## 'It was deep April, and the morn'

It was deep April, and the morn
    Shakspere was born;
The world was on us, pressing sore;
My Love and I took hands and swore,
    Against the world, to be

Poets and lovers evermore,
To laugh and dream on Lethe's shore,
To sing to Charon in his boat,
Heartening the timid souls afloat;
Of judgment never to take heed,
But to those fast-locked souls to speed,
Who never from Apollo fled,
Who spent no hour among the dead;
    Continually
    With them to dwell,
Indifferent to heaven and hell.

MICHAEL FIELD
*Underneath the Bough* (1893)


## Morbidezza

White girl, your flesh is lilies,
Grown 'neath a frozen moon,
So still is
The rapture of your swoon
Of whiteness, snow or lilies.

The virginal revealment,
Your bosom's wavering slope,
Concealment,
'Neath fainting heliotrope,
Of whitest white's revealment,

Is like a bed of lilies,
A jealous-guarded row,
Whose will is
Simply chaste dreams: – but oh,
The alluring scent of lilies!

ARTHUR SYMONS
*Silhouettes* (2nd edition 1896)

## The Destroyer of a Soul

I hate you with a necessary hate.
First, I sought patience: passionate was she:
My patience turned in very scorn of me,
That I should dare forgive a sin so great,
As this, through which I sit disconsolate;
Mourning for that live soul, I used to see;
Soul of a saint, whose friend I used to be:
Till you came by! a cold, corrupting, fate.

Why come you now? You, whom I cannot cease
With pure and perfect hate to hate? Go, ring
The death-bell with a deep, triumphant toll!
Say you, my friend sits by me still? Ah, peace!
Call you this thing my friend? this nameless thing?
This living body, hiding its dead soul?

LIONEL JOHNSON
*Poems* (1895)

## Against My Lady Burton: On Her Burning the Last Writing of Her Dead Husband

'To save his soul', whom narrowly she loved
She did this deed of everlasting shame,
For devils' laughter; and was soulless proved
Heaping dishonour on her scholar's name.
Her lean distrust awoke when he was dead;
Dead, hardly cold; whose life was worn away
In scholarship's high service; from his head
She lightly tore his ultimate crown of bay.
His masterpiece, the ripe fruit of his age,
In art's despite she gave the hungry flame;
Smiled at the death of each laborious page,
Which she read only by the light of shame.

Dying he trusted her: him dead she paid
Most womanly, destroying his life's prize:
So Judas decently his Lord betrayed
With deep dishonour wrought in love's disguise.
With deep dishonour, for her jealous heart
His whole life's work, with light excuse put by
For love of him, or haply, hating art.
Oh Love be this, let us curse Love and die.
Nay! Love forgive: could such a craven thing
Love anywhere? but let her name pass down
Dishonoured through the ages, who did fling
To the rank scented mob a sage's crown,
And offered Fame, Love, Honour, mincingly
To her one God – sterile Propriety!

ERNEST DOWSON
Written 1891
Text from *The Poetical Works of Ernest Dowson* (1967)

## The Price

Terrible is the price
    Of beginning anew, of birth;
For Death has loaded dice.

Men hurry and hide like mice;
    But they cannot evade the Earth,
And Life, Death's fancy price.

A blossom once or twice,
    Love lights on Summer's hearth;
But Winter loads the dice.

In jangling shackles of ice,
    Ragged and bleeding, Mirth
Pays the Piper's price.

The dance is done in a trice:
   Death belts his bony girth;
And struts, and rattles his dice.

Let Virtue play or Vice,
   Beside his sombre firth
Life is the lowest price
Death wins with loaded dice.

JOHN DAVIDSON
*The Last Ballad* (1899)


## Ad Cinerarium

Who in this small urn reposes,
   Celt or Roman, man or woman,
Steel of steel, or rose of roses?

Whose the dust set rustling slightly,
   In its hiding-place abiding,
When this urn is lifted lightly?

Sure some mourner deemed immortal
   What thou holdest and enfoldest,
Little house without a portal!

When the artificers had slowly
   Formed thee, turned thee, sealed thee, burned thee,
Freighted with thy freightage holy,

Sure he thought there's no forgetting
   All the sweetness and completeness
Of his rising, of her setting,

And so bade them grave no token,
   Generation, age, or nation,
On thy round side still unbroken; –

Let them score no cypress verses,
    Funeral glories, prayers, or stories,
Mourner's tears, or mourner's curses,

Round thy brown rim time hath polished, –
    Left thee dumbly cold and comely
As some shrine of gods abolished.

Ah, 'twas well! It scarcely matters
    What is sleeping in the keeping
Of this house of human tatters, –

Steel of steel, or rose of roses,
    Man or woman, Celt or Roman,
If but soundly he reposes!

VICTOR PLARR
*In the Dorian Mood* (1896)

## A Dream of Death

I dreamed that one had died in a strange place
Near no accustomed hand;
And they had nailed the boards above her face,
The peasants of that land,
And, wondering, planted by her solitude
A cypress and a yew:
I came, and wrote upon a cross of wood,
Man had no more to do:
*She was more beautiful than thy first love,*
*This lady by the trees*:
And gazed upon the mournful stars above,
And heard the mournful breeze.

W. B. YEATS
*Poems* (1899)

## Vigilantibus

When Morning, with a hundred wings,
Broke through the curtain-chink; and wept
The earth, at what the day-break brings:
  The body slept.

A little yet the early sky,
With gold and blue, shall be astir
For you; while you are passing by:
  But not for her.

Go! let the voices of your feet
Speak thoughts beyond the tongue's control;
For now, in ways where all things meet,
  Now sleeps the soul.

Go! nor forget the steadfast gaze,
That, loosed in Death, hath pierced the night
Of the great mystery of our days,
  With eyes of light.

HERBERT HORNE
*Diversi Colores* (1891)


## Contradictions

Now, even, I cannot think it true,
My friend, that there is no more you.
Almost as soon were no more I,
Which were, of course, absurdity!
Your place is bare, you are not seen,
Your grave, I'm told, is growing green;

And both for you and me, you know,
There's no Above and no Below.
That you are dead must be inferred,
And yet my thought rejects the word.

AMY LEVY
*A London Plane-Tree* (1889)

## Epitaphium Citharistriae

Stand not uttering sedately
   Trite oblivious praise above her!
Rather say you saw her lately
   Lightly kissing her last lover:

Whisper not, 'There is a reason
   Why we bring her no white blossom:'
Since the snowy bloom's in season
   Strow it on her sleeping bosom:

Oh, for it would be a pity
   To o'erpraise her or to flout her:
She was wild, and sweet, and witty –
   Let's not say dull things about her.

VICTOR PLARR
*In the Dorian Mood* (1896)

## 'I would not die'

I would not die
To meet a goodly company;
I was ever, ever shy,

And have loved to live retired,
That I might con
Some mystery scarce pondered on.
Oh, this I have desired!

No hope to brood
Where harpers wing on wing intrude,
Or bold saints with trumpets rude;
Where four beasts from turning eyne
Watch my strange ways:
But in concealment of deep rays
May some recess be mine!

I never can,
On earth, though quite escaped from man,
Put society under ban:
Buzzing bees swing in a flower,
Gnats drum and dance,
The weasel intercepts my trance,
Birds warble through a bower.

Once Chloe graced
My suit; how fondly we embraced!
Still my arm was round her waist:
Chloe dropt her pretty head
Upon my knee,
And Love was left alone with me
Just while she slumberèd.

And once I lay
In sickness; I had swooned away,
For I wandered as at play;
It was untethered innocence:
Naught of my own
I had, the night was open thrown,
Sound wrought no more offence.

Endowed by thee,
Death, let me enter privacy,
Unmorose and fellowly

To mix, with the free pleasure
Of stars and springs
And magic, unfamiliar things,
My beauteous leisure.

MICHAEL FIELD
*Underneath the Bough* (1893)


## The Last Music

Calmly, breathe calmly all your music, maids!
Breathe a calm music over my dead queen.
All your lives long, you have nor heard, nor seen,
Fairer than she, whose hair in sombre braids
    With beauty overshades
      Her brow, broad and serene.

Surely she hath lain so an hundred years:
Peace is upon her, old as the world's heart.
Breathe gently, music! Music done, depart:
And leave me in her presence to my tears,
    With music in mine ears;
      For sorrow hath its art.

Music, more music, sad and slow! she lies
Dead: and more beautiful, than early morn.
Discrowned am I, and of her looks forlorn:
Alone vain memories immortalize
    The way of her soft eyes,
      Her musical voice low-borne.

The balm of gracious death now laps her round,
As once life gave her grace beyond her peers.
Strange! that I loved this lady of the spheres,
To sleep by her at last in common ground:
    When kindly sleep hath bound
      Mine eyes, and sealed mine ears.

Maidens! make a low music: merely make
Silence a melody, no more. This day,
She travels down a pale and lonely way:
Now, for a gentle comfort, let her take
    Such music, for her sake,
    As mourning love can play.

Holy my queen lies in the arms of death:
Music moves over her still face, and I
Lean breathing love over her. She will lie
In earth thus calmly, under the wind's breath:
    The twilight wind, that saith:
    *Rest! worthy found, to die.*

LIONEL JOHNSON
*Poems* (1895)

## Aedh Pleads with the Elemental Powers

The Powers whose name and shape no living creature knows
Have pulled the Immortal Rose;
And though the Seven Lights bowed in their dance and wept,
The Polar Dragon slept,
His heavy rings uncoiled from glimmering deep to deep:
When will he wake from sleep?

Great Powers of falling wave and wind and windy fire,
With your harmonious choir
Encircle her I love and sing her into peace,
That my old care may cease;
Unfold your flaming wings and cover out of sight
The nets of day and night.

Dim Powers of drowsy thought, let her no longer be
Like the pale cup of the sea,

When winds have gathered and sun and moon burned dim
Above its cloudy rim;
But let a gentle silence wrought with music flow
Whither her footsteps go.

W. B. YEATS
*The Wind Among the Reeds* (1899)

## Love Without Wings

(EIGHT SONGS)

I

I thought: no more the worst endures!
    I die, I end the strife, –
You swiftly took my hands in yours
    And drew me back to life!

II

We sat when shadows darken,
    And let the shadows be:
Each was a soul to hearken,
    Devoid of eyes to see.

You came at dusk to find me;
    I knew you well enough . . .
O lights that dazzle and blind me –
    It is no friend, but Love!

III

How is it possible
    You should forget me,
Leave me for ever
    And never regret me!

I was the soul of you,
    Past love or loathing,
Lost in the whole of you . . .
    Now, am I nothing?

IV

The fallen oak still keeps its yellow leaves
    But all its growth is o'er!
So, at your name, my heart still beats and grieves
    Although I love no more.

V

And so I shall meet you
    Again, my dear;
How shall I greet you?
    What shall I hear?

I, you forgot!
    (But who shall say
You loved me not
    – Yesterday?)

VI

Ah me, do you remember still
    The garden where we strolled together
The empty groves, the little hill
    Starred o'er with pale Italian heather?

And you to me said never a word,
    Nor I a single word to you.
And yet how sweet a thing was heard,
    Resolved, abandoned by us two!

VII

I know you love me not . . . I do not love you
    Only at dead of night
I smile a little, softly dreaming of you
    Until the dawn is bright.

I love you not; you love me not; I know it!
    But when the day is long
I haunt you like the magic of a poet,
    And charm you like a song.

### VIII

O Death of things that are, Eternity
    Of things that seem!
Of all the happy past remains to me,
    To–day, a dream!

Long blessèd days of love and wakening thought,
    All, all are dead;
Nothing endures we did, nothing we wrought,
    Nothing we said.

But once I dreamed I sat and sang with you
    On Ida's hill.
There, in the echoes of my life, we two
    Are singing still.

A. MARY F. ROBINSON
*Lyrics Selected from the Works* (1891)

# 8. FIRE FROM FRANCE

(All the poems in this section are translations)

In the title of his *English Poems* (1892) Richard Le Gallienne declared his position against the French influence; ironically so, for he had earlier exemplified the power of that influence when he introduced the 'Le' into his name. Now he was stolidly English, and in the poem, 'To the Reader', complained to England,

> not of thee this new voice in our ears,
> Music of France that once was of the spheres;
> And not of thee these strange green flowers that spring
> From daisy roots and seem to bear a sting.

Certainly, for good or ill, France was the most potent foreign influence on English writing, both in style and content, at the end of the nineteenth century. Davidson in his *Fleet Street Eclogues* wrote that 'Some have stolen fire from France'. *The Times* called the first volume of *The Yellow Book* a 'combination of English rowdyism and French lubricity'. Words and phrases came from France: *épater les bourgeois*, decadence, *fin de siècle, art nouveau*; many moralists felt that the degenerate morals that they claimed to see came from there too and should be sent back. Lord Alfred Douglas published his *Poèmes* (1896) in both French and English. Even Lionel Johnson wrote an article on contemporary French poetic practice. Both *The Yellow Book* and *The Savoy* published poems in French, the latter translating Verlaine's account of his visit to England where his lecture was heard by most of the aspiring poets. Even when feelings against the French influence ran highest, *The Savoy* under Symons's editorship continued to stress the importance of French literature.

The most frequently remembered of the French writers were Gautier, Baudelaire, Huysmans, Verlaine and Mallarmé. The general effect of their influence was a reinforcement of ideas drawn from English sources, and the stimulus of new ideas both of form and content.

Of the translators, Symons was the most influential since he backed up his translations with perceptive essays on contemporary, usually French, literature. His influence was great on both Eliot and Yeats. Eliot remarked that but for reading Symons (he was referring to *The Symbolist Movement in Literature*) he would never have read Laforgue and the other Symbolists. Yeats seems to have regarded Symons primarily as a translator, since his three selections of his work for *The Oxford Book of Modern Verse* are all translations.

The poets were not blind to work in countries other than France. If most of the writers understood French, many knew German, though they may have viewed it, as Lionel Johnson did, as a 'gross tongue, partially redeemed by Heine'. In *Italian Lyrists of To-day* (1893), G. A. Greene, a member of the Rhymers' Club, translated over thirty contemporary Italian poets, including the young d'Annunzio, the subject of one of Symons's essays and a poet who demonstrates the pervasiveness of the French influence.

For such as Lionel Johnson the Classics came first, and several poems demonstrate a love of Latin, not always the late Latin which des Esseintes favoured and whose 'patches of rouge' had more charm for Mallarmé 'than the rosy flesh of youth'. Johnson, also a member of the Rhymers' Club, which was predominantly Irish, also fell under the influence of Celtic literature, though the pale light of the Celtic Twilight shows more diffused than in direct translation.

## Charleville

The square, with gravel paths and shabby lawns.
Correct, the trees and flowers repress their yawns.
The tradesman brings his favourite conceit,
To air it, while he stifles with the heat.

In the kiosk, the military band.
The shakos nod the time of the quadrilles.
The flaunting dandy strolls about the stand.
The notary, half unconscious of his seals.

On the green seats, small groups of grocermen,
Absorbed, their sticks scooping a little hole
Upon the path, talk market prices; then
Take up a cue: I think, upon the whole . . .

The loutish roughs are larking on the grass.
The sentimental trooper, with a rose
Between his teeth, seeing a baby, grows
More tender, with an eye upon the nurse.

Unbuttoned, like a student, I follow
A couple of girls along the chestnut row.
They know I am following, for they turn and laugh,
Half impudent, half shy, inviting chaff.

I do not say a word. I only stare
At their round, fluffy necks. I follow where
The shoulders drop; I struggle to define
The subtle torso's hesitating line.

Only my rustling tread, deliberate, slow;
The rippled silence from the still leaves drips.
They think I am an idiot, they speak low;
– I feel faint kisses creeping on my lips.

JOHN GRAY
*Silverpoints* (1893)
*From the French of Arthur Rimbaud*

## Pantomime

Pierrot, no sentimental swain,
Washes a pâté down again
    With furtive flagons, white and red.

Cassandre, to chasten his content,
Greets with a tear of sentiment
    His nephew disinherited.

That blackguard of a Harlequin
Pirouettes, and plots to win
    His Colombine that flits and flies.

Colombine dreams, and starts to find
A sad heart sighing in the wind,
    And in her heart a voice that sighs.

ARTHUR SYMONS
*Silhouettes* (2nd edition 1896)
*From the French of Paul Verlaine*

## Fantoches

Scaramouche waves a threatening hand
To Pulcinella, and they stand,
    Two shadows, black against the moon.

The old doctor of Bologna pries
For simples with impassive eyes,
    And mutters o'er a magic rune.

The while his daughter, scarce half-dressed,
Glides slyly 'neath the trees, in quest
    Of her bold pirate lover's sail;

Her pirate from the Spanish main,
Whose passion thrills her in the pain
  Of the loud languorous nightingale.

ARTHUR SYMONS
*Silhouettes* (2nd edition 1896)
*From the French of Paul Verlaine*

## Femmes Damnées

Like moody beasts they lie along the sands;
Look where the sky against the sea-rim clings:
Foot stretches out to foot, and groping hands
Have languors soft and bitter shudderings.

Some, smitten hearts with the long secrecies,
On velvet moss, deep in their bowers' ease,
Prattling the love of timid infancies,
Are tearing the green bark from the young trees.

Others, like sisters, slowly walk and grave;
By rocks that swarm with ghostly legions,
Where Anthony saw surging on the waves
The purple breasts of his temptations.

Some, by the light of crumbling, resinous gums,
In the still hollows of old pagan dens,
Call thee in aid to their deliriums
O Bacchus! cajoler of ancient pains.

And those whose breasts for scapulars are fain
Nurse under their long robes the cruel thong!
These, in dim woods, where huddling shadows throng,
Mix with the foam of pleasure tears of pain.

JOHN GRAY
*Silverpoints* (1893)
*From the French of Charles Baudelaire*

## Colloque Sentimental

Into the lonely park all frozen fast,
Awhile ago there were two forms who passed.

Lo, are their lips fallen and their eyes dead,
Hardly shall a man hear the words they said.

Into the lonely park, all frozen fast,
There came two shadows who recall the past.

'Dost thou remember our old ecstasy?' –
'Wherefore should I possess that memory?' –

'Doth thine heart beat at my sole name alway?
Still dost thou see my soul in visions?' 'Nay!' –

'They were fair days of joy unspeakable,
Whereon our lips were joined?' – 'I cannot tell.' –

'Were not the heavens blue, was not hope high?'
'Hope has fled vanquished down the darkling sky.' –

So through the barren oats they wanderèd,
And the night only heard the words they said.

ERNEST DOWSON
*Decorations* (1899)
*From the French of Paul Verlaine*

## Spleen

Around were all the roses red,
The ivy all around was black.

Dear, so thou only move thine head,
Shall all mine old despairs awake!

Too blue, too tender was the sky,
The air too soft, too green the sea.

Always I fear, I know not why,
Some lamentable flight from thee.

I am so tired of holly-sprays
And weary of the bright box-tree,

Of all the endless country ways;
Of everything alas! save thee.

ERNEST DOWSON
*Decorations* (1899)
*From the French of Paul Verlaine*


## Spleen

The roses every one were red,
And all the ivy leaves were black.

Sweet, do not even stir your head,
Or all of my despairs come back.

The sky is too blue, too delicate:
Too soft the air, too green the sea.

I fear – how long had I to wait! –
That you will tear yourself from me.

The shining box-leaves weary me,
The varnished holly's glistening,

The stretch of infinite country;
So, saving you, does everything.

JOHN GRAY
*Silverpoints* (1893)
*From the French of Paul Verlaine*

## La Destruction

The Devil stirs about me without rest,
And round me floats like noxious air and thin:
I breathe this poison-air which scalds my breast,
And fills me with desires of monstrous sin.

Knowing my love of Art, he sometimes takes
The shape of supple girls supremely fair;
And with a wily, canting lie he makes
My heated lips his shameful potions share.

Then far he leads me from the sight of God,
Crushed with fatigue, to where no man has trod –
To the vague, barren plains where silence sounds,

And hurls into my face his foul construction
Of slimy clothes, and gaping, putrid wounds,
And all the bleeding harness of Destruction!

VINCENT O'SULLIVAN
*Poems* (1896)
*From the French of Charles Baudelaire*

## Harmonie du Soir

*Voici venir le temps*

Now is the hour when, swinging in the breeze,
Each flower, like a censer, sheds its sweet.
The air is full of scents and melodies,
O languorous waltz! O swoon of dancing feet!

Each flower, like a censer, sheds its sweet,
The violins are like sad souls that cry,
O languorous waltz! O swoon of dancing feet!
A shrine of Death and Beauty is the sky.

The violins are like sad souls that cry,
Poor souls that hate the vast black night of Death;
A shrine of Death and Beauty is the sky.
Drowned in red blood, the Sun gives up his breath.

This soul that hates the vast black night of Death
Takes all the luminous past back tenderly.
Drowned in red blood, the Sun gives up his breath.
Thine image like a monstrance shines in me.

LORD ALFRED DOUGLAS
*The City of the Soul* (1899)
*From the French of Charles Baudelaire*

## *Joyful Death*

In a snail-covered earth and rich and deep
    I will dig out for mine own self my grave,
Where I can throw my old tired bones and sleep
    Forgetful as a shark upon the wave.

I hate both wills and tombs; rather, God knows,
    Than ask the world one tear upon my name,
Living, I would far gladlier bid the crows
    Suck out the blood from my uncleanly frame.

O worms! black friends who may not hear or see,
There comes to you a dead man glad and free!
Philosophers! Wise sons of rottenness,

Unpitying crawl from feet to ruined head
And tell me if any pain remains for this
Old soulless body dead among the dead!

THEODORE WRATISLAW
*Love's Memorial* (1892)
*From the French of Charles Baudelaire*

## *Prelude*

As from corrupted flesh the over-bold
Young vines in dense luxuriance rankly grow,
And strange weird plants their horrid buds unfold
O'er the foul rotting of a corpse below;

As spreading crimson flowers with centred gold
Like the fresh blood of recent wounds o'erflow,
Where vile enormous chrysalids are rolled
In the young leaves, and cruel blossoms blow:

E'en so within my heart malignant flowers
Of verse swell forth: the leaves in fearful gloom
Exhale a sinister scent of human breath.

Lured by the radiance of the blood-red bowers,
The unconscious hand is stretched to pluck the bloom,
And the sharp poison fills the veins with death.

G. A. GREENE
*Italian Lyrists of To-day* (1893)
*From the Italian of Gabriele d'Annunzio*

## *Sea-wind*

The flesh is sad, alas! and all the books are read.
Flight, only flight! I feel that birds are wild to tread
The floor of unknown foam, and to attain the skies!
Nought, neither ancient gardens mirrored in the eyes,
Shall hold this heart that bathes in waters its delight,
O nights! nor yet my waking lamp, whose lonely light
Shadows the vacant paper, whiteness profits best,
Nor the young wife who rocks her baby on her breast.
I will depart! O steamer, swaying rope and spar,
Lift anchor for exotic lands that lie afar!

A weariness, outworn by cruel hopes, still clings
To the last farewell handkerchief's last beckonings!
And are not these, the masts inviting storms, not these
That an awakening wind bends over wrecking seas,
Lost, not a sail, a sail, a flowering isle, ere long?
But, O my heart, hear thou, hear thou the sailors' song!

ARTHUR SYMONS
*Images of Good and Evil* (1899)
*From the French of Stéphane Mallarmé*

## Carmen CI

By ways remote and distant waters sped,
Brother, to thy sad grave-side am I come,
That I may give the last gifts to the dead,
And vainly parley with thine ashes dumb:
Since she who now bestows and now denies
Hath ta'en thee, hapless brother, from mine eyes.

But lo! these gifts, the heirlooms of past years,
Are made sad things to grace thy coffin shell,
Take them, all drenchèd with a brother's tears,
And, brother, for all time, hail and farewell!

AUBREY BEARDSLEY
In *The Savoy* (1896)
*From the Latin of Catullus*

# 9. POEMS AND BALLADS

Though the organization of this section was designed to be loose enough to provide space for those poems which did not fall into the narrower categories of the other sections, the poems can be divided into two groups: those that deal, usually impressionistically, with traditional subject matter, and those written in the ballad tradition.

The impressions record, with the expected exception of one of Symons's poems, what John Gray calls 'the strait allure of simple things'. The love of the city was not so strong as to exclude all natural beauty; indeed, Yeats's 'Innisfree', among the most famous poems of nostalgia for the simple life, comes directly out of his homesickness in the midst of Fleet Street. Even Symons in 'A Causerie from a Castle in Ireland'[1] wrote that 'if I lived here too long I should forget that I am a Londoner and remember that I am a Cornishman . . . I must come back to London; for I have perceived the insidious danger of idealism ever since I came to these ascetic regions'. Nature must always possess something of that attraction which Housman so beautifully, and in appearance so simply, caught.

The style of these poems is not that of the earlier Victorians. Under the influence of Pater, who wrote that for Dante Gabriel Rossetti the 'first condition of the poetic way of seeing and presenting things is particularisation',[2] poets began to aim at exactly fixing the impression, in catching, like the later Degas, mood without narrative. Yeats explained that 'the revolt against Victorianism meant to the young poet a revolt against irrelevant descriptions of nature, the scientific and moral discursiveness of *In Memoriam* . . . the political eloquence of Swinburne, the psychological curiosity of Browning, and the poetical diction of everybody'. 'For in truth,' Pater had written in *Appreciations,* 'all art does but consist in the removal of surplusage.' The precision and detail of these poems, in many ways

1. In *The Savoy*, 6 (October 1896).
2. *Appreciations* (1889).

like that striving for exactness of another of Pater's pupils, Gerard Manley Hopkins, are what resulted. Some of the features that Symons in 'The Decadent Movement in Literature'[3] saw as elements of that style describe effectively Hopkins's attempts to depict the last fine shade: 'an intense self consciousness, a restless curiosity in research, an over-subtilising refinement upon refinement'. The clarity of the impression is also in a sense Imagistic. Pound praised the pure Imagism of Johnson's line from 'April', 'Clear lie the fields, and fade into blue air', and it is the 1890s poet who began, as Yeats recorded, 'that search for hard positive subject-matter.'[4]

The ballad is a more specific but still a fairly loose form, large enough to include writers as different as Wilde, Kipling and Housman, each of whom included an execution among his subjects ('The Ballad of Reading Gaol', 'Danny Deever' and *A Shropshire Lad*: 9). And Yeats and Davidson, despite their fierce mutual dislike, found parallel themes in 'The Ballad of Father Gilligan' and 'A Ballad of a Nun'. The ballad tends to imply traditional subject matter, the heroic event, the national myth, even the melodramatic story, and it is not surprising that Yeats, an Irishman, Davidson, a Scot, and the more jingoistic of the English poets, wrote ballads. Mary Robinson even claimed that the ballad was a special women's form. 'We women', she said in *Collected Poems* (1902), 'have a privilege in these matters . . . We have always been the prime makers of ballads and love songs.'

Anthologies can usually afford to be kinder to lyric poets than to writers of ballads, and those ballads we include do little more than suggest the production in this popular genre; for we omit some of the best-known story-poems that come from this period like Newbolt's 'Drake's Drum' and 'He Fell Among Thieves', and Kipling's 'Ballad of East and West' and 'The Road to Mandalay'.

3. In *Harper's New Monthly Magazine*, 87 (November 1893).
4. *The Oxford Book of Modern Verse*, p. xxxix.

## At Dieppe

### AFTER SUNSET

The sea lies quieted beneath
  The after-sunset flush
That leaves upon the heaped grey clouds
  The grape's faint purple blush.

Pale, from a little space in heaven
  Of delicate ivory,
The sickle-moon and one gold star
  Look down upon the sea.

ARTHUR SYMONS
*Silhouettes* (2nd edition 1896)


## A Song

Last night I met my own true love
  Walking in Paradise;
A halo shone above his hair,
  A glory in his eyes.

We sat and sang in alleys green
  And heard the angels play;
Believe me, this was true last night
  Though it is false to-day.

A. MARY F. ROBINSON
*Lyrics Selected from the Works* (1891)

## *Paradise Fancies*

### I.

Through Paradise garden
  A minstrel strays,
An old golden viol
  For ever he plays.

Birds fly to his head,
  Beasts lie at his feet,
For none of God's angels
  Make music so sweet.

And here, far from Eden,
  And lonely and mute,
I listen and long:
  For my heart is the lute!

### II.

On the topmost branch of the Tree of Life
  There hung a ripe red apple,
The angels singing underneath
  All praised its crimson dapple.

They plucked it once to play at ball,
  But 'mid the shouts and laughter
The apple fell o'er Heaven's edge,
  Sad angels looking after.

And while they smiled to see it rest
  Beside a peaceful chapel,
An old priest flung it farther still,
  'Bah, what a battered apple!'

### III.

Sing, oh the flowers in Paradise:
  Rose, lily and girasole!
In all the fields of Paradise
  Every flower is a soul.

A climbing bindweed you are there
 With petals lily-fine,
Around my rose-bush pink and fair
 Your curling tendrils twine.

Too close those slender tendrils cling,
 So close I cannot breathe!
Till o'er my dead red roses swing,
 Your lilies wreath on wreath.

A. MARY F. ROBINSON
*Lyrics Selected from the Works* (1891)

## A Shropshire Lad

2

Loveliest of trees, the cherry now
Is hung with bloom along the bough,
And stands about the woodland ride
Wearing white for Eastertide.

Now, of my threescore years and ten,
Twenty will not come again,
And take from seventy springs a score,
It only leaves me fifty more.

And since to look at things in bloom
Fifty springs are little room,
About the woodlands I will go
To see the cherry hung with snow.

A. E. HOUSMAN
*A Shropshire Lad* (1896)

## Pastel

The light of our cigarettes
   Went and came in the gloom:
   It was dark in the little room.

Dark, and then, in the dark,
   Sudden, a flash, a glow,
   And a hand and a ring I know.

And then, through the dark, a flush
   Ruddy and vague, the grace –
   A rose – of her lyric face.

ARTHUR SYMONS
*Silhouettes* (2nd edition 1896)

## The Lake Isle of Innisfree

I will arise and go now, and go to Innisfree,
And a small cabin build there, of clay and wattles made;
Nine bean rows will I have there, a hive for the honey bee,
And live alone in the bee-loud glade.

And I shall have some peace there, for peace comes dropping slow,
Dropping from the veils of the morning to where the cricket sings;
There midnight's all a glimmer, and noon a purple glow,
And evening full of the linnet's wings.

I will arise and go now, for always night and day
I hear lake water lapping with low sounds by the shore;
While I stand on the roadway, or on the pavements gray,
I hear it in the deep heart's core.

W. B. YEATS
*Poems* (1899)

## *April*

A pleasant heat breathes off the scented grass,
  From bright green blades, and shining daisies:
Now give we joy, who sometime cried, Alas!
Now set we forth our melodies, and sing
  Soft praises to the spring,
    Musical praises.

The flying winds are lovely with the sun:
  Now all in sweet and dainty fashion
Goes life: for royal seasons are begun.
Now each new day and each new promise add
  Fresh cause of being glad,
    With vernal passion.

Few leaves upon the branches dare the spring:
  But many buds are making ready,
Trusting the sun, their perfect summer king.
Likewise we put away our wintry cares:
  We hear but happy airs;
    Our hopes are steady.

Cold were the crystal rivers, bitter cold;
  And snows upon the iron mountains;
And withering leaves upon the trodden mould.
Hark to the crystal voices of the rills,
  Falling among the hills,
    From secret fountains!

Long not for June with roses: nor for nights
  Loud with tumultuary thunder:
Those hours wax heavy with their fierce delights.
But April is all bright, and gives us first,
  Before the roses burst,
    Her joy and wonder.

Clear lie the fields, and fade into blue air:
  Here, sweet concerted birds are singing
Around this lawn of sweet grass, warm and fair.

And holy music, through the waving trees,
    Comes gently down the breeze,
        Where bells are ringing.

LIONEL JOHNSON
*Poems* (1895)

## Poem

Geranium, houseleek, laid in oblong beds
On the trim grass. The daisies' leprous stain
Is fresh. Each night the daisies burst again,
Though every day the gardener crops their heads.

A wistful child, in foul unwholesome shreds,
Recalls some legend of a daisy chain
That makes a pretty necklace. She would fain
Make one, and wear it, if she had some threads.

Sun, leprous flowers, foul child. The asphalt burns.
The garrulous sparrows perch on metal Burns.
Sing! Sing! they say, and flutter with their wings.
He does not sing, he only wonders why
He is sitting there. The sparrows sing. And I
Yield to the strait allure of simple things.

JOHN GRAY
*Silverpoints* (1893)

## In Romney Marsh

As I went down to Dymchurch Wall,
    I heard the South sing o'er the land;
I saw the yellow sunlight fall
    On knolls where Norman churches stand.

And ringing shrilly, taut and lithe,
  Within the wind a core of sound,
The wire from Romney town to Hythe
  Alone its airy journey wound.

A veil of purple vapour flowed
  And trailed its fringe along the Straits;
The upper air like sapphire glowed;
  And roses filled Heaven's central gates.

Masts in the offing wagged their tops;
  The swinging waves pealed on the shore;
The saffron beach, all diamond drops
  And beads of surge, prolonged the roar.

As I came up from Dymchurch Wall,
  I saw above the Downs' low crest
The crimson brands of sunset fall,
  Flicker and fade from out the west.

Night sank: like flakes of silver fire
  The stars in one great shower came down;
Shrill blew the wind; and shrill the wire
  Rang out from Hythe to Romney town.

The darkly shining salt sea drops
  Streamed as the waves clashed on the shore;
The beach, with all its organ stops
  Pealing again, prolonged the roar.

JOHN DAVIDSON
*Ballads and Songs* (1894)


## The Badge of Men

'In shuttered rooms let others grieve,
  And coffin thought in speech of lead;
I'll tie my heart upon my sleeve:
  It is the Badge of Men,' he said.

His friends forsook him: 'Who was he!'
   Even beggars passed him with a grin:
Physicians called it lunacy;
   And priests, the unpardonable sin.

He strove, he struck for standing-ground:
   They beat him humbled from the field;
For though his sword was keen, he found
   His mangled heart a feeble shield.

He slunk away, and sadly sought
   The wilderness – false friend of woe.
'Man is The Enemy,' he thought;
   But Nature proved a fiercer foe:

The vampire sucked, the vulture tore,
   And the old dragon left its den,
Agape to taste the thing he wore –
   The ragged, bleeding Badge of Men.

'Against the Fates there steads no charm,
   For every force takes its own part:
I'll wear a buckler on my arm,
   And in my bosom hide my heart!'

But in his bosom prisoned fast
   It pained him more than when it beat
Upon his sleeve; and so he cast
   His trouble to the ghouls to eat.

Back to the city, there and then
   He ran; and saw, through all disguise,
On every sleeve the Badge of Men:
   For truth appears to cruel eyes.

Straight with his sword he laid about,
   And hacked and pierced their hearts, until
The beaten terror-stricken rout
   Begged on their knees to know his will.

He said, 'I neither love nor hate;
  I would command in everything.'
They answered him, 'Heartless and great!
  Your slaves we are: be you our king!'

JOHN DAVIDSON
*The Last Ballad* (1899)

## A Ballad of a Nun

From Eastertide to Eastertide
  For ten long years her patient knees
Engraved the stones – the fittest bride
  Of Christ in all the diocese.

She conquered every earthly lust;
  The abbess loved her more and more;
And, as a mark of perfect trust,
  Made her the keeper of the door.

High on a hill the convent hung,
  Across a duchy looking down,
Where everlasting mountains flung
  Their shadows over tower and town.

The jewels of their lofty snows
  In constellations flashed at night;
Above their crests the moon arose;
  The deep earth shuddered with delight.

Long ere she left her cloudy bed,
  Still dreaming in the orient land,
On many a mountain's happy head
  Dawn lightly laid her rosy hand.

The adventurous sun took Heaven by storm;
  Clouds scattered largesses of rain;
The sounding cities, rich and warm,
  Smouldered and glittered in the plain.

Sometimes it was a wandering wind,
   Sometimes the fragrance of the pine,
Sometimes the thought how others sinned,
   That turned her sweet blood into wine.

Sometimes she heard a serenade
   Complaining sweetly far away:
She said, 'A young man woos a maid';
   And dreamt of love till break of day.

Then would she ply her knotted scourge
   Until she swooned; but evermore
She had the same red sin to purge,
   Poor, passionate keeper of the door!

For still night's starry scroll unfurled,
   And still the day came like a flood:
It was the greatness of the world
   That made her long to use her blood.

In winter-time when Lent drew nigh,
   And hill and plain were wrapped in snow,
She watched beneath the frosty sky
   The nearest city nightly glow.

Like peals of airy bells outworn
   Faint laughter died above her head
In gusts of broken music borne:
   'They keep the Carnival,' she said.

Her hungry heart devoured the town:
   'Heaven save me by a miracle!
Unless God sends an angel down,
   Thither I go though it were Hell.'

She dug her nails deep in her breast,
   Sobbed, shrieked, and straight withdrew the bar:
A fledgling flying from the nest,
   A pale moth rushing to a star.

Fillet and veil in strips she tore;
   Her golden tresses floated wide;
The ring and bracelet that she wore
   As Christ's betrothed, she cast aside.

'Life's dearest meaning I shall probe;
   Lo! I shall taste of love at last!
Away!' She doffed her outer robe,
   And sent it sailing down the blast.

Her body seemed to warm the wind;
   With bleeding feet o'er ice she ran:
'I leave the righteous God behind;
   I go to worship sinful man.'

She reached the sounding city's gate;
   No question did the warder ask:
He passed her in: 'Welcome, wild mate!'
   He thought her some fantastic mask.

Half-naked through the town she went;
   Each footstep left a bloody mark;
Crowds followed her with looks intent;
   Her bright eyes made the torches dark.

Alone and watching in the street
   There stood a grave youth nobly dressed;
To him she knelt and kissed his feet;
   Her face her great desire confessed.

Straight to his house the nun he led:
   'Strange lady, what would you with me?'
'Your love, your love, sweet lord,' she said;
   'I bring you my virginity.'

He healed her bosom with a kiss;
   She gave him all her passion's hoard;
And sobbed and murmured ever, 'This
   Is life's great meaning, dear, my lord.

'I care not for my broken vow;
  Though God should come in thunder soon,
I am sister to the mountains now,
  And sister to the sun and moon.'

Through all the towns of Belmarie
  She made a progress like a queen.
'She is,' they said, 'whate'er she be,
  The strangest woman ever seen.

'From fairyland she must have come,
  Or else she is a mermaiden.'
Some said she was a ghoul, and some
  A heathen goddess born again.

But soon her fire to ashes burned;
  Her beauty changed to haggardness;
Her golden hair to silver turned;
  The hour came of her last caress.

At midnight from her lonely bed
  She rose, and said, 'I have had my will.'
The old ragged robe she donned, and fled
  Back to the convent on the hill.

Half-naked as she went before,
  She hurried to the city wall,
Unnoticed in the rush and roar
  And splendour of the carnival.

No question did the warder ask:
  Her ragged robe, her shrunken limb,
Her dreadful eyes! 'It is no mask;
  It is a she-wolf, gaunt and grim!'

She ran across the icy plain;
  Her worn blood curdled in the blast;
Each footstep left a crimson stain;
  The white-faced moon looked on aghast.

She said between her chattering jaws,
   'Deep peace is mine, I cease to strive;
Oh, comfortable convent laws,
   That bury foolish nuns alive!

'A trowel for my passing-bell,
   A little bed within the wall,
A coverlet of stones; how well
   I there shall keep the Carnival!'

Like tired bells chiming in their sleep,
   The wind faint peals of laughter bore;
She stopped her ears and climbed the steep,
   And thundered at the convent door.

It opened straight: she entered in,
   And at the wardress' feet fell prone:
'I come to purge away my sin;
   Bury me, close me up in stone.'

The wardress raised her tenderly;
   She touched her wet and fast-shut eyes:
'Look, sister; sister, look at me;
   Look; can you see through my disguise?'

She looked and saw her own sad face,
   And trembled, wondering, 'Who art thou?'
'God sent me down to fill your place:
   I am the Virgin Mary now.'

And with the word, God's mother shone:
   The wanderer whispered, 'Mary, hail!'
The vision helped her to put on
   Bracelet and fillet, ring and veil.

'You are sister to the mountains now,
   And sister to the day and night;
Sister to God.' And on the brow
   She kissed her thrice, and left her sight.

While dreaming in her cloudy bed,
     Far in the crimson orient land
On many a mountain's happy head
     Dawn lightly laid her rosy hand.

JOHN DAVIDSON
*Ballads and Songs* (1894)


## The Ballad of Father Gilligan

The old priest Peter Gilligan
Was weary night and day;
For half his flock were in their beds,
Or under green sods lay.

Once, while he nodded on a chair,
At the moth-hour of eve,
Another poor man sent for him,
And he began to grieve.

'I have no rest, nor joy, nor peace,
'For people die and die';
And after cried he, 'God forgive!
'My body spake, not I!'

And then, half-lying on the chair
He knelt, prayed, fell asleep;
And the moth-hour went from the fields,
And stars began to peep.

They slowly into millions grew,
And leaves shook in the wind;
And God covered the world with shade,
And whispered to mankind.

Upon the time of sparrow chirp
When the moths came once more,
The old priest Peter Gilligan
Stood upright on the floor.

'Mavrone, mavrone! the man has died,
'While I slept on the chair';
He roused his horse out of its sleep,
And rode with little care.

He rode now as he never rode,
By rocky lane and fen;
The sick man's wife opened the door:
'Father! you come again!'

'And is the poor man dead?' he cried.
'He died an hour ago.'
The old priest Peter Gilligan
In grief swayed to and fro.

'When you were gone, he turned and died
'As merry as a bird.'
The old priest Peter Gilligan
He knelt him at that word.

'He who hath made the night of stars
'For souls, who tire and bleed,
'Sent one of His great angels down
'To help me in my need.

'He who is wrapped in purple robes,
'With planets in His care,
'Had pity on the least of things
'Asleep upon a chair.'

W. B. YEATS
*Poems* (1899)

## *A Shropshire Lad*

### 9

On moonlit heath and lonesome bank
  The sheep beside me graze;
And yon the gallows used to clank
  Fast by the four cross ways.

A careless shepherd once would keep
  The flocks by moonlight there,[1]
And high amongst the glimmering sheep
  The dead man stood on air.

They hang us now in Shrewsbury jail:
  The whistles blow forlorn,
And trains all night groan on the rail
  To men that die at morn.

There sleeps in Shrewsbury jail to-night,
  Or wakes, as may betide,
A better lad, if things went right,
  Than most that sleep outside.

And naked to the hangman's noose
  The morning clocks will ring
A neck God made for other use
  Than strangling in a string.

And sharp the link of life will snap,
  And dead on air will stand
Heels that held up as straight a chap
  As treads upon the land.

So here I'll watch the night and wait
  To see the morning shine,
When he will hear the stroke of eight
  And not the stroke of nine;

---

1. Hanging in chains was called keeping sheep by moonlight.

And wish my friend as sound a sleep
    As lads' I did not know,
That shepherded the moonlit sheep
    A hundred years ago.

A. E. HOUSMAN
*A Shropshire Lad* (1896)


## Admirals All

### A SONG OF SEA KINGS

Effingham, Grenville, Raleigh, Drake,
    Here's to the bold and free!
Benbow, Collingwood, Byron, Blake,
    Hail to the Kings of the Sea!
Admirals all, for England's sake,
    Honour be yours and fame!
And honour, as long as waves shall break,
    To Nelson's peerless name!

> *Admirals all, for England's sake,*
>     *Honour be yours and fame!*
> *And honour, as long as waves shall break,*
>     *To Nelson's peerless name!*

Essex was fretting in Cadiz Bay
    With the galleons fair in sight;
Howard at last must give him his way,
    And the word was passed to fight.
Never was schoolboy gayer than he,
    Since holidays first began:
He tossed his bonnet to wind and sea,
    And under the guns he ran.

Drake nor devil nor Spaniard feared,
    Their cities he put to the sack;
He singed His Catholic Majesty's beard,
    And harried his ships to wrack;

He was playing at Plymouth a rubber of bowls
   When the great Armada came;
But he said, 'They must wait their turn, good souls,'
   And he stooped, and finished the game.

Fifteen sail were the Dutchmen bold,
   Duncan he had but two;
But he anchored them fast where the Texel shoaled,
   And his colours aloft he flew.
'I've taken the depth to a fathom,' he cried,
   'And I'll sink with a right good will:
For I know when we're all of us under the tide
   My flag will be fluttering still.'

Splinters were flying above, below,
   When Nelson sailed the Sound:
'Mark you, I wouldn't be elsewhere now,'
   Said he, 'for a thousand pound!'
The Admiral's signal bade him fly,
   But he wickedly wagged his head:
He clapped the glass to his sightless eye,
   And 'I'm damned if I see it!' he said.

Admirals all, they said their say,
   (The echoes are ringing still).
Admirals all, they went their way
   To the haven under the hill.
But they left us a kingdom none can take –
   The realm of the circling sea –
To be ruled by the rightful sons of Blake,
   And the Rodneys yet to be.

     *Admirals all, for England's sake,*
      *Honour be yours and fame!*
     *And honour, as long as waves shall break,*
      *To Nelson's peerless name!*

HENRY NEWBOLT
*Admirals All, and Other Verses* (1897)

## *The Barber*

### 1

I dreamed I was a barber; and there went
Beneath my hand, oh! manes extravagant.
Beneath my trembling fingers, many a mask
Of many a pleasant girl. It was my task
To gild their hair, carefully, strand by strand;
To paint their eyebrows with a timid hand;
To draw a bodkin, from a vase of kohl,
Through the closed lashes; pencils from a bowl
Of sepia to paint them underneath;
To blow upon their eyes with a soft breath.
They lay them back and watched the leaping bands.

### 2

The dream grew vague. I moulded with my hands
The mobile breasts, the valley; and the waist
I touched; and pigments reverently placed
Upon their thighs in sapient spots and stains,
Beryls and crysolites and diaphanes,
And gems whose hot harsh names are never said.
I was a masseur; and my fingers bled
With wonder as I touched their awful limbs.

### 3

Suddenly, in the marble trough, there seems
O, last of my pale mistresses, Sweetness!
A twylipped scarlet pansie. My caress
Tinges thy steelgray eyes to violet.
Adown thy body skips the pit-a-pat
Of treatment once heard in a hospital
For plagues that fascinate, but half appal.

### 4

So, at the sound, the blood of me stood cold.
Thy chaste hair ripened into sullen gold.

The throat, the shoulders, swelled and were uncouth.
The breasts rose up and offered each a mouth.
And on the belly pallid blushes crept,
That maddened me, until I laughed and wept.

JOHN GRAY<br>
Silverpoints (1893)

## The Ballad of a Barber

Here is the tale of Carrousel,
The barber of Meridian Street.
He cut, and coiffed, and shaved so well,
That all the world was at his feet.

The King, the Queen, and all the Court,
To no one else would trust their hair,
And reigning belles of every sort
Owed their successes to his care.

With carriage and with cabriolet
Daily Meridian Street was blocked,
Like bees about a bright bouquet
The beaux about his doorway flocked.

Such was his art he could with ease
Curl wit into the dullest face;
Or to a goddess of old Greece
Add a new wonder and a grace.

All powders, paints, and subtle dyes,
And costliest scents that men distil,
And rare pomades, forgot their price
And marvelled at his splendid skill.

The curling irons in his hand
Almost grew quick enough to speak,
The razor was a magic wand
That understood the softest cheek.

Yet with no pride his heart was moved;
He was so modest in his ways!
His daily task was all he loved,
And now and then a little praise.

An equal care he would bestow
On problems simple or complex;
And nobody had seen him show
A preference for either sex.

How came it then one summer day,
Coiffing the daughter of the King,
He lengthened out the least delay
And loitered in his hairdressing?

The Princess was a pretty child,
Thirteen years old, or thereabout.
She was as joyous and as wild
As spring flowers when the sun is out.

Her gold hair fell down to her feet
And hung about her pretty eyes;
She was as lyrical and sweet
As one of Schubert's melodies.

Three times the barber curled a lock,
And thrice he straightened it again;
And twice the irons scorched her frock,
And twice he stumbled in her train.

His fingers lost their cunning quite,
His ivory combs obeyed no more;
Something or other dimmed his sight,
And moved mysteriously the floor.

He leant upon the toilet table,
His fingers fumbled in his breast;
He felt as foolish as a fable,
And feeble as a pointless jest.

He snatched a bottle of Cologne,
And broke the neck between his hands;
He felt as if he was alone,
And mighty as a king's commands.

The Princess gave a little scream,
Carrousel's cut was sharp and deep;
He left her softly as a dream
That leaves a sleeper to his sleep.

He left the room on pointed feet;
Smiling that things had gone so well.
They hanged him in Meridian Street.
You pray in vain for Carrousel.

AUBREY BEARDSLEY
In *The Savoy* (1896)


## Glamour of Gold

The white hands of my lady's maid
Move deftly through the shining hair!
How my heart falters half afraid
Lest they should hurt a thing so fair
    As my sweet lady's head!
And how I wish that I stood there
    Twisting the strands instead!

Fortunate fingers those, that hold
The handles of the steels that fret
And dent each heavy tress of gold . . .
Till all the golden mass is set
    With waves bewildering,
Where fire and dusk together met
    Rival day's sunsetting!

Or so at least it seems to me
While gazing on my lady's face!
And when with leaping heart I see

Her soft shy breathing 'neath the lace
   That falls even to her feet . . .
The curves of her slim body trace –
   See her supremely sweet –

Ah! then love swoons too satisfied
Too passionate for words of praise
With but one prayer, to abide
Safely at her sweet side always!
   Even as that maiden there
That staid and silent still delays
   Winding the long gold hair! . . .

OLIVE CUSTANCE
*Opals* (1897)

## The Cap and Bells

The jester walked in the garden:
The garden had fallen still;
He bade his soul rise upward
And stand on her window-sill.

It rose in a straight blue garment,
When owls began to call:
It had grown wise-tongued by thinking
Of a quiet and light footfall;

But the young queen would not listen;
She rose in her pale night gown;
She drew in the heavy casement
And pushed the latches down.

He bade his heart go to her,
When the owls called out no more;
In a red and quivering garment
It sang to her through the door.

It had grown sweet-tongued by dreaming,
Of a flutter of flower-like hair;
But she took up her fan from the table
And waved it off on the air.

'I have cap and bells' he pondered,
'I will send them to her and die;'
And when the morning whitened
He left them where she went by.

She laid them upon her bosom,
Under a cloud of her hair,
And her red lips sang them a love song:
Till stars grew out of the air.

She opened her door and her window,
And the heart and the soul came through,
To her right hand came the red one,
To her left hand came the blue.

They set up a noise like crickets,
A chattering wise and sweet,
And her hair was a folded flower
And the quiet of love in her feet.

W. B. YEATS
*The Wind Among the Reeds* (1899)

## Daisy

Where the thistle lifts a purple crown
　　Six foot out of the turf,
And the harebell shakes on the windy hill –
　　O the breath of the distant surf! –

The hills look over on the South,
　　And southward dreams the sea;
And, with the sea-breeze hand in hand,
　　Came innocence and she.

Where 'mid the gorse the raspberry
  Red for the gatherer springs,
Two children did we stray and talk
  Wise, idle, childish things.

She listened with big-lipped surprise,
  Breast-deep mid flower and spine:
Her skin was like a grape, whose veins
  Run snow instead of wine.

She knew not those sweet words she spake,
  Nor knew her own sweet way;
But there's never a bird, so sweet a song
  Thronged in whose throat that day!

Oh, there were flowers in Storrington
  On the turf and on the spray;
But the sweetest flower on Sussex hills
  Was the Daisy-flower that day!

Her beauty smoothed earth's furrowed face!
  She gave me tokens three: –
A look, a word of her winsome mouth,
  And a wild raspberry.

A berry red, a guileless look,
  A still word, – strings of sand!
And yet they made my wild, wild heart
  Fly down to her little hand.

For standing artless as the air,
  And candid as the skies,
She took the berries with her hand,
  And the love with her sweet eyes.

The fairest things have fleetest end:
  Their scent survives their close,
But the rose's scent is bitterness
  To him that loved the rose!

She looked a little wistfully,
    Then went her sunshine way: –
The sea's eye had a mist on it,
    And the leaves fell from the day.

She went her unremembering way,
    She went and left in me
The pang of all the partings gone,
    And partings yet to be.

She left me marvelling why my soul
    Was sad that she was glad;
At all the sadness in the sweet,
    The sweetness in the sad.

Still, still I seemed to see her, still
    Look up with soft replies,
And take the berries with her hand,
    And the love with her lovely eyes.

Nothing begins, and nothing ends,
    That is not paid with moan;
For we are born in others' pain,
    And perish in our own.

FRANCIS THOMPSON
*Poems* (1893)


## Sir Eldric

Sir Eldric rode by field and fen
To reach the haunts of heathen men.

    About the dusk he came into
        A wood of birchen grey,
    And on the other side he knew
        The heathen country lay.

' 'Tis but a night (he sang) to ride,
And Christ shall reach the other side!'

The moon came peering thro' the trees
   And found him undismayed,
For still he sang his litanies
   And as he rode he prayed.

He looked as young, as pure and glad
As ever looked Sir Galahad.

   About the middle of the night
      He came upon the brink,
   Of running waters cool and white
      And lighted there to drink.

And as he knelt a hidden foe
Crept from behind and smote him so.

   He turned; he felt his heart's blood run;
      He sought his enemy:
   'And shall I leave my deeds undone,
      And die for such as thee?'

And since a Knight was either man,
They wrestled till the dawn began.

   Then in the dim and rustling place
      Amid the thyme and dew,
   Sir Eldric dealt the stroke of grace,
      And sank a-dying too,

And thought upon that other's plight
Who was not sure of Heaven that night.

   He dipped his fingers in his breast;
      He sought in vain to rise;
   He leaned across his foe at rest,
      And murmured, 'I baptize!'

When lo! the sun broke overhead:
There, at his side, *Himself* lay dead!

A. MARY F. ROBINSON
*Lyrics Selected from the Works* (1891)

## The Priest of Love

In Sicily in the days of art
  A painter prince held sway,
Who loved one lady with all his heart
  And dreamed of her night and day.

She was a girl of scarce thirteen,
  And he was but a youth;
Yet he sware none other should be his queen,
  And kept his oath with truth.

And still as she grew he built her a home,
  That the years less long might seem,
Out on an island, girt with the foam,
  Beautiful as a dream.

And he called the masters from every part,
  Of temper, and tint, and tone,
Who moulded in metal miraculous art,
  Or wrought it in colour or stone,

All carvers of wood and silver and gold,
  All weavers that loved the loom,
To make her a palace of perfect mould,
  And fill it with tender bloom.

And he sent for marbles out of the isles,
  Rose-red and white as snow,
And made a dome that shone for miles
  In the ruddy evening glow.

And the palace grew, and the maiden grew
  In stature and beauty and grace
Year by year – for shape and for hue,
  A wonderful woman's face.

And ever of marbles from far-off isles,
  Like music soft and slow,
Rose fluted pillars and fretted piles,
  And hung in the wave below,

With many a cupola poised above,
   And many a sculptured frieze,
That filled with anguish of hopeless love
   The amorous ocean breeze.

And he hung rich arras about the place,
   Wrought in a distant clime,
With love, and passion, and war, and the chase,
   And gods of the olden time;

And he steeped his brush in the hues of love,
   His soul in the poet's themes,
And filled the walls and the ceilings above
   With forms as fair as dreams;

And he melted his heart to heavenly hues,
   And bathed the grainèd glass
In burning reds and beautiful blues,
   And greens as soft as grass;

And he fetched rare marbles from far-off isles
   For the sculptors, as white as snow,
Who made them smile immortal smiles,
   With love immortal glow.

And the palace grew and the maiden grew
   In beauty side by side;
And when both were perfect in form and hue,
   And ready – the maiden died.

Then he shut himself up in the palace alone,
   With the statues and his despair,
And his young dead bride as cold as stone,
   And fired it, and perished there.

And the red flame shone to the far-off isles
   Over the ocean-flow,
And the sky was red for miles and miles,
   And the sea lay red below.

JOHN BARLAS
*Selections from 'Songs of a Bayadere' and*
*'Songs of a Troubadour'* (1893)

## Sir Lancelot's Bride

Soft blows the breeze, the sun shines bright,
 The birds sing loud and gay;
But from the castle on the height
 Sounds forth a blither lay.

The hall is decked with flowerets fair,
 The gates are opened wide,
To welcome home that youthful pair,
 Sir Lancelot and his bride.

The lingering hours pass slowly by,
 The blossoms droop and fade;
And many a bright impatient eye
 Looks down the rocky glade.

'Look forth, my son, adown the height,'
 Outspeaks a harper old;
'Methought I saw a helmet bright
 Flash back the sunset's gold.'

'Sir Lancelot's band draw nigh, my sire,
 Their hundred helmets gleam,
And like a line of living fire
 They ford the shallow stream.

'Hurrah! hurrah! they come, they come!
 But why so slow and sad?
Why march they not to beat of drum,
 With shouts and laughter glad?

'Oh, sweet and sad their music streams,
 In cadence low and long;
More like a funeral dirge it seems
 Than a gay bridal song.'

'Look forth again,' the old man said,
 'Thy sight is strong and clear;
What bear they on that narrow bed,
 That looks so like a bier?'

'I see the gleam of golden hair,
    As slowly on they ride:
For weird in beauty, strangely fair,
    They bring Sir Lancelot's bride.

'They bear her through the rocky dale;
    Methinks they sigh and weep:
My lady's cheek is deadly pale –
    Oh, say, can that be *sleep?*

'She lies in all her loveliness,
    A fair yet awful sight;
And that is not her bridal dress,
    That gleams so ghastly white.

'The light falls on her lily cheek,
    And on her golden head –
Oh, hush, or but in whispers speak:
    Say not – that she is dead!

'Alas, alas! in deep despair
    Sir Lancelot's head is bowed:
He hides his face; he cannot bear
    To see the snow-white shroud.'

Within the hall the flowerets fair
    Ere now have drooped and died;
Fit welcome to that mournful pair,
    Sir Lancelot and his bride.

The morn shall come with brighter flowers,
    The lark shall warble gay;
But never more shall Lancelot's towers
    Send forth a gladsome lay.

CONSTANCE NADEN
*Complete Poetical Works* (1894)

## A Ballad of John Nicholson

It fell in the year of Mutiny,
    At darkest of the night,
John Nicholson by Jalándhar came,
    On his way to Delhi fight.

And as he by Jalándhar came,
    He thought what he must do,
And he sent to the Rajah fair greeting,
    To try if he were true.

'God grant your Highness length of days,
    And friends when need shall be;
And I pray you send your Captains hither,
    That they may speak with me.'

On the morrow through Jalándhar town
    The Captains rode in state;
They came to the house of John Nicholson,
    And stood before the gate.

The chief of them was Mehtab Singh,
    He was both proud and sly;
His turban gleamed with rubies red,
    He held his chin full high.

He marked his fellows how they put
    Their shoes from off their feet;
'Now wherefore make ye such ado
    These fallen lords to greet?

'They have ruled us for a hundred years,
    In truth I know not how,
But though they be fain of mastery
    They dare not claim it now.'

Right haughtily before them all
    The durbar hall he trod,
With rubies red his turban gleamed,
    His feet with pride were shod.

They had not been an hour together,
    A scanty hour or so,
When Mehtab Singh rose in his place
    And turned about to go.

Then swiftly came John Nicholson
    Between the door and him,
With anger smouldering in his eyes,
    That made the rubies dim.

'You are over-hasty, Mehtab Singh,' –
    Oh, but his voice was low!
He held his wrath with a curb of iron
    That furrowed cheek and brow.

'You are over-hasty, Mehtab Singh,
    When that the rest are gone,
I have a word that may not wait
    To speak with you alone.'

The Captains passed in silence forth
    And stood the door behind;
To go before the game was played
    Be sure they had no mind.

But there within John Nicholson
    Turned him on Mehtab Singh,
'So long as the soul is in my body
    You shall not do this thing.

'Have ye served us for a hundred years
    And yet ye know not why?
We brook no doubt of our mastery,
    We rule until we die.

'Were I the one last Englishman
    Drawing the breath of life,
And you the master-rebel of all
    That stir this land to strife –

'Were I,' he said, 'but a Corporal,
   And you a Rajput King,
So long as the soul was in my body
   You should not do this thing.

'Take off, take off, those shoes of pride,
   Carry them whence they came;
Your Captains saw your insolence,
   And they shall see your shame.'

When Mehtab Singh came to the door
   His shoes they burned his hand,
For there in long and silent lines
   He saw the Captains stand.

When Mehtab Singh rode from the gate
   His chin was on his breast:
The Captains said, 'When the strong command
   Obedience is best.'

HENRY NEWBOLT
*Admirals All* (1897)

## Gunga Din

You may talk o' gin and beer
When you're quartered safe out 'ere,
An' you're sent to penny-fights an' Aldershot it;
But when it comes to slaughter
You will do your work on water,
An' you'll lick the bloomin' boots of 'im that's got it.
Now in Injia's sunny clime,
Where I used to spend my time
A-servin' of 'Er Majesty the Queen,
Of all them blackfaced crew
The finest man I knew
Was our regimental bhisti, Gunga Din.
    He was 'Din! Din! Din!

'You limpin' lump o' brick-dust, Gunga Din!
  'Hi! slippery *hitherao!*
  'Water, get it! *Panee lao!*[1]
'You squidgy-nosed old idol, Gunga Din.'

The uniform 'e wore
Was nothin' much before,
An' rather less than 'arf o' that be'ind,
For a piece o' twisty rag
An' a goatskin water-bag
Was all the field-equipment 'e could find.
When the sweatin' troop-train lay
In a sidin' through the day,
Where the 'eat would make your bloomin' eyebrows crawl,
We shouted 'Harry By!'[2]
Till our throats were bricky-dry,
Then we wopped 'im 'cause 'e couldn't serve us all.
    It was 'Din! Din! Din!
  'You 'eathen, where the mischief 'ave you been?
    'You put some *juldee*[3] in it
    'Or I'll *marrow*[4] you this minute
  'If you don't fill up my helmet, Gunga Din!'

'E would dot an' carry one
Till the longest day was done;
An' 'e didn't seem to know the use o' fear.
If we charged or broke or cut,
You could bet your bloomin' nut,
'E'd be waitin' fifty paces right flank rear.
With 'is mussick[5] on 'is back,
'E would skip with our attack,
An' watch us till the bugles made 'Retire,'
An' for all 'is dirty 'ide
'E was white, clear white, inside
When 'e went to tend the wounded under fire!
    It was 'Din! Din! Din!'

1. Bring water swiftly.   2. Mr Atkins's equivalent for 'O brother'.
3. Be quick.   4. Hit you.   5. Water-skin.

With the bullets kickin' dust-spots on the green.
    When the cartridges ran out,
    You could hear the front-files shout,
  'Hi! ammunition-mules an' Gunga Din!'

I sha'n't forgit the night
When I dropped be'ind the fight
With a bullet where my belt-plate should 'a' been.
I was chokin' mad with thirst,
An' the man that spied me first
Was our good old grinnin', gruntin' Gunga Din.
'E lifted up my 'ead,
An' he plugged me where I bled,
An' 'e guv me 'arf-a-pint o' water-green:
It was crawlin' and it stunk,
But of all the drinks I've drunk,
I'm gratefullest to one from Gunga Din.
    It was 'Din! Din! Din!
  'Ere's a beggar with a bullet through 'is spleen;
    'E's chawin' up the ground,
    'An' 'e's kickin' all around;
  'For Gawd's sake git the water, Gunga Din!'

'E carried me away
To where a dooli lay,
An' a bullet come an' drilled the beggar clean.
'E put me safe inside,
An' just before 'e died,
'I 'ope you liked your drink,' sez Gunga Din.
So I'll meet 'im later on
At the place where 'e is gone –
Where it's always double drill and no canteen;
'E'll be squattin' on the coals
Givin' drink to poor damned souls,
An' I'll get a swig in hell from Gunga Din!
    Yes, Din! Din! Din!

You Lazarushian-leather Gunga Din!
  Though I've belted you and flayed you,
  By the livin' Gawd that made you,
You're a better man than I am, Gunga Din!

RUDYARD KIPLING
*Barrack-Room Ballads* (1892)


## The Ballad of Reading Gaol

In Memoriam

C. T. W.

Sometime Trooper of the Royal Horse Guards.
Obiit H.M. Prison, Reading, Berkshire,
July 7th, 1896.

I

He did not wear his scarlet coat,
  For blood and wine are red,
And blood and wine were on his hands
  When they found him with the dead,
The poor dead woman whom he loved,
  And murdered in her bed.

He walked amongst the Trial Men
  In a suit of shabby gray;
A cricket cap was on his head,
  And his step seemed light and gay;
But I never saw a man who looked
  So wistfully at the day.

I never saw a man who looked
  With such a wistful eye
Upon that little tent of blue
  Which prisoners call the sky,
And at every drifting cloud that went
  With sails of silver by.

I walked, with other souls in pain,
    Within another ring,
And was wondering if the man had done
    A great or little thing,
When a voice behind me whispered low,
    '*That fellow's got to swing.*'

Dear Christ! the very prison walls
    Suddenly seemed to reel,
And the sky above my head became
    Like a casque of scorching steel;
And, though I was a soul in pain,
    My pain I could not feel.

I only knew what hunted thought
    Quickened his step, and why
He looked upon the garish day
    With such a wistful eye;
The man had killed the thing he loved,
    And so he had to die.

Yet each man kills the thing he loves,
    By each let this be heard,
Some do it with a bitter look,
    Some with a flattering word,
The coward does it with a kiss,
    The brave man with a sword!

Some kill their love when they are young,
    And some when they are old;
Some strangle with the hands of Lust,
    Some with the hands of Gold:
The kindest use a knife, because
    The dead so soon grow cold.

Some love too little, some too long,
    Some sell, and others buy;
Some do the deed with many tears,

And some without a sigh:
For each man kills the thing he loves,
   Yet each man does not die.

He does not die a death of shame
   On a day of dark disgrace,
Nor have a noose about his neck,
   Nor a cloth upon his face,
Nor drop feet foremost through the floor
   Into an empty space.

He does not sit with silent men
   Who watch him night and day;
Who watch him when he tries to weep,
   And when he tries to pray;
Who watch him lest himself should rob
   The prison of its prey.

He does not wake at dawn to see
   Dread figures throng his room,
The shivering Chaplain robed in white,
   The Sheriff stern with gloom,
And the Governor all in shiny black,
   With the yellow face of Doom.

He does not rise in piteous haste
   To put on convict-clothes,
While some coarse-mouthed Doctor gloats, and notes
   Each new and nerve-twitched pose,
Fingering a watch whose little ticks
   Are like horrible hammer-blows.

He does not know that sickening thirst
   That sands one's throat, before
The hangman with his gardener's gloves
   Slips through the padded door,
And binds one with three leathern thongs,
   That the throat may thirst no more.

He does not bend his head to hear
　　The Burial Office read,
Nor, while the terror of his soul
　　Tells him he is not dead,
Cross his own coffin, as he moves
　　Into the hideous shed.

He does not stare upon the air
　　Through a little roof of glass:
He does not pray with lips of clay
　　For his agony to pass;
Nor feel upon his shuddering cheek
　　The kiss of Caiaphas.


II

Six weeks our guardsman walked the yard,
　　In the suit of shabby gray:
His cricket cap was on his head,
　　And his step seemed light and gay,
But I never saw a man who looked
　　So wistfully at the day.

I never saw a man who looked
　　With such a wistful eye
Upon that little tent of blue
　　Which prisoners call the sky,
And at every wandering cloud that trailed
　　Its ravelled fleeces by.

He did not wring his hands, as do
　　Those witless men who dare
To try to rear the changeling Hope
　　In the cave of black Despair:
He only looked upon the sun,
　　And drank the morning air.

He did not wring his hands nor weep,
　　Nor did he peek or pine,
But he drank the air as though it held

Some healthful anodyne;
With open mouth he drank the sun
    As though it had been wine!

And I and all the souls in pain,
    Who tramped the other ring,
Forgot if we ourselves had done
    A great or little thing,
And watched with gaze of dull amaze
    The man who had to swing.

And strange it was to see him pass
    With a step so light and gay,
And strange it was to see him look
    So wistfully at the day,
And strange it was to think that he
    Had such a debt to pay.

For oak and elm have pleasant leaves
    That in the spring-time shoot:
But grim to see is the gallows-tree,
    With its adder-bitten root,
And, green or dry, a man must die
    Before it bears its fruit!

The loftiest place is that seat of grace
    For which all worldlings try:
But who would stand in hempen band
    Upon a scaffold high,
And through a murderer's collar take
    His last look at the sky?

It is sweet to dance to violins
    When Love and Life are fair:
To dance to flutes, to dance to lutes
    Is delicate and rare:
But it is not sweet with nimble feet
    To dance upon the air!

So with curious eyes and sick surmise
  We watched him day by day,
And wondered if each one of us
  Would end the self-same way,
For none can tell to what red Hell
  His sightless soul may stray.

At last the dead man walked no more
  Amongst the Trial Men,
And I knew that he was standing up
  In the black dock's dreadful pen,
And that never would I see his face
  In God's sweet world again.

Like two doomed ships that pass in storm
  We had crossed each other's way:
But we made no sign, we said no word,
  We had no word to say;
For we did not meet in the holy night,
  But in the shameful day.

A prison wall was round us both,
  Two outcast men we were:
The world had thrust us from its heart,
  And God from out His care:
And the iron gin that waits for Sin
  Had caught us in its snare.

### III

In Debtors' Yard the stones are hard,
  And the dripping wall is high,
So it was there he took the air
  Beneath the leaden sky,
And by each side a Warder walked,
  For fear the man might die.

Or else he sat with those who watched
  His anguish night and day;
Who watched him when he rose to weep,
  And when he crouched to pray;
Who watched him lest himself should rob
  Their scaffold of its prey.

The Governor was strong upon
  The Regulations Act:
The Doctor said that Death was but
  A scientific fact:
And twice a day the Chaplain called,
  And left a little tract.

And twice a day he smoked his pipe,
  And drank his quart of beer:
His soul was resolute, and held
  No hiding-place for fear;
He often said that he was glad
  The hangman's hands were near.

But why he said so strange a thing
  No Warder dared to ask:
For he to whom a watcher's doom
  Is given as his task,
Must set a lock upon his lips,
  And make his face a mask.

Or else he might be moved, and try
  To comfort or console:
And what should Human Pity do
  Pent up in Murderers' Hole?
What word of grace in such a place
  Could help a brother's soul?

With slouch and swing around the ring
  We trod the Fools' Parade!
We did not care: we knew we were

The Devil's Own Brigade:
And shaven head and feet of lead
    Make a merry masquerade.

We tore the tarry rope to shreds
    With blunt and bleeding nails;
We rubbed the doors, and scrubbed the floors,
    And cleaned the shining rails:
And, rank by rank, we soaped the plank,
    And clattered with the pails.

We sewed the sacks, we broke the stones,
    We turned the dusty drill:
We banged the tins, and bawled the hymns,
    And sweated on the mill:
But in the heart of every man
    Terror was lying still.

So still it lay that every day
    Crawled like a weed-clogged wave:
And we forgot the bitter lot
    That waits for fool and knave,
Till once, as we tramped in from work,
    We passed an open grave.

With yawning mouth the yellow hole
    Gaped for a living thing;
The very mud cried out for blood
    To the thirsty asphalte ring:
And we knew that ere one dawn grew fair
    Some prisoner had to swing.

Right in we went, with soul intent
    On Death and Dread and Doom:
The hangman, with his little bag,
    Went shuffling through the gloom:
And each man trembled as he crept
    Into his numbered tomb.

❧

That night the empty corridors
  Were full of forms of Fear,
And up and down the iron town
  Stole feet we could not hear,
And through the bars that hide the stars
  White faces seemed to peer.

He lay as one who lies and dreams
  In a pleasant meadow-land,
The watchers watched him as he slept,
  And could not understand
How one could sleep so sweet a sleep
  With a hangman close at hand.

But there is no sleep when men must weep
  Who never yet have wept:
So we – the fool, the fraud, the knave –
  That endless vigil kept,
And through each brain on hands of pain
  Another's terror crept.

Alas! it is a fearful thing
  To feel another's guilt!
For, right within, the sword of Sin
  Pierced to its poisoned hilt,
And as molten lead were the tears we shed
  For the blood we had not spilt.

The Warders with their shoes of felt
  Crept by each padlocked door,
And peeped and saw, with eyes of awe,
  Gray figures on the floor,
And wondered why men knelt to pray
  Who never prayed before.

All through the night we knelt and prayed,
  Mad mourners of a corse!
The troubled plumes of midnight were

The plumes upon a hearse:
And bitter wine upon a sponge
   Was the savour of Remorse.

The gray cock crew, the red cock crew,
   But never came the day:
And crooked shapes of Terror crouched,
   In the corners where we lay:
And each evil sprite that walks by night
   Before us seemed to play.

They glided past, they glided fast,
   Like travellers through a mist:
They mocked the moon in a rigadoon
   Of delicate turn and twist,
And with formal pace and loathsome grace
   The phantoms kept their tryst.

With mop and mow, we saw them go,
   Slim shadows hand in hand:
About, about, in ghostly rout
   They trod a saraband:
And the damned grotesques made arabesques,
   Like the wind upon the sand!

With the pirouettes of marionettes,
   They tripped on pointed tread:
But with flutes of Fear they filled the ear,
   As their grisly masque they led,
And loud they sang, and long they sang,
   For they sang to wake the dead.

'*Oho!*' they cried, '*The world is wide,*
   *But fettered limbs go lame!*
*And once, or twice, to throw the dice*
   *Is a gentlemanly game,*
*But he does not win who plays with Sin*
   *In the secret House of Shame.*'

No things of air these antics were,
    That frolicked with such glee:
To men whose lives were held in gyves,
    And whose feet might not go free,
Ah! wounds of Christ! they were living things,
    Most terrible to see.

Around, around, they waltzed and wound;
    Some wheeled in smirking pairs;
With the mincing step of a demirep
    Some sidled up the stairs:
And with subtle sneer, and fawning leer,
    Each helped us at our prayers.

The morning wind began to moan,
    But still the night went on:
Through its giant loom the web of gloom
    Crept till each thread was spun:
And, as we prayed, we grew afraid
    Of the Justice of the Sun.

The moaning wind went wandering round
    The weeping prison-wall:
Till like a wheel of turning steel
    We felt the minutes crawl:
O moaning wind! what had we done
    To have such a seneschal?

At last I saw the shadowed bars,
    Like a lattice wrought in lead,
Move right across the whitewashed wall
    That faced my three-plank bed,
And I knew that somewhere in the world
    God's dreadful dawn was red.

At six o'clock we cleaned our cells,
    At seven all was still,
But the sough and swing of a mighty wing
    The prison seemed to fill,
For the Lord of Death with icy breath
    Had entered in to kill.

He did not pass in purple pomp,
    Nor ride a moon-white steed.
Three yards of cord and a sliding board
    Are all the gallows' need:
So with rope of shame the Herald came
    To do the secret deed.

We were as men who through a fen
    Of filthy darkness grope:
We did not dare to breathe a prayer,
    Or to give our anguish scope:
Something was dead in each of us,
    And what was dead was Hope.

For Man's grim Justice goes its way,
    And will not swerve aside:
It slays the weak, it slays the strong,
    It has a deadly stride:
With iron heel it slays the strong,
    The monstrous parricide!

We waited for the stroke of eight:
    Each tongue was thick with thirst:
For the stroke of eight is the stroke of Fate
    That makes a man accursed,
And Fate will use a running noose
    For the best man and the worst.

We had no other thing to do,
   Save to wait for the sign to come:
So, like things of stone in a valley lone,
   Quiet we sat and dumb:
But each man's heart beat thick and quick,
   Like a madman on a drum!

With sudden shock the prison-clock
   Smote on the shivering air,
And from all the gaol rose up a wail
   Of impotent despair,
Like the sound that frightened marshes hear
   From some leper in his lair.

And as one sees most fearful things
   In the crystal of a dream,
We saw the greasy hempen rope
   Hooked to the blackened beam,
And heard the prayer the hangman's snare
   Strangled into a scream.

And all the woe that moved him so
   That he gave that bitter cry,
And the wild regrets, and the bloody sweats,
   None knew so well as I:
For he who lives more lives than one
   More deaths than one must die.

IV

There is no chapel on the day
   On which they hang a man:
The Chaplain's heart is far too sick,
   Or his face is far too wan,
Or there is that written in his eyes
   Which none should look upon.

So they kept us close till high on noon,
    And then they rang the bell,
And the Warders with their jingling keys
    Opened each listening cell,
And down the iron stair we tramped,
    Each from his separate Hell.

Out into God's sweet air we went,
    But not in wonted way,
For this man's face was white with fear,
    And that man's face was gray,
And I never saw sad men who looked
    So wistfully at the day.

I never saw sad men who looked
    With such a wistful eye
Upon that little tent of blue
    We prisoners called the sky,
And at every careless cloud that passed
    In happy freedom by.

But there were those amongst us all
    Who walked with downcast head,
And knew that, had each got his due,
    They should have died instead:
He had but killed a thing that lived,
    Whilst they had killed the dead.

For he who sins a second time
    Wakes a dead soul to pain,
And draws it from its spotted shroud,
    And makes it bleed again,
And makes it bleed great gouts of blood,
    And makes it bleed in vain!

Like ape or clown, in monstrous garb
    With crooked arrows starred,
Silently we went round and round

  The slippery asphalte yard;
Silently we went round and round,
  And no man spoke a word.

Silently we went round and round,
  And through each hollow mind
The Memory of dreadful things
  Rushed like a dreadful wind,
And Horror stalked before each man,
  And Terror crept behind.

The Warders strutted up and down,
  And kept their herd of brutes,
Their uniforms were spick and span,
  And they wore their Sunday suits,
But we knew the work they had been at,
  By the quicklime on their boots.

For where a grave had opened wide,
  There was no grave at all:
Only a stretch of mud and sand
  By the hideous prison-wall,
And a little heap of burning lime,
  That the man should have his pall.

For he has a pall, this wretched man,
  Such as few men can claim:
Deep down below a prison-yard,
  Naked for greater shame,
He lies, with fetters on each foot,
  Wrapt in a sheet of flame!

And all the while the burning lime
  Eats flesh and bone away,
It eats the brittle bone by night,
  And the soft flesh by day,
It eats the flesh and bone by turns,
  But it eats the heart alway.

For three long years they will not sow
    Or root or seedling there:
For three long years the unblessed spot
    Will sterile be and bare,
And look upon the wondering sky
    With unreproachful stare.

They think a murderer's heart would taint
    Each simple seed they sow.
It is not true! God's kindly earth
    Is kindlier than men know,
And the red rose would but blow more red,
    The white rose whiter blow.

Out of his mouth a red, red rose!
    Out of his heart a white!
For who can say by what strange way,
    Christ brings His will to light,
Since the barren staff the pilgrim bore
    Bloomed in the great Pope's sight?

But neither milk-white rose nor red
    May bloom in prison air;
The shard, the pebble, and the flint,
    Are what they give us there:
For flowers have been known to heal
    A common man's despair.

So never will wine-red rose or white,
    Petal by petal, fall
On that stretch of mud and sand that lies
    By the hideous prison-wall,
To tell the men who tramp the yard
    That God's Son died for all.

Yet though the hideous prison-wall
   Still hems him round and round,
And a spirit may not walk by night
   That is with fetters bound,
And a spirit may but weep that lies
   In such unholy ground,

He is at peace – this wretched man –
   At peace, or will be soon:
There is no thing to make him mad,
   Nor does Terror walk at noon,
For the lampless Earth in which he lies
   Has neither Sun nor Moon.

They hanged him as a beast is hanged:
   They did not even toll
A requiem that might have brought
   Rest to his startled soul,
But hurriedly they took him out,
   And hid him in a hole.

They stripped him of his canvas clothes,
   And gave him to the flies:
They mocked the swollen purple throat,
   And the stark and staring eyes:
And with laughter loud they heaped the shroud
   In which their convict lies.

The Chaplain would not kneel to pray
   By his dishonoured grave:
Nor mark it with that blessed Cross
   That Christ for sinners gave,
Because the man was one of those
   Whom Christ came down to save.

Yet all is well; he has but passed
   To Life's appointed bourne:
And alien tears will fill for him

Pity's long-broken urn,
For his mourners will be outcast men,
    And outcasts always mourn.


V


I know not whether Laws be right,
    Or whether Laws be wrong;
All that we know who lie in gaol
    Is that the wall is strong;
And that each day is like a year,
    A year whose days are long.

But this I know, that every Law
    That men have made for Man,
Since first Man took his brother's life,
    And the sad world began,
But straws the wheat and saves the chaff
    With a most evil fan.

This too I know – and wise it were
    If each could know the same –
That every prison that men build
    Is built with bricks of shame,
And bound with bars lest Christ should see
    How men their brothers maim.

With bars they blur the gracious moon,
    And blind the goodly sun:
And they do well to hide their Hell,
    For in it things are done
That Son of God nor son of Man
    Ever should look upon!

The vilest deeds like poison weeds
    Bloom well in prison-air:
It is only what is good in Man

That wastes and withers there:
Pale Anguish keeps the heavy gate,
   And the Warder is Despair.

For they starve the little frightened child
   Till it weeps both night and day:
And they scourge the weak, and flog the fool,
   And gibe the old and gray,
And some grow mad, and all grow bad,
   And none a word may say.

Each narrow cell in which we dwell
   Is a foul and dark latrine,
And the fetid breath of living Death
   Chokes up each grated screen,
And all, but Lust, is turned to dust
   In Humanity's machine.

The brackish water that we drink
   Creeps with a loathsome slime,
And the bitter bread they weigh in scales
   Is full of chalk and lime,
And Sleep will not lie down, but walks
   Wild-eyed, and cries to Time.

But though lean Hunger and green Thirst
   Like asp with adder fight,
We have little care of prison fare,
   For what chills and kills outright
Is that every stone one lifts by day
   Becomes one's heart by night.

With midnight always in one's heart,
   And twilight in one's cell,
We turn the crank, or tear the rope,
   Each in his separate Hell,
And the silence is more awful far
   Than the sound of a brazen bell.

And never a human voice comes near
   To speak a gentle word:
And the eye that watches through the door
   Is pitiless and hard:
And by all forgot, we rot and rot,
   With soul and body marred.

And thus we rust Life's iron chain
   Degraded and alone:
And some men curse, and some men weep,
   And some men make no moan:
But God's eternal Laws are kind
   And break the heart of stone.

And every human heart that breaks,
   In prison-cell or yard,
Is as that broken box that gave
   Its treasure to the Lord,
And filled the unclean leper's house
   With the scent of costliest nard.

Ah! happy they whose hearts can break
   And peace of pardon win!
How else may man make straight his plan
   And cleanse his soul from Sin?
How else but through a broken heart
   May Lord Christ enter in?

And he of the swollen purple throat,
   And the stark and staring eyes,
Waits for the holy hands that took
   The Thief to Paradise;
And a broken and a contrite heart
   The Lord will not despise.

The man in red who reads the Law
  Gave him three weeks of life,
Three little weeks in which to heal
  His soul of his soul's strife,
And cleanse from every blot of blood
  The hand that held the knife.

And with tears of blood he cleansed the hand,
  The hand that held the steel:
For only blood can wipe out blood,
  And only tears can heal:
And the crimson stain that was of Cain
  Became Christ's snow-white seal.

VI

In Reading gaol by Reading town
  There is a pit of shame,
And in it lies a wretched man
  Eaten by teeth of flame,
In a burning winding-sheet he lies,
  And his grave has got no name.

And there, till Christ call forth the dead,
  In silence let him lie:
No need to waste the foolish tear,
  Or heave the windy sigh:
The man had killed the thing he loved,
  And so he had to die.

And all men kill the thing they love,
  By all let this be heard,
Some do it with a bitter look,
  Some with the flattering word,
The coward does it with a kiss,
  The brave man with a sword!

C.3.3. (OSCAR WILDE)
*The Ballad of Reading Gaol* (2nd edition 1898)

# 10. THE ROSES FALL

Poet after poet seems to have found a complex comfort in the prospect of defeat, decline and death, an attitude summed up by Mallarmé in his prose-poem 'Plainte d'Automne', where he says that 'I have loved all that is summed up in the word "fall".' There were those who found this attitude objectionable, called it effeteness and effeminacy, and, as Yeats recalls Davidson did, demanded 'blood and guts'. But the feeling was none the less there, and the dying fall, the gentle, somewhat pallid languor, the exquisite boredom, are rightly thought of as characteristic of a good deal of 1890s poetry. Many of the poets could have written of 'the tired taste and jaded sensibilities of our end of the century'. The description is in fact Richard Le Gallienne's, in a review of John Davidson's *The Wonderful Mission of Earl Lavender* (1895), the Proem to which ends:

> Though our thoughts turn ever Doomwards,
>> Though our sun is well-nigh set,
> Though our Century totters tombwards,
>> We may laugh a little yet.

Even the laughter was a little wry. Max Beerbohm, seeing that Paterian experiences 'gave nothing but lassitude to those who had gained them through suffering', retired from the fray to rest on his laurels: 'I, who crave no knighthood, shall write no more. I shall write no more. Already I feel myself to be a trifle outmoded. I belong to the Beardsley period.' In the same year (1896) he published his *Works,* and reached the ripe age of twenty-four.

Other ages have affected melancholy, and other young men have felt this falling of the petals before the buds have opened, but in the 1890s the feeling had a new importance. Its origins are complex. The century, whether one believed in the idea of centuries decaying or not, seemed to be dying in more than the simple numerical sense; the old queen was obviously near the end of her reign; frequent parallels were drawn between the Roman Empire in decline and the

British Empire, politically, artistically and morally; the old order was changing, the old gods falling. Some sort of cataclysmic event seemed to be looming ahead; events in retrospect seemed to be leading inevitably to the shattering changes of the First World War. The writers saw, in Frank Kermode's words in *The Sense of an Ending*, the '*fin de siècle*', where all the elements of the apocalyptic paradigm clearly co-exist'. Yeats, talking of Pater's *Marius the Epicurean* in *Autobiographies* wondered whether this book 'had not caused the disasters of my friends. It taught us to walk upon a rope, tightly stretched through serene air, and we were left to keep our feet upon a swaying rope in a storm'. Even the Celtic Renaissance encouraged the feeling of decline, directed as it was at the time by Arnold's essay 'On the Study of Celtic Literature'. Arnold characterized the Celtic sensibility by quoting from Ossian, 'They went forth to the war, but they always fell', and he felt fairly sure that English poetry got much of its melancholy from a Celtic source. This seems likely in the case of Lionel Johnson, determined to be Irish without much support from his ancestry, whose 'Mystic and Cavalier' obviously owes much to Arnold.

Wherever they originated, perhaps in the very sensibility that recognized them, 'the weariness, the fever and the fret' that affected Keats, were still oppressing poets of the 1890s. But the 'wings of poesy' were there too, and it was ironically Hardy, who has been accused of a variety of gloomy philosophies, who saw at the very turn of the century, in a thrush instead of a nightingale, the possibilities of hope.

Hope was more characteristic of women writers, who found a new counter to pessimism in the progress of science, and they refused to accept this vision of decline. The fact that women had always been associated with nature made it easier for them to accept evolution, and they used Darwinian theory to imagine a future in which they would come into their own in literary, social and political spheres. They viewed the end of the century with anticipation rather than despair.

## *Vitae summa brevis spem nos vetat incohare longam*

They are not long, the weeping and the laughter,
    Love and desire and hate:
I think they have no portion in us after
        We pass the gate.

They are not long, the days of wine and roses:
    Out of a misty dream
Our path emerges for a while, then closes
        Within a dream.

ERNEST DOWSON
*Verses* (1896)

## The Sad Shepherd

There was a man whom Sorrow named his friend,
And he, of his high comrade Sorrow dreaming,
Went walking with slow steps along the gleaming
And humming sands, where windy surges wend:
And he called loudly to the stars to bend
From their pale thrones and comfort him, but they
Among themselves laugh on and sing alway:
And then the man whom Sorrow named his friend
Cried out, *Dim sea, hear my most piteous story!*
The sea swept on and cried her old cry still,
Rolling along in dreams from hill to hill;
He fled the persecution of her glory
And, in a far-off, gentle valley stopping,
Cried all his story to the dewdrops glistening,
But naught they heard, for they are always listening,
The dewdrops, for the sound of their own dropping.

And then the man whom Sorrow named his friend,
Sought once again the shore, and found a shell
And thought, *I will my heavy story tell*
*Till my own words, re-echoing, shall send*
*Their sadness through a hollow, pearly heart;*
*And my own tale again for me shall sing,*
*And my own whispering words be comforting*
*And lo! my ancient burden may depart.*
Then he sang softly nigh the pearly rim;
But the sad dweller by the sea-ways lone
Changed all he sang to inarticulate moan
Among her wildering whirls, forgetting him.

W. B. YEATS
*Poems* (1899)


## Sorrow's Importunity

### 1

When Sorrow first came wailing to my door,
    April rehearsed the madrigal of May;
And, as I ne'er had seen her face before,
    I kept on singing, and she went her way.


### 2

When next came Sorrow, life was winged with scent
    Of glistening laurel and full-blossoming bay:
I asked, but understood not, what she meant,
    Offered her flowers, and she went her way.


### 3

When yet a third time Sorrow came, we met
    In the ripe silence of an Autumn day:
I gave her fruit I had gathered, and she ate,
    Then seemed to go unwillingly away.

4

When last came Sorrow, around barn and byre
  Wind-carven snow, the Year's white sepulchre, lay.
'Come in,' I said, 'and warm you by the fire.'
  And there she sits, and never goes away.

ALFRED AUSTIN
*The Conversion of Winckelmann, and Other Poems* (1897)

## Plainte Eternelle

The sun sinks down, the tremulous day-light dies,
  (Down their long shafts the weary sun-beams glide)
  The white-winged ships drift with the falling tide.
Come back, my love, with pity in your eyes!

The tall white ships drift with the falling tide.
  (Far, far away I hear the seamews' cries)
  Come back, my love, with pity in your eyes!
There is no room now in my heart for pride,

Come back, come back! with pity in your eyes,
  (The night is dark, the sea is fierce and wide)
  There is no room now in my heart for pride,
Though I become the scorn of all the wise.

I have no place now in my heart for pride.
  (The moon and stars have fallen from the skies)
  Though I become the scorn of all the wise,
Thrust, if you will, sharp arrows in my side.

Let me become the scorn of all the wise.
  (Out of the East I see the morning ride)
  Thrust, if you will, sharp arrows in my side,
Play with my tears and feed upon my sighs.

Wound me with swords, put arrows in my side,
  (On the white sea the haze of noon-day lies)
  Play with my tears and feed upon my sighs,
But come, my love, before my heart has died.

Drink my salt tears and feed upon my sighs,
  (Westward the evening goes with one red stride)
  Come back, my love, before my heart has died,
Down sinks the sun, the tremulous day-light dies.

Come back! my love, before my heart has died,
  (Out of the South I see the pale moon rise)
  Down sinks the sun, the tremulous day-light dies,
The white-winged ships drift with the falling tide.

LORD ALFRED DOUGLAS
*Poèmes* (1896)

## The Rose of Battle

Rose of all Roses, Rose of all the World!
The tall thought-woven sails, the flap unfurled
Above the tide of hours, trouble the air,
And God's bell buoyed to be the water's care;
While hushed from fear, or loud with hope, a band
With blown, spray-dabbled hair gather at hand.
*Turn if you may from battles never done,*
I call, as they go by me one by one,
*Danger no refuge holds, and war no peace,*
*For him who hears love sing and never cease,*
*Beside her clean-swept hearth, her quiet shade;*
*But gather all for whom no love hath made*
*A woven silence, or but came to cast*
*A song into the air, and singing past*
*To smile on the pale dawn; and gather you,*
*Who have sought more than is in rain or dew,*
*Or in the sun and moon, or on the earth,*
*Or sighs amid the wandering, starry mirth,*
*Or comes in laughter from the sea's sad lips;*
*And wage God's battles in the long gray ships.*

*The sad, the lonely, the insatiable,*
*To these Old Night shall all her mystery tell;*
*God's bell has claimed them by the little cry*
*Of their sad hearts, that may not live nor die.*

Rose of all Roses, Rose of all the World!
You, too, have come where the dim tides are hurled
Upon the wharves of sorrow, and heard ring
The bell that calls us on: the sweet far thing.
Beauty grown sad with its eternity
Made you of us, and of the dim gray sea.
Our long ships loose thought-woven sails and wait,
For God has bid them share an equal fate;
And when at last defeated in His wars,
They have gone down under the same white stars,
We shall no longer hear the little cry
Of our sad hearts, that may not live nor die.

W. B. YEATS
*Poems* (1899)

## A Lane in February

I wandered up this way last year;
    Unchanged, unmoved, it may not be
    Unlike what then it seemed to me;
The same dull ivied trees, and here
    The same black hedges that gird in
    Downs barren as the breasts of sin,
The same still wearied atmosphere.

And then as now I slowly passed
    Along the steep divided slope,
    With aching heart and without hope,
Scarce caring in what shape the last
    Blow fell upon my beaten brow,
    With eyes foreseeing then as now
The future blacker than the past.

What has the year left with me? One
    Sad love destroyed through time and scorn;
    A summer of delight forlorn;
Memories of sorrows that are gone
    With grey and desolated hours;
    And this dry handful of spoilt flowers
That died as I laid hand thereon.

THEODORE WRATISLAW
*Love's Memorial* (1892)

## Into the Twilight

Out-worn heart, in a time out-worn,
Come clear of the nets of wrong and right;
Laugh heart again in the gray twilight,
Sigh, heart, again in the dew of the morn.

Your mother Erie is always young,
Dew ever shining and twilight gray;
Though hope fall from you and love decay,
Burning in fires of a slanderous tongue.

Come, heart, where hill is heaped upon hill:
For there the mystical brotherhood
Of sun and moon and hollow and wood
And river and stream work out their will;

And God stands winding His lonely horn,
And time and the world are ever in flight;
And love is less kind than the gray twilight,
And hope is less dear than the dew of the morn.

W. B. YEATS
*The Wind Among the Reeds* (1899)

## By the Pool at the Third Rosses

I heard the sighing of the reeds
In the grey pool in the green land,
The sea-wind in the long reeds sighing
Between the green hill and the sand.

I heard the sighing of the reeds
Day after day, night after night;
I heard the whirring wild ducks flying,
I saw the sea-gull's wheeling flight.

I heard the sighing of the reeds
Night after night, day after day,
And I forgot old age, and dying,
And youth that loves, and love's decay.

I heard the sighing of the reeds
At noontide and at evening,
And some old dream I had forgotten
I seemed to be remembering.

I hear the sighing of the reeds:
Is it in vain, is it in vain
That some old peace I had forgotten
Is crying to come back again?

ARTHUR SYMONS
*Images of Good and Evil* (1899)


## A Last Word

Let us go hence: the night is now at hand;
  The day is overworn, the birds all flown;
  And we have reaped the crops the gods have sown;
Despair and death; deep darkness o'er the land,

Broods like an owl; we cannot understand
   Laughter or tears, for we have only known
   Surpassing vanity: vain things alone
Have driven our perverse and aimless band.

Let us go hence, somewhither strange and cold,
   To Hollow Lands where just men and unjust
   Find end of labour, where's rest for the old,
Freedom to all from love and fear and lust.
Twine our torn hands! O pray the earth enfold
Our life-sick hearts and turn them into dust.

ERNEST DOWSON
*Decorations* (1899)


## Nihilism

Among immortal things not made with hands;
Among immortal things, dead hands have made:
Under the Heavens, upon the Earth, there stands
Man's life, my life: of life I am afraid.

Where silent things, and unimpassioned things,
Where things of nought, and things decaying, are:
I shall be calm soon, with the calm, death brings.
The skies are gray there, without any star.

Only the rest! the rest! Only the gloom,
Soft and long gloom! The pausing from all thought!
My life, I cannot taste: the eternal tomb
Brings me the peace, which life has never brought.

For all the things I do, and do not well;
All the forced drawings of a mortal breath:
Are as the hollow music of a bell,
That times the slow approach of perfect death.

LIONEL JOHNSON
*Ireland, with Other Poems* (1897)

## A Shropshire Lad

### 54

With rue my heart is laden
    For golden friends I had,
For many a rose-lipt maiden
    And many a lightfoot lad.

By brooks too broad for leaping
    The lightfoot boys are laid;
The rose-lipt girls are sleeping
    In fields where roses fade.

A. E. HOUSMAN
*A Shropshire Lad* (1896)


## The Garden of Shadow

Love heeds no more the sighing of the wind
Against the perfect flowers: thy garden's close
Is grown a wilderness, where none shall find
One strayed, last petal of one last year's rose.

O bright, bright hair! O mouth like a ripe fruit!
Can famine be so nigh to harvesting?
Love, that was songful, with a broken lute
In grass of graveyards goeth murmuring.

Let the wind blow against the perfect flowers,
And all thy garden change and glow with spring:
Love is grown blind with no more count of hours,
Nor part in seed-time nor in harvesting.

ERNEST DOWSON
*Verses* (1896)

## The Falling of the Leaves

Autumn is over the long leaves that love us,
And over the mice in the barley sheaves;
Yellow the leaves of the rowan above us,
And yellow the wet wild-strawberry leaves.

The hour of the waning of love has beset us,
And weary and worn are our sad souls now;
Let us part, ere the season of passion forget us,
With a kiss and a tear on thy drooping brow.

W. B. YEATS
*Poems* (1899)

## Ennui

Alas! and oh that Spring should come again
Upon the soft wings of desired days,
And bring with her no anodyne to pain,
And no discernment of untroubled ways.
There was a time when her yet distant feet,
Guessed by some prescience more than half divine,
Gave to my listening ear such happy warning,
        That fresh, serene, and sweet,
My thoughts soared up like larks into the morning,
From the dew-sprinkled meadows crystalline.

Soared up into the heights celestial,
And saw the whole world like a ball of fire,
Fashioned to be a monster playing ball
For the enchantment of my young desire.
And yesterday they flew to this black cloud,
(Missing the way to those ethereal spheres.)

And saw the earth a vision of affright,
     And men a sordid crowd,
And felt the fears and drank the bitter tears,
And saw the empty houses of Delight.

The sun has sunk into a moonless sea,
And every road leads down from Heaven to Hell,
The pearls are numbered on youth's rosary,
I have outlived the days desirable.
What is there left? And how shall dead men sing
Unto the loosened strings of Love and Hate,
Or take strong hands to Beauty's ravishment?
     Who shall devise this thing,
To give high utterance to Miscontent,
Or make Indifference articulate?

LORD ALFRED DOUGLAS
*The City of the Soul* (1899)

## Michael Robartes Bids his Beloved be at Peace

I hear the Shadowy Horses, their long manes a-shake,
Their hoofs heavy with tumult, their eyes glimmering white;
The North unfolds above them clinging, creeping night,
The East her hidden joy before the morning break,
The West weeps in pale dew and sighs passing away,
The South is pouring down roses of crimson fire:
O vanity of Sleep, Hope, Dream, endless Desire,
The Horses of Disaster plunge in the heavy clay:
Beloved, let your eyes half close, and your heart beat
Over my heart, and your hair fall over my breast,
Drowning love's lonely hour in deep twilight of rest,
And hiding their tossing manes and their tumultuous feet.

W. B. YEATS
*The Wind Among the Reeds* (1899)

## *Mystic and Cavalier*

Go from me: I am one of those, who fall.
What! hath no cold wind swept your heart at all,
In my sad company? Before the end,
    Go from me, dear my friend!

Yours are the victories of light: your feet
Rest from good toil, where rest is brave and sweet.
But after warfare in a mourning gloom,
    I rest in clouds of doom.

Have you not read so, looking in these eyes?
Is it the common light of the pure skies,
Lights up their shadowy depths? The end is set:
    Though the end be not yet.

When gracious music stirs, and all is bright,
And beauty triumphs through a courtly night;
When I too joy, a man like other men:
    Yet, am I like them, then?

And in the battle, when the horsemen sweep
Against a thousand deaths, and fall on sleep:
Who ever sought that sudden calm, if I
    Sought not? Yet, could not die.

Seek with thine eyes to pierce this crystal sphere:
Canst read a fate there, prosperous and clear?
Only the mists, only the weeping clouds:
    Dimness, and airy shrouds.

Beneath, what angels are at work? What powers
Prepare the secret of the fatal hours?
See! the mists tremble, and the clouds are stirred:
    When comes the calling word?

The clouds are breaking from the crystal ball,
Breaking and clearing: and I look to fall.
When the cold winds and airs of portent sweep,
    My spirit may have sleep.

O rich and sounding voices of the air!
Interpreters and prophets of despair:
Priests of a fearful sacrament! I come,
    To make with you mine home.

LIONEL JOHNSON
*Poems* (1895)

## Dregs

The fire is out, and spent the warmth thereof,
(This is the end of every song man sings!)
The golden wine is drunk, the dregs remain,
Bitter as wormwood and as salt as pain;
And health and hope have gone the way of love
Into the drear oblivion of lost things.
Ghosts go along with us until the end;
This was a mistress, this, perhaps, a friend.
With pale, indifferent eyes, we sit and wait
For the dropt curtain and the closing gate:
This is the end of all the songs man sings.

ERNEST DOWSON
*Decorations* (1899)

## A Shropshire Lad

### 7

When smoke stood up from Ludlow,
  And mist blew off from Teme,
And blithe afield to ploughing
  Against the morning beam
  I strode beside my team,

The blackbird in the coppice
    Looked out to see me stride,
And hearkened as I whistled
    The trampling team beside,
    And fluted and replied:

'Lie down, lie down, young yeoman;
    What use to rise and rise?
Rise man a thousand mornings
    Yet down at last he lies,
    And then the man is wise.'

I heard the tune he sang me,
    And spied his yellow bill;
I picked a stone and aimed it,
    And threw it with a will:
    Then the bird was still.

Then my soul within me
    Took up the blackbird's strain,
And still beside the horses
    Along the dewy lane
    It sang the song again:

'Lie down, lie down, young yeoman;
    The sun moves always west;
The road one treads to labour
    Will lead one home to rest,
    And that will be the best.'

A. E. HOUSMAN
*A Shropshire Lad* (1896)

## The Darkling Thrush

I leant upon a coppice gate
    When Frost was spectre-gray,
And Winter's dregs made desolate
    The weakening eye of day.

The tangled bine-stems scored the sky
  Like strings from broken lyres,
And all mankind that haunted nigh
    Had sought their household fires.

The land's sharp features seemed to be
    The Century's corpse outleant,
His crypt the cloudy canopy,
    The wind his death-lament.
The ancient pulse of germ and birth
    Was shrunken hard and dry,
And every spirit upon earth
    Seemed fervourless as I.

At once a voice outburst among
    The bleak twigs overhead
In a full-hearted evensong
    Of joy illimited;
An aged thrush, frail, gaunt, and small,
  In blast-beruffled plume,
Had chosen thus to fling his soul
    Upon the growing gloom.

So little cause for carollings
    Of such ecstatic sound
Was written on terrestrial things
    Afar or nigh around,
That I could think there trembled through
    His happy good-night air
Some blessed Hope, whereof he knew
    And I was unaware.
*December 1900*

THOMAS HARDY
*Poems of the Past and Present* (1902)

## Darwinism

When first the unflowering Fern-forest
  Shadowed the dim lagoons of old,
A vague, unconscious, long unrest
  Swayed the great fronds of green and gold.

Until the flexible stem grew rude,
  The fronds began to branch and bower,
And lo! upon the unblossoming wood
  There breaks a dawn of apple-flower.

Then on the fruitful forest-boughs
  For ages long the unquiet ape
Swung happy in his airy house
  And plucked the apple, and sucked the grape.

Until at length in him there stirred
  The old, unchanged, remote distress,
That pierced his world of wind and bird
  With some divine unhappiness.

Not love, nor the wild fruits he sought,
  Nor the fierce battles of his clan
Could still the unborn and aching thought,
  Until the brute became the man.

Long since; and now the same unrest
  Goads to the same invisible goal,
Till some new gift, undream'd, unguess'd,
  End the new travail of the soul.

A. MARY F. ROBINSON
*Lyrics Selected from the Works* (1891)

## Scientific Wooing

I was a youth of studious mind,
Fair Science was my mistress kind,
   And held me with attraction chemic;
No germs of Love attacked my heart,
Secured as by Pasteurian art
   Against that fatal epidemic.

For when my daily task was o'er
I dreamed of $H_2SO_4$,
   Whilst stealing through my slumbers placid
Came Iodine, with violet fumes,
And Sulphur, with its yellow blooms,
   And whiffs of Hydrochloric Acid.

My daily visions, thoughts, and schemes
With wildest hope illumed my dreams,
   The daring dreams of trustful twenty:
I might accomplish my desire,
And set the river Thames on fire
   If but Potassium were in plenty!

Alas! that yearnings so sublime
Should all be blasted in their prime
   By hazel eyes and lips vermilion!
Ye gods! restore the halcyon days
While yet I walked in Wisdom's ways,
   And knew not Mary Maud Trevylyan!

Yet nay! the sacrilegious prayer
Was not mine own, oh fairest fair!
   Thee, dear one, will I ever cherish;
Thy worshipped image small remain
In the grey thought-cells of my brain
   Until their form and function perish.

Away with books, away with cram
For Intermediate Exam.!
   Away with every college duty!

Though once Agnostic to the core,
A virgin Saint I now adore,
    And swear belief in Love and Beauty.

Yet when I meet her tranquil gaze,
I dare not plead, I dare not praise,
    Like other men with other lasses;
She's never kind, she's never coy,
She treats me simply as a boy,
    And asks me how I like my classes!

I covet not her golden dower –
Yet surely Love's attractive power
    Directly as the mass must vary –
But ah! inversely as the square
Of distance! shall I ever dare
    To cross the gulf, and gain my Mary?

So chill she seems – and yet she might
Welcome with radiant heat and light
    My courtship, if I once began it;
For is not e'en the palest star
That gleams so coldly from afar
    A sun to some revolving planet?

My Mary! be a solar sphere!
Envy no comet's mad career,
    No arid, airless lunar crescent!
Oh for a spectroscope to show
That in thy gentle eyes doth glow
    Love's vapour, pure and incandescent!

Bright fancy! can I fail to please
If with similitudes like these
    I lure the maid to sweet communion?
My suit, with Optics well begun,
By Magnetism shall be won,
    And closed at last in Chemic union!

At this I'll aim, for this I'll toil,
And this I'll reach – I will, by Boyle,
    By Avogadro, and by Davy!

When every science lends a trope
To feed my love, to fire my hope,
  Her maiden pride must cry '*Peccavi!*'

I'll sing a deep Darwinian lay
Of little birds with plumage gay,
  Who solved by courtship Life's enigma;
I'll teach her how the wild-flowers love,
And why the trembling stamens move,
  And how the anthers kiss the stigma.

Or Mathematically true
With rigorous Logic will I woo,
  And not a word I'll say at random;
Till urged by Syllogistic stress,
She falter forth a tearful 'Yes,'
  A sweet '*Quod erat demonstrandum!*'

CONSTANCE NADEN
*Complete Poetical Works* (1894)

## Woman's Future

Complacent they tell us, hard hearts and derisive,
  In vain is our ardour: in vain are our sighs:
Our intellects, bound by a limit decisive,
  To the level of Homer's may never arise.
We heed not the falsehood, the base innuendo,
  The laws of the universe, these are our friends,
Our talents shall rise in a mighty crescendo,
  We trust Evolution to make us amends!

But ah, when I ask you for food that is mental,
  My sisters, you offer me ices and tea!
You cherish the fleeting, the mere accidental,
  At cost of the True, the Intrinsic, the Free.

Your feelings, compressed in Society's mangle,
    Are vapid and frivolous, pallid and mean.
To slander you love; but you don't care to wrangle;
    You bow to Decorum, and cherish Routine.

Alas, is it woolwork you take for your mission,
    Or Art that your fingers so gaily attack?
Can patchwork atone for the mind's inanition?
    Can the soul, oh my sisters, be fed on a *plaque?*
Is this your vocation? My goal is another,
    And empty and vain is the end you pursue.
In antimacassars the world you may smother;
    But intellect marches o'er them and o'er you.

On Fashion's vagaries your energies strewing,
    Devoting your days to a rug or a screen,
Oh, rouse to a lifework – do something worth doing!
    Invent a new planet, a flying-machine.
Mere charms superficial, mere feminine graces,
    That fade or that flourish, no more you may prize;
But the knowledge of Newton will beam from your faces,
    The soul of a Spencer will shine in your eyes.


ENVOY

Though jealous exclusion may tremble to own us,
    Oh, wait for the time when our brains shall expand!
When once we're enthroned, you shall never dethrone
    us –
    The poets, the sages, the seers of the land!

MAY KENDALL
*Dreams to Sell* (1887)

## *Envoy*

Go, songs, for ended is our brief, sweet play;
  Go, children of swift joy and tardy sorrow:
And some are sung, and that was yesterday,
  And some unsung, and that may be to-morrow.

Go forth; and if it be o'er stony way,
  Old joy can lend what newer grief must borrow:
And it was sweet, and that was yesterday,
  And sweet is sweet, though purchasèd with sorrow.

Go, songs, and come not back from your far way:
  And if men ask you why ye smile and sorrow,
Tell them ye grieve, for your hearts know To-day,
  Tell them ye smile, for your eyes know To-morrow.

FRANCIS THOMPSON
*New Poems* (1897)

# BIOGRAPHICAL AND
# BIBLIOGRAPHICAL NOTES

The following notes provide a short account of each poet's life and
a brief bibliography. In order to keep this within reasonable bounds
of size we restrict ourselves to a chronological list of the author's
main books of poems under (a), and a select number of books or
articles which will provide a starting point for critical or biographical
study under (b). We have omitted the frequent addition to titles of
the words 'and other poems' in the interests of space and only note
place of publication when it is other than London. Many of these
minor poets have no monograph devoted to them and information
should be sought in the books listed in the general section.

ALFRED AUSTIN (1835–1913) was born in Leeds, graduated from
London University, and was called to the Bar in 1857. He abandoned
law for literature in 1858, and thereafter as poet, novelist, critic,
editor and journalist, he won enough support to earn him the
Laureateship in 1896, although critics have consistently, and by and
large justifiably, felt that his successes are few and mostly in prose.

(a) *Interludes* (1872)
   *Soliloquies in Song* (1882)
   *At the Gate of the Convent* (1885)
   *Love's Widowhood* (1889)
   *Lyrical Poems* (1891)
   *Narrative Poems* (1891)
   *Songs of England* (1891)
   *England's Darling* (1896)
   *The Conversion of Winckelmann* (2md edn, 1897)
   *A Tale of True Love* (1902)
   *Victoria the Wise* (1903)
   *Sacred and Profane Love* (1908)
(b) *The Autobiography of Alfred Austin, Poet Laureate, 1835–1910*
   (1911)
   Norton B. Crowell, *Alfred Austin: Victorian* (1955)

JOHN EVELYN BARLAS (1860–1914) published under the pseudo-nym 'Evelyn Douglas'. Born in Burma and educated at New College, Oxford, he took posts as a teacher while pursuing in his own time his twin enthusiasms, poetry and socialism. He took part in the violent socialist demonstrations in the 1880s and it may have been a blow received at one of these that led the way to his insanity. In a letter of February 1892 Dowson reported he had been 'lately run in for shooting the House of Commons'; he had fired a revolver near the Speaker's residence to show his contempt for the House. Wilde guaranteed half of the £200 for which he was bound over to keep the peace. He spent most of his later years in an asylum and died in Gartnavel Royal Hospital.

(a) *Poems, Lyrical and Dramatic* (1884)
   *Bird-Notes* (Chelmsford, 1887)
   *Dream-Fugues* (Chelmsford, 1887)
   *Holy of Holies* (1887)
   *Love Sonnets* (Chelmsford, 1889)
   *Selections from 'Songs of a Bayadere' and 'Songs of a Troubadour'* (Dundee, 1893)
   H. S. Salt, ed., *Selections from the Poems of John E. Barlas* (1925)
   Ian Fletcher, ed., *Six Sonnets* (1981)
(b) Henry S. Salt, 'John Barlas's Poetry', *The Yellow Book*, XI (1896), 80–90
   David Lowe, *John Barlas, Sweet Singer and Socialist* (Cupar, 1915)


AUBREY BEARDSLEY (1872–98), primarily a draughtsman, rose rapidly to fame after his designs for *Morte d'Arthur* in 1893. Art editor for the first four volumes of *The Yellow Book* (1894–5) and for *The Savoy* (1896), and designer of covers and decorations for many books which caught the public eye, he had achieved an influential body of work before he died, a convert to Roman Cath-olicism, in Menton. The three poems here are virtually the sum of his achievement in verse.

(a) *Under the Hill, and Other Essays in Prose and Verse* (1904)
(b) Stanley Weintraub, *Beardsley* (1967)
   Brian Reade, *Beardsley* (1967)
   Henry Maas, J. L. Duncan and W. G. Good, eds, *The Letters*

    *of Aubrey Beardsley* (1970)

    Malcolm Easton, *Aubrey Beardsley and the Dying Lady* (1972)

    Brigid Brophy, *Beardsley and his World* (1976)

    Miriam J. Benkovitz, *Aubrey Beardsley: An Account of his Life* (1981)

    Ian Fletcher, *Aubrey Beardsley* (Boston, 1988)

    Robert Langenfeld, ed., *Reconsidering Aubrey Beardsley* (Ann Arbor, 1989)

    Mark Samuels Lasner, *A Selective Checklist of the Published Work of Aubrey Beardsley* (Boston, 1995)

ROBERT LAURENCE BINYON (1869–1943), poet, art-historian and critic, was born in Lancaster. He won the Newdigate Prize with *Persephone* (Oxford, 1890), and edited Elkin Mathews's *Shilling Garland* series of poetry books. He became Keeper of Prints and Drawings in the British Museum, where he worked for forty years, establishing himself as an authority on Oriental art, but always considering himself primarily a poet.

(a) *Lyric Poems* (1894)
    *Poems* (Oxford, 1895)
    *The Praise of Life* (1896)
    *First Book of London Visions* (1896)
    *Porphyrion* (1898)
    *Second Book of London Visions* (1899)
    *Odes* (1901)
    *The Death of Adam* (1904)
    *England* (1909)
    *Auguries* (1913)
    *The Cause* (1917)
    *For the Fallen* (1917)
    *The New World* (1918)
    *The Secret* (1920)
    *Collected Poems* (2 vols, 1931)
    *The North Star* (1941)

MATHILDE BLIND (1841–96) was from a German Jewish family which fled to England after the suppression of the Baden insurrection of 1848–9 in which her stepfather was involved. She remained a revolutionary. She was familiar with the Pre-Raphaelites – she lived for long periods with the Madox Browns in Manchester. She lived the independent life of the New Woman, supporting women's suffrage and promoting women's education (she left her estate to Newnham College). She edited Shelley (1872) and wrote biographies of George Eliot (1883) and Madame Roland (1886), as well as poems which are in key with her feminist energies. Her strongest friendships were with Eleanor Marx and the novelist Mona Caird.

(a) *Poems* (1867, under the pseudonym of 'Claude Lake')
    *The Prophecy of Saint Oran and other Poems* (1881)
    *The Heather on Fire* (1886)
    *The Ascent of Man* (1889)
    *Dramas in Miniature* (1891)
    *Songs and Sonnets* (1893)
    *Birds of Passage: Songs of the Orient and Occident* (1895)
    *The Poetical Works of Mathilde Blind*, ed. Arthur Symons (1900)

OLIVE ELEANOR CUSTANCE (1874–1944) was the daughter of a marriage of two aristocratic families. Passionate for literature, she fell in love with John Gray (who advised her sensibly), contributed to eight volumes of *The Yellow Book* and corresponded with poets and artists. She became Lady Alfred Douglas after a runaway marriage in 1902 and had a son who became a point of contention between her husband and her father. She and Lord Alfred separated after eleven years, but they remained on good terms.

(a) *Opals* (1897)
    *Rainbows* (1902)
    *The Blue Bird* (1905)
    *The Inn of Dreams* (1911)
    Brocard Sewell, ed., *The Selected Poems of Olive Custance* (1995)
    R. K. R. Thornton and Ian Small, introduction, *Opals 1897
    with Rainbows 1902* (Woodstock reprint, Poole, 1996).
(b) Nancy J. Hawkey, 'Olive Custance Douglas: an Annotated
    Bibliography of Writings About Her', *English Literature in Tran-
    sition*, 15 (1972), 49–56
    Brocard Sewell, *Olive Custance: Her Life and Work* (1975)
    Brocard Sewell, *Like Black Swans, Some People and Themes*
    (Padstow, 1982)

JOHN DAVIDSON (1857–1909), the son of a minister of the Evangelical Union, held a variety of jobs (like teacher, chemical analyst, clerk) in Scotland before he left to make a living by his pen in London. There he wrote plays, novels, poems and criticism, trying to retain the quality of his art against the demands of making a livelihood through journalism, which he despised. A member of the Rhymers' Club, he was none the less hostile to the less vigorous elements of the age. Though he achieved some popularity with his *Fleet Street Eclogues,* he always found difficulty in supporting his family. His stance became increasingly Nietzschean and assertive. He drowned himself in 1909.

(a) *In a Music-Hall* (1891)
    *Fleet Street Eclogues* (1893)
    *Ballads and Songs* (1894)
    *A Second Series of Fleet Street Eclogues* (1896)
    *New Ballads* (1897)
    *The Last Ballad* (1899)
    *The Testament of a Vivisector* (1901)
    *The Testament of a Man Forbid* (1901)
    *The Testament of an Empire-Builder* (1901)
    *The Testament of a Prime Minister* (1904)
    *Holiday* (1906)
    *The Testament of John Davidson* (1908)
    *Fleet Street* (1909)
    Maurice Lindsay, ed., *John Davidson, a Selection of his Poems* (1961)
    Andrew Turnbull, ed., *The Poems of John Davidson* (2 vols, Edinburgh, 1973)
    R. K. R. Thornton and Ian Small, introduction, *In a music-hall 1891 with Ballads and songs 1894* (Woodstock reprint, Oxford, 1993)
(b) James Benjamin Townsend, *John Davidson, Poet of Armageddon* (New Haven, 1961)
    Carroll V. Peterson, *John Davidson* (Boston, 1972)
    Mary O'Connor, *John Davidson* (Edinburgh, 1987)

RICHARD WATSON DIXON (1833–1900), son of a Methodist minister, was an Anglican minister in Northumberland and Cumberland. At Oxford he knew Burne-Jones, Morris and Rossetti. His poetry and his writing on ecclesiastical history are not as well known as his friendship and correspondence with Gerard Manley Hopkins.

(a) *Christ's Company* (1861)
   *Mano* (1883)
   *Odes and Eclogues* (Oxford, 1884)
   *Lyrical Poems* (Oxford, 1887)
   *Songs and Odes* (1896)
   *The Last Poems of Richard Watson Dixon 3 D.D.* (1905)
   *Poems* (1909)
   Shirley M. C. Johnson and Todd K. Bender, eds, *The Collected Poems of Canon Richard Watson Dixon, 1833–1900* (NY, 1989)
(b) Claude C. Abbott, ed., *The Correspondence of Gerard Manley Hopkins and Richard Watson Dixon* (Oxford, 1955)
   (Arthur) James Sambrook, *A Poet Hidden* (1962)

LORD ALFRED DOUGLAS (1870–1945), son of the 8th Marquess of Queensberry, educated at Winchester and Magdalen College, Oxford, is popularly known for his involvement with Oscar Wilde. He married Olive Custance in 1902. His name is usually associated with that of Wilde, but his verse is worthy of consideration in its own right, and his prickly autobiographical work is of interest.

(a) *Poèmes* (Paris, 1896)
   *The City of the Soul* (1899)
   *Sonnets* (1909)
   *Collected Poems* (1919)
   *Collected Satires of Lord Alfred Douglas* (1926)
   *Complete Poems* (1928)
   *Lyrics* (1935)
   *Sonnets* (1935)
   R. K. R. Thornton and Ian Small, introduction, *The city of the soul* (Woodstock reprint, Poole, 1996)
(b) *The Autobiography of Lord Alfred Douglas* (1929)
   William Freeman, *The Life of Lord Alfred Douglas: Spoilt Child of Genius* (1948)
   Rupert Croft-Cooke, *Bosie* (1963)
   Gary H. Paterson, 'Lord Alfred Douglas: An Annotated

Bibliography of Writing About Him', *English Literature in Transition*, 23 (1980), 168–200

Mary Hyde, ed., *Bernard Shaw and Alfred Douglas: A Correspondence* (1982)

H. Montgomery Hyde, *Lord Alfred Douglas* (1984)

ERNEST CHRISTOPHER DOWSON (1867–1900), son of the owner of a dry-dock, had an irregular education, frequently on the continent. He gave up his course at Queen's College, Oxford, and for a time mixed work in his father's declining business with associating with other writers, notably at the Rhymers' Club. He always moved freely between England and France, and was until his death from consumption always on good terms with his fellow poets and translators. His unreturned devotion to a young girl is an important but often exaggerated feature of his life.

(a) *Verses* (1896)
*The Pierrot of the Minute* (1897)
*Decorations* (1899)
Mark Longaker, ed., *The Poems of Ernest Dowson* (Philadelphia, 1962)
Desmond Flower, ed., *The Poetical Works of Ernest Dowson* (3rd edition, 1967)
R. K. R. Thornton and Ian Small, introduction, *Verses 1896 with Decorations 1899* (Woodstock reprint, Oxford, 1994)
(b) Victor Plarr, *Ernest Dowson 1888–1897: Reminiscences, Unpublished Letters and Marginalia* (1914)
Thomas B. Swann, *Ernest Dowson* (New York, 1964)
Desmond Flower and Henry Maas, eds, *The Letters of Ernest Dowson* (1967)
Mark Longaker, *Ernest Dowson* (3rd edition, 1967)
Jonathan Ramsey, 'Ernest Dowson: An Annotated Bibliography of Writings about Him', *English Literature in Transition*, 14 (1971), 17–42 and 18 (1975), 54–8
G. A. Cevasco, *Three Decadent Poets, Ernest Dowson, John Gray, and Lionel Johnson: An Annotated Bibliography* (1990)
Jean-Jacques Chardin, *Ernest Dowson (1867–1900) et la crise fin de siècle anglaise* (Paris, 1995)

MICHAEL FIELD is the pseudonym of Katharine Harris Bradley (1846–1914) and her niece Edith Emma Cooper (1862–1913). Bradley was born in Birmingham to a tobacco manufacturer, and became mother and sister, as well as aunt, to Cooper, when the girl's real mother died. Later she also became her lover. Bradley studied at Newnham College, Cambridge for a while, and in 1878 both women went to study at Bristol, where they cut the figure of the New Woman. Their jointly-composed and jointly-published poetry was pagan, sensual and Sapphic. After the death of their beloved Chow dog, which was partly responsible for their conversion to Catholicism in 1906, their poetry was almost all religious. Both died of cancer, Katharine succumbing soon after Edith's death. Robert Browning was a close friend, and they met most of the literary figures of the day, giving colourful descriptions of these encounters in their journals. They also wrote many dramas.

(a) *The New Minnesinger* by Arran Leigh [i.e. Bradley] (1875)
    *Bellerophôn* by Arran and Isla Leigh [i.e. Bradley and Cooper] (1881)
    *Long Ago* (1889)
    *Sight and Song* (1892)
    *Underneath the Bough* (1893)
    *Wild Honey from Various Thyme* (1908)
    *Poems of Adoration* (1912)
    *Mystic Trees* (1913)
    *Whym Chow: Flame of Love* (1914)
    *Dedicated* (1914)
    T. Sturge Moore, ed., *A Selection from the Poems* (1923)
    *The Wattlefold: Unpublished Poems* (Oxford, 1930)
    R. K. R. Thornton and Ian Small, introduction, *Sight and song 1892 with Underneath the Bough 1893* (Woodstock reprint, Oxford, 1993)
(b) Mary C. Sturgeon, *Michael Field* (1922)
    T. and D. C. Sturge Moore, eds, *Works and Days: From the Journals of Michael Field* (1933)
    David J. Moriarty, ' "Michael Field" (Edith Cooper and Katherine Bradley) and Their Male Critics', *Nineteenth-Century Women Writers of the English-Speaking World* (1986)
    Christine White, ' "Poets and Lovers Evermore": Interpreting

Female Love in the Poetry and Journals of Michael Field',
*Textual Practice*, 4 (1990)

Holly Laird, 'Contradictory Legacies: Michael Field and Feminist Restoration', *Victorian Poetry*, 33 (1995)

Yopie Prins, 'A Metaphorical Field: Katherine Bradley and
Edith Cooper', *Victorian Poetry*, 33 (1995)

Yopie Prins, 'Sappho Doubled: Michael Field', *Yale Journal of
Criticism* (1995)

JOHN GRAY (1866–1934) sought for an identity all his life. Son of
a man who rose to be inspector of stores at Woolwich Arsenal, Gray
worked assiduously at his own education. He held positions in the
General Post Office and the Foreign Office for a while. He was
helped by Ricketts and Shannon and met Oscar Wilde, who signed
a contract to pay for Gray's exquisite *Silverpoints* (1893) – though
it was in the end published at the publisher's expense. Gray rejected
the exaggerated pose of that volume and that life not only to write
predominantly religious poetry, but also to take orders; he had
become a Roman Catholic in 1890. He was ordained in 1901 and
performed his duties mostly in Edinburgh, where he lived with his
friend André Raffalovich.

(a) *Silverpoints* (1893)
*Spiritual Poems* (1896)
*Ad Matrem* (1904)
*Vivis* (Ditchling, Sussex, 1922)
*The Long Road* (1926)
*Poems, 1931* (1931)
Ian Fletcher, ed., *The Poems of John Gray* (Greensboro, NC,
1988)
R. K. R. Thornton and Ian Small, introduction, *Silverpoints 1893
with Spiritual poems 1896* (Woodstock reprint, Oxford, 1994)

(b) Brocard Sewell, ed., *Two Friends: John Gray and André Raffalov-
ich* (Aylesford, 1963)
Brocard Sewell, *Footnote to the Nineties* (1968)
G. A. Cevasco, *John Gray* (Boston, 1982)
Brocard Sewell, *In the Dorian Mode: A Life of John Gray, 1866–
1934* (Padstow, 1983)
G. A. Cevasco, *Three Decadent Poets, Ernest Dowson, John Gray,*

*and Lionel Johnson: An Annotated Bibliography* (1990)
Jerusha Hull McCormack, *John Gray: Poet, Dandy, and Priest*
(Hanover, NH, 1991)
Jerusha Hull McCormack, ed., *The Selected Prose of John Gray*
(Greensboro, NC, 1992)

GEORGE ARTHUR GREENE (1853–1921) was born and educated in
Florence, though he was of Anglo-lrish stock. After his first in
modern literature at Trinity College Dublin, he held a variety of
lecturing and examining posts. He was one of several Irishmen in
the Rhymers' Club and served as its unofficial secretary, helping to
organize its two anthologies. He was active in Irish matters, becoming
vice chairman of the Irish Literary Society and working for the Irish
Texts Society.

(a) *Italian Lyrists of To-day* (1893)
   *Dantesques* (1903)
   *Songs of the Open Air* (1912)

THOMAS HARDY (1840–1928) was born in Dorset. The son of a
builder, he trained and for a short time practised as an architect.
His novels brought him increasing fame and financial security but,
after the predominantly hostile reception of *Jude the Obscure* (1895),
he increasingly devoted his attentions to poetry, for which in any
case he had a lifelong love. He received the OM in 1910.

(a) *Wessex Poems* (1898)
   *Poems of the Past and Present* (1902)
   *Time's Laughingstocks* (1909)
   *Satires of Circumstance* (1914)
   *Moments of Vision* (1917)
   *Late Lyrics and Earlier* (1922)
   *Human Shows, Far Phantasies* (1925)
   *Winter Words* (1928)
   James Gibson, ed., *The Variorum Edition of the Complete Poems*
   (1979)
   Samuel Hynes, ed., *The Complete Poetical Works* (2 vols, Oxford,
   1982–4)
   R. K. R. Thornton and Ian Small, introduction, *Wessex poems
   1898* (Woodstock reprint, Oxford, 1994)

(b) 'Florence E. Hardy', *The Early Life of Thomas Hardy, 1840–91* (1928) and *The Later Years of Thomas Hardy, 1892–1928* (1930), combined as *The Life of Thomas Hardy* (1962)

F. B. Pinion, *A Hardy Companion* (1968, 1974)

Michael Millgate, *Thomas Hardy: a Biography* (Oxford, 1982)

William E. Buckler, *The Poetry of Thomas Hardy, a Study in Art and Ideas* (1983)

Simon Gattrell, *Hardy the Creator: A Textual Biography* (Oxford, 1988)

WILLIAM ERNEST HENLEY (1849–1903) was born in Gloucester the son of a bookseller. He was a cripple from boyhood, losing one foot from tubercular arthritis and in danger of losing the other until he placed himself under Lister's care in Edinburgh Infirmary. He was the model for Long John Silver for his friend Robert Louis Stevenson, with whom he collaborated on four plays before a bitter quarrel separated them in 1888. He was editor of several papers, including the *Scots Observer*, later the *National Observer*, the *Magazine of Art* and the *New Review*. The honest modernity of his poetry perhaps comes from the balance of his vigorous style and attitude set against his constrained and painful existence.

(a) *A Book of Verses* (1888)

*The Song of the Sword* (1892)

*London Voluntaries* (1893)

*Poems* (1898)

*London Types* (1898)

*For England's Sake* (1900)

*Hawthorn and Lavender* (1901)

*A Song of Speed* (1903)

*The Works of W. E. Henley* (7 vols, 1908)

*The Works of William Ernest Henley* (2 vols, 1921)

R. K. R. Thornton and Ian Small, introduction, *Poems 1898* (Woodstock reprint, Oxford, 1993)

(b) Jerome H. Buckley, *William Ernest Henley* (Princeton, 1945)

John Connell, *W. E. Henley* (1949)

Joseph M. Flora, *William Ernest Henley* (New York, 1970)

Edward H. Cohen, *The Henley-Davidson Quarrel* (Gainesville, Fla., 1974)

HERBERT PERCY HORNE (1864–1916), art-historian, architect, typographer, designer, art-collector and poet, was involved in the foundation of the Century Guild and in the editing of its magazines, the *Century Guild Hobby Horse* and the *Hobby Horse*. A permanent guest at the Rhymers' Club, Horne became an art connoisseur and later lived in Italy, where the Museo Horne, in which he established his collection, still exists, though some of its pieces have gone to the Uffizi.

(a) *Diversi Colores* (1891)
   *Amata Loquitur* (1961)
   R. K. R. Thornton and Ian Small, introduction, *Selwyn Image Poems and carols 1894 with Herbert Horne Diversi colores 1891* (Woodstock reprint, Oxford, 1995).
(b) Frank Kermode, *Forms of Attention* (1985)
   Ian Fletcher, *Rediscovering Herbert Horne: Poet, Architect, Typographer, Art Historian* (Greensboro, NC, 1990)

ALFRED EDWARD HOUSMAN (1859–1936) was born near Bromsgrove, Worcestershire. Despite initial failure in his degree at Oxford, he returned to university life in 1892, after ten years in the Patent Office, to take the Chair of Latin at University College London, from which he moved to a similar chair at Cambridge in 1911. A meticulous editor of Manilius and other writers, a witty and severe critic, he is best known for his small corpus of poems, the ideas behind which can be seen in his *The Name and Nature of Poetry* (Cambridge, 1933). His poetry gains power from the emotional pressure of his repressed homosexual feelings.

(a) *A Shropshire Lad* (1896)
   *Last Poems* (1922)
   *More Poems* (1936)
   John W. Carter, ed., *The Collected Poems of A. E. Housman* (1939)
   Tom Burns Haber, ed., *The Manuscript Poems* (Minneapolis, 1955)
   Christopher Ricks, ed., *Collected Poems and Selected Prose* (1988, 1989)
   R. K. R. Thornton and Ian Small, introduction, *A Shropshire lad 1896* (Woodstock reprint, Oxford, 1994)

(b) Tom Burns Haber, *A. E. Housman* (New York, 1967)
Christopher Ricks, ed., *A. E. Housman*, Twentieth Century
Views (Englewood Cliffs, NJ, 1968)
B. J. Leggett, *Housman's Land of Lost Content* (1970)
Henry Maas, ed., *The Letters of A. E. Housman* (1971)
B. J. Leggett, *The Poetic Art of A. E. Housman* (1978)
John Carter and John Sparrow, *A. E. Housman: A Bibliography*
(2nd edn revd by William White, Godalming, 1982)
Norman Page, *A. E. Housman: A Critical Biography* (1983)
John Bayley, *Housman's Poems* (Oxford, 1992)

SELWYN IMAGE (1849–1930) was the second son of the vicar of
Bodiam in Sussex. When the family moved to Brighton he was
inspired to become an architect by the building of St Michael's,
with its Burne-Jones west window. He went to Marlborough and
New College, Oxford, was ordained, but, after a period as curate in
Tottenham, left the Church to become scholar, artist, designer,
decorator and poet. He co-founded the Century Guild with Arthur
Mackmurdo and helped in the production of the *Century Guild
Hobby Horse*. With Stewart Headlam he founded the Church and
Stage Guild. The house at 20 Fitzroy Street which he occupied
until 1917 was, in the 1890s, a centre for artistic activity. He devoted
himself religiously to art, and was Slade Professor of Fine Arts at
Oxford from 1910 to 1916.

(a) *Poems and Carols* (1894)
Arthur H. Mackmurdo, ed., *The Poems of Selwyn Image*
(1932)
R. K. R. Thornton and Ian Small, introduction, *Selwyn Image
Poems and carols 1894 with Herbert Horne Diversi colores 1891*
(Woodstock reprint, Oxford, 1995)
(b) Arthur H. Mackmurdo, ed., *Selwyn Image, Letters* (1932)
S. E. (Lisa) Tickner, *Selwyn Image: His Life, Work and Associ-
ations* (unpublished Ph.D. thesis, University of Reading, 1970)

LIONEL PIGOT JOHNSON (1867–1902) was born at Broadstairs
and educated at Winchester and New College, Oxford. He was a
scholar and a traditionalist, influenced by Celticism, the Classics
and Catholicism, his adopted religion. His criticism, of the school
of Arnold and Pater, is revealing and incisive; his poems are cold

and clear. Yeats in *Autobiographies* and 'In Memory of Major Robert Gregory' remembers this fellow-member of the Rhymers' Club, and Pound refers to Johnson in 'Hugh Selwyn Mauberley'.

(a) *Poems* (1895)
    *Ireland* (1897)
    Ezra Pound, ed., *Poetical Works* (1915)
    Ian Fletcher, ed., *The Complete Poems of Lionel Johnson* (1953, revd edn, New York, 1982)
    R. K. R. Thornton and Ian Small, introduction, *Poems 1895* (Woodstock reprint, Oxford, 1993)
    R. K. R. Thornton and Ian Small, introduction, *Ireland 1897* (Woodstock reprint, Poole, 1996)
(b) Arthur W. Patrick, *Lionel Johnson, poète et critique* (Paris, 1939)
    G. A. Cevasco, *Three Decadent Poets, Ernest Dowson, John Gray, and Lionel Johnson: An Annotated Bibliography* (1990)

MAY KENDALL (1861–?1931) was born Emma Goldworth Kendall in Bridlington, daughter of a Wesleyan minister. She spent most of her life in Liverpool and Birmingham, and published novels as well as her witty and ironic satires. She abandoned authorship at the end of the century to work for social reform and among the poor, but in 1913 she helped to liven up a study of the rural poor: *How the Labourer Lives. A Study of the Rural Labour Problem* (with B. Seebohm Rowntree). She returned to a late flowering of stories and poems in the *Cornhill* in the last years of her life.

(a) *That Very Mab* (with Andrew Lang, 1885)
    *Dreams to Sell* (1887)
    *Songs from Dreamland* (1894)
(b) Roger Lancelyn Green, *Andrew Lang: A Critical Biography* (1946)
    Asa Briggs, *Social Thought and Social Action: A Study of the Work of B. Seebohm Rowntree* (1961)

RUDYARD KIPLING (1865–1936), born in Bombay but educated in England, returned to India in 1882 to become a journalist, but had achieved a name as a writer of verse and short stories by the time of his return to England in 1889. He was awarded the Nobel Prize for Literature in 1907, but his verse, with its patriotism and rather brass-band style, has only recently returned to some critical praise.

(a) *Departmental Ditties* (Lahore, 1886)
   *Barrack-Room Ballads* (1892)
   *The Seven Seas* (1896)
   *Recessional, and Other Poems* (1899)
   *The Five Nations* (1903)
   *Songs from Books* (1913)
   *The Years Between* (1918)
   *Rudyard Kipling's Verse. Definitive Edition* (1940)
   T. S. Eliot, ed., *A Choice of Kipling's Verse* (1941)
   R. K. R. Thornton and Ian Small, introduction, *Barrack-room ballads 1892* (Woodstock reprint, Oxford, 1993)
(b) Charles Carrington, *Rudyard Kipling: His Life and Work* (1955, 3rd edn 1970)
   James McG. Stewart, ed. A. W. Yeats, *Rudyard Kipling: A Bibliographical Catalogue* (Toronto, 1959)
   Roger Lancelyn Green, *Kipling: The Critical Heritage* (1971)
   Angus Wilson, *The Strange Ride of Rudyard Kipling* (1977)
   Earl of Birkenhead, *Rudyard Kipling* (1978)

RICHARD LE GALLIENNE (1866–1947) was born in Liverpool, where he trained for a short time as an accountant. He made his name in the 1890s as poet, critic and belle-lettrist; he was associated with the Rhymers' Club, and he was influential as reviewer and as reader for the firm of Mathews and Lane. He moved to America in the new century and to France in 1930. He wrote too much and never regained the position he had in the 1890s, a period with which he reaffirmed his connection in his recollections of *The Romantic '90s* (1925).

(a) *My Ladies' Sonnets* (Liverpool, 1887)
   *Volumes in Folio* (1889)
   *English Poems* (1892)
   *Robert Louis Stevenson, an Elegy* (1895)
   *Rubáiyát of Omar Khayyám: a Paraphrase* (1897)
   *New Poems* (1910)
   *The Lonely Dancer* (1914)
   *The Silk-Hat Soldier* (1915)

*The Junk-Man* (1920)
*A Jongleur Strayed* (1922)
R. K. R. Thornton and Ian Small, introduction, *Robert Louis Stevenson and other poems 1895* (Woodstock reprint, Poole, 1996)
(b) Geoffrey Smerdon and Richard Whittington-Egan, *The Quest of the Golden Boy* (1960)
Wendell Harris and Rebecca Larsen, 'Richard Le Gallienne: A Bibliography of Writings about Him', *English Literature in Transition*, 19 (1976), 111–32

EUGENE LEE-HAMILTON (1845–1907) spent his early life mainly on the continent and was privately educated. Having won a scholar-ship to Oxford to study modern languages, he went down after two years without taking a degree. After six years in the Civil Service, he resigned in 1875 because of an illness (probably psychosomatic) which kept him bedridden for twenty years. The disease may well have been in part an escape from life, but he was cured and married in the 1890s. He was the half-brother of Vernon Lee (Violet Paget).

(a) *Poems and Transcripts* (1878)
*Gods, Saints and Men* (1880)
*The New Medusa* (1882)
*Apollo and Marsyas* (1884)
*Imaginary Sonnets* (1888)
*Sonnets of the Wingless Hours* (1894)
*Forest Notes* (with his wife, Annie E. Holdsworth, 1899)
*Gods, Saints and Men, The New Medusa and Sonnets of the Wingless Hours* (Garland reprint, 1984)
(b) Peter Gunn, *Vernon Lee: Violet Paget 1856–1935* (1964)

AMY LEVY (1861–89), daughter of an editor, was educated at Brighton and Newnham College, Cambridge, where she was the first Jewish student. She stayed only four terms before returning to her parents' home in London. She published poems in journals and in her own collections, wrote novels, wrote on Jewish and socialist subjects and was active in support of the poor. She was close friends with Clementina Black, the socialist and suffragist, and knew writers like Vernon Lee, Eleanor Marx (who translated her novel *Reuben Sachs* into German) and Olive Schreiner. Deafness, depression and

perhaps the sense of the impossibility of a woman succeeding as a
writer, drove to her suicide in 1889.

(a) *Xantippe* (Cambridge, 1881)
   *A Minor Poet* (1884)
   *A London Plane-Tree* (1889)
   *A Ballad of Religion and Marriage* (1915)
   Melvyn New, ed., *Selected Writings of Amy Levy, 1861–1889*
   (Gainsville, Fla., 1993)

CAROLINE BLANCHE ELIZABETH, LADY LINDSAY (1844–1912)
was the only daughter of Hannah Mayer Rothschild and the MP
Henry Fitzroy. Her marriage to Sir Henry Coutts Lindsay lasted
from 1864 to the 1880s, when she separated from him and began
her writing career, which included poetry, novels, plays and verses
for children. Caroline Lindsay also wrote a pamphlet on *The Art of
Poetry with Regard to Women Writers* (1899).

(a) *Lyrics* (1890)
   *A String of Beads* (1892)
   *The King's Last Vigil* (1894)
   *The Flower Seller* (1896)
   *The Christmas of the Sorrowful* (1898)
   *The Apostle of the Ardennes* (1899)
   *For England* (1900)
   *The Prayer of St. Scholastica* (1900)
   *From a Venetian Balcony and Other Poems of Venice and the Near
   Lands* (1903)
   *Godfrey's Quest: a fantastic poem* (1905)
   *Lays and Lyrics* (Venice, 1907)
   *Poems of Love and Death* (1907)
   *From a Venetian Calle* (1908)
   *Within Hospital Walls* (1910)

ALICE CHRISTIANA MEYNELL (1847–1922), née Thompson, married Wilfrid Meynell in 1877 and helped him to edit *Merry England*.
A Catholic convert in the 1870s, she was familiar with many Catholic
writers of the 1890s like Katharine Tynan and Francis Thompson
or of an earlier period like Coventry Patmore, though she counted
other writers like George Meredith among her friends. She not only

wrote poems and numerous essays but also had a family of eight children and found time for political action as a staunch supporter of the non-militant suffragists.

(a) *Preludes* (1875)
   *Poems* (1893)
   *Other Poems* (1896)
   *Later Poems* (1902)
   *The Shepherdess* (1914)
   *A Father of Women* (1917)
   *The Last Poems of Alice Meynell* (1923)
   *The Poems of Alice Meynell*, Oxford Standard Authors (1940)
   F. P., V. M., O. S. and F. M., eds, *Alice Meynell Prose and Poetry* with a biographical and critical introduction by V. Sackville-West (1947)
(b) Viola Meynell, *Alice Meynell: A Memoir* (1929)
   Terence L. Connolly, ed., *Alice Meynell Centenary Tribute, 1847–1947* (Boston, 1948)
   Beverly Ann Schlack, 'The Poetess of poets: Alice Meynell Rediscovered', *Women's Studies*, 7 (1980), 111–26
   June Badeni, *The Slender Tree: A Life of Alice Meynell* (Padstow, 1981)

CONSTANCE CAROLINE WOODHILL NADEN (1858–89) was born in Birmingham. Her mother died a fortnight later and Constance was brought up by her mother's parents. She was a brilliant student and impressed in many different disciplines when she enrolled at the new Mason Science College. Espousing scientific and evolutionary theories, she wrote for the *Journal of Science* and the *Agnostic Journal* and lectured widely. Her own theory of Hylo-Idealism, which aimed at reconciling mind with matter, was noticed by Oscar Wilde, who used it in his short story 'The Canterville Ghost: A Hylo-Idealistic Romance', as well as by the Aristotelian Society, which elected her a member. Throughout her life she was active in the women's movement – from presiding over women's debating societies to lecturing on women's suffrage. Her poetry bears the stamp of her combined scientific, philosophical and feminist interests, and is characterized by a satirical tone. In an article in *The Speaker* of 1890, William Gladstone ranked her poetry alongside that of Christina

Rossetti and Elizabeth Barrett Browning. A promising career was cut short as she died, soon after moving to London, at the age of thirty-one.

(a) *Songs and Sonnets of Springtime* (1881)
   *A Modern Apostle, the Elixir of Life and Other Poems* (1887)
   *Selections from the Philosophical and Poetical Works of Constance C. W. Naden*, compiled by Emily and Edith Hughes (1893)
   *The Complete Poetical Works of Constance Naden*, with a foreword by Robert Lewins (1894)

(b) William R. Hughes, *Constance Naden: A Memoir* (1890)
   Philip E. and Susan Harris Smith, 'Constance Naden: Late Victorian Feminist, Poet and Philosopher', *Victorian Poetry*, 15 (1977), 367–70
   Philip E. Smith II, 'Robert Lewins, Constance Naden, and Hylo-Idealism', *Notes and Queries*, 223 (1978)
   James R. Moore, 'The Erotics of Evolution: Constance Naden and Hylo-Idealism' in *One Culture: Essays in Science and Literature*, ed. George Levine (1987)
   Marion Thain, *Constance Naden and a Feminist Poetics* (unpublished M.Phil. thesis, University of Birmingham, 1995)

EDITH NESBIT (1858–1924) was the youngest of five and most famous for her children's writing, which she began in the 1890s. She spent much of her youth on the continent with her consumptive sister. She felt herself to be a poet in spite of the popularity of her books like *The Railway Children* (1906), and considered herself most clearly represented by her socialist poems. She was involved in the founding of the Fabians, and lived in an unconventional and bohemian household, married to the Fabian, philanderer and incestuous paedophile, Hubert Bland, but receiving into the house her husband's mistress and children and herself having a number of lovers who often accompanied her on family holidays. She married again in 1917.

(a) *Lays and Legends* (1886)
   *Leaves of Life* (1888)
   *Lays and Legends (second series)* (1892)
   *A Pomander of Verse* (1895)
   *Songs of Love and Empire* (1898)

    *The Rainbow and the Rose* (1905)
    *Ballads and Lyrics of Socialism 1883–1908* (1908)
    *Ballads and Verses of the Spiritual Life* (1911)
    *Many Voices* (1922)
(b) Julia Briggs, *A Woman of Passion: The Life of E. Nesbit* (1987, 1989)

HENRY JOHN NEWBOLT (1862–1938), barrister, editor, author and poet, was born at Bilston and educated at Clifton and Corpus Christi, Oxford. He practised law for some years, but continued to write, achieving an immediate popularity with his poems about the sea, which are still familiar both as recitation and song. He edited the *Monthly Review* for the first four years of the twentieth century. He was co-author of the official naval history of the First World War. He was knighted in 1915.

(a) *Admirals All* (1897)
    *The Island Race* (1898)
    *The Sailing of the Long Ships* (1902)
    *Songs of the Sea* (1904)
    *Clifton Chapel* (1908)
    *Songs of Memory and Hope* (1909)
    *Collected Poems, 1897–1907* (1910)
    *Poems: New and Old* (1912)
    *St George's Day* (1918)
    *A Perpetual Memory* (1939)
    Patrick Dickinson, ed., *Selected Poems* (1981)
    R. K. R. Thornton and Ian Small, introduction, *The island race 1898* (Woodstock reprint, Oxford, 1995)
(b) *My World as in My Time: Memoirs of Sir Henry Newbolt* (1932)
    Margaret Newbolt, ed., *The Later Life and Letters of Sir Henry Newbolt* (1942)
    Michael Bright, 'Remembering Sir Henry Newbolt: An Essay and Bibliography', *English Literature in Transition*, 33 (1990), 155–78
    Vanessa Furse Jackson, *The Poetry of Henry Newbolt* (Greensboro, NC, 1994)

VINCENT O'SULLIVAN (1868–1940) was born in New York, the son of an Irish immigrant who had made a fortune as a coffee-broker.

He was educated at Columbia Grammar School in New York, at Oscott and at Exeter College, Oxford, where he did not graduate. His work was published by Elkin Mathews and Leonard Smithers, and O'Sullivan was familiar with many of the authors they published, like Wilde, Dowson and Beardsley. After the First World War he lectured at Rennes University, travelled, wrote, was injured in a street accident in 1932 and, though he had once been wealthy, died in poverty in Paris.

(a) *Poems* (1896)
   *The Houses of Sin* (1897)
   R. K. R. Thornton and Ian Small, introduction, *The houses of sin 1897 with Poems 1896* (Woodstock reprint, Oxford, 1995)
(b) Carey McWilliams, 'Vincent O'Sullivan', *South Atlantic Quarterly*, 30, no. 41 (1931)
   Alan Anderson, introduction, *Opinions* (1959)

STEPHEN PHILLIPS (1864–1915), son of the Precentor of Peterborough Cathedral, was educated at a variety of places, and abandoned his studies for the Civil Service in order to join Sir Frank Benson's company. His stage experience made his poetic dramas more successful in the theatre than most of his Victorian predecessors', and he seemed to be entering the new century with great promise. It was not fulfilled, though he wrote several pieces. From 1913 to 1915 he edited the *Poetry Review*.

(a) *Orestes* (1884)
   in *Primavera* (1890)
   *Eremus* (1894)
   *Christ in Hades* (1897)
   *Poems* (1898)
   *New Poems* (1908)
   *The New Inferno* (1911)
   *Lyrics and Dramas* (1913)
   *Panama* (1915)
(b) Peter Frost, 'The Rise and Fall of Stephen Phillips', *English Literature in Transition*, 25 (1982), 225–31

VICTOR GUSTAVE PLARR (1863–1929) was born near Strasburg, his father Alsatian, his mother English. The family moved to England after the Franco-Prussian war and Plarr studied modern history at Worcester College, Oxford. Though he continued his connections with poets and poetry (he had been in the Rhymers' Club), he balanced that side of his work by his cataloguing and biographical works for the Royal College of Surgeons of England, whose librarian he was. Pound pictures him there as 'Monsieur Verog' in 'Hugh Selwyn Mauberley'.

(a) *In the Dorian Mood* (1896)
   ed. and contrib., *The Garland of New Poetry* (1896)
   *The Tragedy of Asgard* (1905)
   Ian Fletcher, ed., *The Collected Poems of Victor Plarr* (1974)
   R. K. R. Thornton and Ian Small, introduction, *In the Dorian mood 1896* (Woodstock reprint, Oxford, 1995)
(b) *Ernest Dowson, 1888–1897: Reminiscences, Unpublished Letters and Marginalia* (1914)

MAY PROBYN (dates unknown). Little is known except that she was the daughter of Julian Probyn of Longhope, Gloucestershire, lived in Weybridge and London, published in magazines, and was a friend of Katharine Tynan. She wrote a novel called *Once! Twice! Thrice! And Away!* (1878) and a story, *Who Killed Cock Robin?* (1880), and her second book of poems is dedicated to Tennyson. She was received into the Roman Catholic Church in 1883.

(a) *Poems* (1881)
   *A Ballad of the Road* (1883)
   *Pansies. A Book of Poems* (1895)

DOLLIE RADFORD (1858–1920) was born Caroline Maitland in Worcester, and was educated there, at Malvern and at Queen's College London. A member of the Fabian Society, she had a lifelong interest in socialism, spending a good deal of time in the home of Karl Marx. She wrote for several magazines on artistic and literary topics. She married Ernest Radford in 1883.

(a) *A Light Load* (1891)
   *Songs for Somebody* (1893)
   *Good Night* (1895)
   *Songs and Other Verses* (1895)

*A Ballad of Victory* (1907)
*Poems* (1910)

ERNEST RADFORD (1857–1919) was born in Plymouth, went to
Trinity Hall, Cambridge, and was called to the Bar in 1880. Though
his poetry frequently reflects his legal background, he was known
as an art critic and lecturer. He moved in socialist and literary
circles, was a member of the Rhymers' Club, and later knew Pound
and Lawrence.

(a) *Translations from Heine* (1882)
    *Measured Steps* (1884)
    *Chambers Twain* (1890)
    *Old and New* (1895)
    *A Collection of Poems* (1906)
    *Songs in the Whirlwind* (with A. Radford, 1918)
(b) Ian Fletcher, 'Letters to Herbert Horne, Ernest Radford and
    Elkin Mathews', *Yeats Studies*, 1 (1971), 203–8

ERNEST PERCIVAL RHYS (1859–1946) was born in Islington, and
qualified and practised as a mining engineer before going to London
in 1886 to begin a career as editor and publisher, whose most
remarkable achievement is the editing of Everyman's Library. He
was the only sign in the Rhymers' Club of a Welsh branch of the
Celtic revival, and he recalls the period in his autobiographical work.

(a) *A London Rose* (1894)
    *Welsh Ballads* (1898)
    *The Leaf Burners* (1918)
    *Rhymes for Everyman* (1933)
    *Song of the Sun* (1937)
(b) *Everyman Remembers* (1931)
    *Letters from Limbo* (1936)
    *Wales England Wed* (1940)
    J. Kimberley Roberts, *Ernest Rhys* (Cardiff, 1983)

AGNES MARY FRANCES ROBINSON (1857–1944) was born in
Leamington, the daughter of a church architect. She was educated
at home, at school in Brussels, in Italy and for seven years at
University College London, where she studied Greek. She had, by

way of her parents' well-attended parties, a wide literary acquaint-
ance in England, including an intimate relationship with Vernon
Lee. In France, after her marriage in 1888 to James Darmesteter,
Professor of Persian in Paris, she cultivated her own literary salon,
which became one of the fashionable intellectual centres in Paris.
After Darmesteter's death in 1894, she married Émile Duclaux, a
French scientist, and continued to live in France after his death in
1904. As well as poetry, she wrote novels, biographies and made
translations.

(a) *A Handful of Honeysuckle* (1878)
   *The Crowned Hippolytus* (1881)
   *The New Arcadia* (1884)
   *An Italian Garden: A Book of Songs* (1886)
   *Songs, Ballads and a Garden Play* (1888)
   *Lyrics Selected from the Works of A. Mary F. Robinson (Madame
   James Darmesteter)* (1891)
   *Retrospect* (1893)
   *The Collected Poems, Lyrical and Narrative of A. Mary F. Robinson
   (Madame Duclaux)* (1902)
   *The Return to Nature: Songs and Symbols* (1904)
   *Images and Meditations: Poems* (1923)
(b) Hannah Lynch, 'A. Mary F. Robinson', *The Fortnightly Review*,
   LXXI, new series (1902)
   Vernon Lee (Violet Paget), *Vernon Lee's Letters* (privately printed
   1937)
   Daniel Halévy, ed., *Mary Duclaux et Maurice Barrès: Lettres
   Échangées* (Paris, 1959)
   Ruth Van Zuyle Holmes, 'Mary Duclaux (1856–1944): Primary
   and Secondary Checklists', *English Literature in Translation*, 10,
   1 (1967), 27–46; supplemented in *ELT* 16, 1(1973), 71–94, and
   in *ELT* 18, 1 (1975), 58–9
   Peter Gunn, *Vernon Lee: Violet Paget 1856–1935* (1984)

ARTHUR WILLIAM SYMONS (1865–1945) educated himself by
writing and lived by his pen. Having written a book (still of interest)
on Browning when he was twenty-one, he rose rapidly to an influential position in the movements of the time, publishing poems,
translations, essays, reviews and editing among other things *The*

*Savoy* (1896). A mental breakdown in 1908 substantially limited his abilities, but his influence as trendsetter and introducer of foreign ideas had already had its effect.

(a) *Days and Nights* (1889)
   *Silhouettes* (1892; 2nd edn, 1896)
   *London Nights* (1895; 2nd edn, 1897)
   *Amoris Victima* (1897)
   *Images of Good and Evil* (1899)
   *Poems* (2 vols, 1902)
   *The Fool of the World* (1906)
   *Knave of Hearts* (1913)
   *Lesbia* (New York, 1920)
   *Love's Cruelty* (1923)
   *Collected Works* (1924, only 9 vols published)
   *Jezebel Mort* (1931)
   R. V. Holdsworth, ed., *Poetry and Prose* (Cheadle, 1974)
   R. K. R. Thornton and Ian Small, introduction, *Silhouettes 1896 with London nights 1897* (Woodstock reprint, Oxford, 1993)
   R. K. R. Thornton and Ian Small, introduction, *Images of good and evil 1899* (Woodstock reprint, Poole, 1996)
(b) John M. Munro, *Arthur Symons* (1969)
   Karl Beckson, ed., *The Memoirs of Arthur Symons* (1977)
   Lawrence W. Markert, *Arthur Symons: Critic of the Seven Arts* (Ann Arbor, 1985)
   Karl Beckson, *Arthur Symons: A Life* (1987)
   Karl Beckson and John M. Munro, eds, *Arthur Symons: Selected Letters* (Iowa City, 1989)
   Karl Beckson, Ian Fletcher, Lawrence W. Markert and John Stokes, *Arthur Symons: A Bibliography* (Greensboro, NC, 1990)

FRANCIS THOMPSON (1859–1907) was born in Preston, the son of a physician. Intended first for the Roman Catholic priesthood and then for his father's profession, he failed to qualify for either. Having followed De Quincey's path into opium and squalor in London, he was befriended by the Meynells who provided both material and spiritual help. His irregular Muse failing after the early 'nineties, he wrote mainly reviews which are of a high standard.

(a) *Poems* (1893)
   *Sister Songs* (1895)
   *New Poems* (1897)
   *The Works of Francis Thompson* (3 vols, 1913)
   R. K. R. Thornton and Ian Small, introduction, *Poems 1894*
   (Woodstock reprint, Oxford, 1993)
(b) John E. Walsh, *Strange Harp, Strange Symphony* (1968)
   John E. Walsh, ed., *The Letters of Francis Thompson* (New York,
   1969)
   Brigid M. Boardman, *Between Heaven and Charing Cross: The
   Life of Francis Thompson* (New Haven, 1988)

OSCAR FINGALL O'FLAHERTIE WILLS WILDE (1854–1900) was
the son of an Irish eye surgeon and the nationalist poet who called
herself Speranza. He was a brilliant classical scholar at Trinity
College Dublin, and then a successful student at Oxford, where he
won the Newdigate Prize. Wilde's acquisition of social celebrity,
with his tour of America advertising Gilbert and Sullivan's *Patience*
and his editing of *Woman's World,* masks his steady work in criticism,
fiction, drama and poetry to earn himself a place as a literary giant,
rather than a mere convenient decadent myth. His society comedies,
his association with Lord Alfred Douglas and his sentence in 1895
to two years' imprisonment with hard labour for gross indecency
are well known. *The Ballad of Reading Gaol* is his only major piece
of writing after he left gaol in 1897. He died in Paris in 1900.

(a) *Ravenna* (Newdigate Prize poem, Oxford, 1881)
   *Poems* (1881)
   *The Ballad of Reading Gaol* (1898)
   R. K. R. Thornton and Ian Small, introduction, *Poems 1892*
   (Woodstock reprint, Poole, 1995)
   R. K. R. Thornton and Ian Small, introduction, *The ballad of
   Reading gaol 1898* (Woodstock reprint, Poole, 1995)
(b) Rupert Hart-Davis, ed., *The Letters of Oscar Wilde* (1963)
   Karl Beckson, *Oscar Wilde: The Critical Heritage* (1970)
   Rupert Hart-Davis, ed., *More Letters of Oscar Wilde* (1985)
   Richard Ellmann, *Oscar Wilde* (1987)
   Regenia Gagnier, *Idylls of the Marketplace: Oscar Wilde and the
   Victorian Public* (Aldershot, 1987)

Peter Raby, *Oscar Wilde* (1988)
Ian Small, *Oscar Wilde Revalued* (1993)

THEODORE WILLIAM GRAF WRATISLAW (1871–1933) was born
and educated at Rugby, and became a solicitor like his father. He
tried to give that up for a literary career in 1893, but found that,
though he contributed to *The Yellow Book* and *The Savoy* and wrote
two books of poems, his writing would not support him. He became
a Civil Servant in 1895, working in the Estate Office at Somerset
House, but he published only one new poem in the twentieth
century.

(a) *Love's Memorial* (Rugby, 1892)
   *Some Verses* (Rugby, 1892)
   *Caprices* (1893)
   *Orchids* (1896)
   John Gawsworth, ed., *Selected Poems* (1935)
   R. K. R. Thornton and Ian Small, introduction, *Caprices 1893
   with Orchids 1896* (Woodstock reprint, Oxford, 1994)
(b) Karl Beckson, introduction, *Oscar Wilde, A Memoir* (1979)

WILLIAM BUTLER YEATS (1865–1939) was born at Sandymount,
near Dublin. His life, from his early experiences of Ireland and
London, his art school training, his love for Maud Gonne, to his
winning of the Nobel Prize for Literature, appointment to the
Irish Senate and death at Cap Martin, has been well documented.
Indisputably one of the great poets of the twentieth century: the
significance of the 1890s in his development is that it was a period
of searching for a stance, a style, a mask, a period of forming his
ideas, and of course a time when he was learning his trade.

(a) *The Wanderings of Oisin* (1889)
   *The Countess Kathleen, and Various Legends and Lyrics* (1892)
   *Poems* (1895; revd 1899)
   *The Secret Rose* (1897)
   *The Wind Among the Reeds* (1899)
   *In the Seven Woods* (1903)
   *The Green Helmet* (1910)
   *Responsibilities* (1914)
   *The Wild Swans at Coole* (Dundrum, 1917)

*Michael Robartes and the Dancer* (Dundrum, 1920)
*Later Poems* (1922)
*The Tower* (1928)
*The Winding Stair* (1933)
*Last Poems* (1939)
Richard J. Finneran, ed., *W. B. Yeats, The Poems: Revised* (1989)
R. K. R. Thornton and Ian Small, introduction, *Poems 1895* (Woodstock reprint, Oxford, 1994)
R. K. R. Thornton and Ian Small, introduction, *The wind among the reeds 1895* (Woodstock reprint, Oxford, 1994)
(b) Harold Bloom, *Yeats* (New York, 1970)
John Kelly and Eric Domville, eds., *The Collected Letters of W. B. Yeats* (vols 1–3, Oxford, 1986–94)
Ian Fletcher, *Yeats and his Contemporaries* (Brighton, 1987)
A. N. Jeffares, *W. B. Yeats: A New Biography* (1988)
Stan Smith, *W. B. Yeats: A Critical Introduction* (1990)
Roy Foster, *W. B. Yeats: A Life*, vol. 1: *The Apprentice Mage 1865–1914* (Oxford, 1997)

## ANTHOLOGIES AND REFERENCE BOOKS

Karl Beckson, ed., *Aesthetes and Decadents of the 1890's* (New York, 1966, 1993)
Jennifer Breen, ed., *Victorian Women Poets 1830–1901: An Anthology* (1994)
G. A. Cevasco, ed., *The 1890s: An Encyclopedia of British Literature, Art, and Culture* (New York, 1993)
Linda Dowling, *Aestheticism and Decadence: A Selective Annotated Bibliography* (New York, 1967)
Angela Leighton and Margaret Reynolds, eds, *Victorian Women Poets: An Anthology* (1995)
Alfred H. Miles, ed., *The Poets and Poetry of the Century* (10 vols, 1891–7)
Catherine W. Reilly, *Late Victorian Poetry 1880–1899: An Annotated Biobibliography* (1994)
Eric S. Robertson, *English Poetesses: A Series of Critical Biographies, with Illustrative Extracts* (1883)
Martin Secker, ed., *The Eighteen Nineties* (1948)

Ian Small, ed., *The Aesthetes: A Sourcebook* (1979)
Derek Stanford, *Writing of the 'Nineties* (1971)
A. J. A. Symons, ed., *An Anthology of 'Nineties Verse* (1928)

## CRITICAL WORKS

Isobel Armstrong, *Victorian Poetry: Poetry, Poetics and Politics* (1993)
Karl Beckson, *London in the 1890s* (1992)
Bernard Bergonzi, *The Turn of a Century* (1973)
Jerome Hamilton Buckley, *The Triumph of Time: A Study of the Victorian Concepts of Time, History, Progress, and Decadence* (Cambridge, Mass., 1966)
Osbert Burdett, *The Beardsley Period* (1925)
A. E. Carter, *The Idea of Decadence in French Literature, 1830–1900* (Toronto, 1958)
J. E. Chamberlin, *Ripe Was the Drowsy Hour* (New York, 1977)
J. A. V. Chapple, *Documentary and Imaginative Literature 1880–1920* (1970)
Barbara Charlesworth, *Dark Passages: The Decadent Consciousness in Victorian Literature* (Madison, Wis., 1965)
Rupert Croft-Cooke, *Feasting With Panthers* (1968)
David Daiches, *Some Late Victorian Attitudes* (1969)
Linda Dowling, *Language and Decadence in the Victorian Fin de Siècle* (Princeton, 1986)
Richard Ellmann, ed., *Edwardians and Late Victorians* (New York, 1959)
B. Ifor Evans, *English Poetry in the Later Nineteenth Century* (revd edn 1966)
Albert J. Farmer, *Le mouvement esthétique ed 'décadent' en Angleterre (1873–1900)* (Paris, 1931)
Ian Fletcher, ed., *Romantic Mythologies* (1967)
Ian Fletcher and Malcolm Bradbury, eds, *Decadence and the 1890s* (1979)
Joann Gardner, *Yeats and the Rhymers' Club* (New York, 1989)
Graham Hough, *The Last Romantics* (1949)
Luce Irigaray, *This Sex Which is Not One*, translated by Catherine Porter with Carolyn Burke (Ithaca, NY, 1985)
Holbrook Jackson, *The Eighteen Nineties* (1913)

Frank Kermode, *Romantic Image* (1957)

J. W. Lambert and Michael Ratcliffe, *The Bodley Head 1887–1987* (1987)

Angela Leighton, *Victorian Women Poets: Writing Against the Heart* (1992)

John A. Lester, Jr., *Journey Through Despair* (Princeton, 1968)

Katherine L. Mix, *A Study in Yellow: The Yellow Book and its Contributors* (1960)

John M. Munro, *The Decadent Poetry of the Eighteen-Nineties* (Beirut, 1970)

James G. Nelson, *The Early Nineties: A View from the Bodley Head* (Cambridge, Mass., 1971)

Jean Pierrot, *The Decadent Imagination 1880–1900* (1981)

Murray Pittock, *Spectrum of Decadence: The Literature of the 1890s* (1993)

Mario Praz, *The Romantic Agony* (1933)

Elaine Showalter, ed., *Daughters of Decadence: Women Writers of the Fin de Siècle* (1990)

Elaine Showalter, *Sexual Anarchy: Gender and Culture at the Fin de Siècle* (1990)

John Stokes, *In the Nineties* (1989)

Koenrad W. Swart, *The Sense of Decadence in Nineteenth Century France* (The Hague, 1964)

Ruth Z. Temple, *The Critic's Alchemy* (1953)

R. K. R. Thornton, *The Decadent Dilemma* (1983)

W. B. Yeats, *Autobiographies* (1926)

# INDEX OF POETS

# INDEX OF TITLES
# AND FIRST LINES